Advance Praise for *Every Season Sacred*

Every Season Sacred is a perfect blend of storytelling and liturgy, inviting us to slow down, stay present, and reorient our eyes to the love of God, even in the midst of a distracted, busy world. Filled with charming stories and poetic prayers, this book is a must-read for the whole family.

ASHLEE GADD
Founder of Coffee + Crumbs and author of *Create Anyway: The Joy of Pursuing Creativity in the Margins of Motherhood*

In *Every Season Sacred*, Kayla Craig does not offer us something new but something ancient—inviting us to embrace the rhythms of the created world as gifts that are meant to orient us toward a life rooted in the love of God. Instead of asking us to fill our lives with more, she gently invites us to embrace what's already been given— the unforced rhythms of grace.

DREW JACKSON
Poet and author of *God Speaks through Wombs* and *Touch the Earth*

Kayla has written the book I have been in search of. Her words invite us into a space of exhale in a way that is accessible even for a mom like me. I know I will be dipping into this book often for many years to come, likely for the rest of my life. I hope it is welcomed into the homes of every family.

HEATHER AVIS
New York Times bestselling author and narrative shifter

Every Season Sacred sets me up to more fully know the life-giving presence of God, inch by inch and moment by moment. What a gift.

JUSTIN McROBERTS
Author of *Sacred Strides: The Journey to Belovedness in Rest and Work*

Flexible, poignant, and (best of all) practical, *Every Season Sacred* reminds us that the Holy Spirit is working in and through our families and invites us to join in on that holy and nurturing work.

ERIN MOON
Cohost of *The Bible Binge* podcast

I've so often prayed Kayla Craig's words over my life, family, home, and community that the books have become dog-eared companions by now. In this new book of prayers and blessings, she gives us language for the nuance, delight, tragedy, and beauty of being alive right now.

SARAH BESSEY
New York Times bestselling author of *A Rhythm of Prayer* and *Jesus Feminist*

At turns tender and funny, thoughtful and profound, this practical guide makes the seasons of the church year accessible for today's families, with prayers for all ages, relatable reflections, and engaging questions for faith conversations. *Every Season Sacred* draws from real-life stories and diverse voices to offer an enduring gift for parents, children, and communities of faith.

LAURA KELLY FANUCCI
Author of *Everyday Sacrament: The Messy Grace of Parenting* and *To Bless Our Callings: Prayers, Poems, and Hymns to Celebrate Vocation*

Kayla sees our everyday as the very place we meet God, and in this book, she shares with us how we might too. But the best part is that she's offering us this lens not for ourselves alone but for the children we're raising.

MEREDITH MILLER
Pastor and author of *Woven: Nurturing a Faith Your Kid Doesn't Have to Heal From*

Kayla has the unique ability to capture these moments—the great and the mundane—and give perspective and words to the celebrations and the memorializations. If your heart needs words, you will find them in *Every Season Sacred*.

JONATHAN PITTS
Pastor at Church of the City and president of For Girls Like You ministries

I am thrilled Kayla's words will grace the kitchen counters, bedside tables, and hearts of thousands. We need her grace-filled hope, prayers, and encouragement in every season.

ANJULI PASCHALL
Author of *Stay* and *Awake*

Kayla Craig compassionately takes us by the hand and invites us to remember that the Creator of the universe walks with us through each and every season. With stunning prose, heartfelt prayers, and deeply rooted contemplative rhythms, *Every Season Sacred* is an invaluable resource for families. I cannot recommend it highly enough.

AUNDI KOLBER, MA, LPC
Therapist and author of *Try Softer* and *Strong like Water*

Every Season Sacred poignantly and profoundly meets us in the messy middle of life: a place few, if any, find comfort, but as parents, it's where we most often reside. These pages filled with meaningful prompts, prayers, and reflections are sure to nurture my family while nourishing this weary mama's soul.

PATRICIA A. TAYLOR
Writer and anti-racism educator

Reflections, Prayers, and Invitations to Nourish Your Soul
and Nurture Your Family throughout the Year

Every
Season Sacred

KAYLA CRAIG

TYNDALE
MOMENTUM®

A Tyndale nonfiction imprint

Visit Tyndale online at tyndale.com.

Visit Tyndale Momentum online at tyndalemomentum.com.

Visit the author at kaylacraig.com.

Tyndale, Tyndale's quill logo, *Tyndale Momentum*, and the Tyndale Momentum logo are registered trademarks of Tyndale House Ministries. Tyndale Momentum is a nonfiction imprint of Tyndale House Publishers, Carol Stream, Illinois.

Edited by Stephanie Rische

Published in association with the literary agency of Gardner Literary LLC. www.gardner-literary.com.

For information about special discounts for bulk purchases, please contact Tyndale House Publishers at csresponse@tyndale.com, or call 1-855-277-9400.

Library of Congress Cataloging-in-Publication Data

A catalog record for this book is available from the Library of Congress.

ISBN 978-1-4964-7711-8

Printed in China

29	28	27	26	25	24	23
9	8	7	6	5	4	3

"Sacramental moments can occur at any moment,
at any place, and to anybody."

FREDERICK BUECHNER

To my kids:
Our stories have converged,
and now we write a new book,
moment by moment, day by day.
No matter what, we are together.
Today, tomorrow, for all the days to come,
with Christ alongside me and before me,
I will love you to the end.

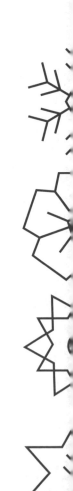

Contents

Introduction

I HOLD MY SON ABRAM'S HAND as we climb to the top of the waterslide. After a day at the pool, his squishy fingers are wrinkled. I squint into the sun, feeling its hot rays warm my shoulders. I wonder if I remembered the sunscreen.

The Midwest humidity hangs thick in the air, mixing with the smell of chlorine. We stand together, warm and content, waiting our turn to plummet down the twists and turns. I soak in my son's blond curls and ocean-blue eyes. He looks lost in thought. With his surfer vibe and laid-back attitude, it seems like God made him for summer.

"Mom," he says, squeezing my hand, "will it be winter soon? I love snow!"

Parenting brings us in and out of seasons. Babies turn into big kids; big kids turn into teens. Change is gradual yet seems to happen all at once. As my husband and I raise our four children, we spend our years journeying through a cycle of four distinct weather seasons, helping us mark the passage of time.

Just as nature follows the rhythm of autumn fading into winter, winter bursting into spring, spring breaking forth into summer, and summer easing into autumn, we also transition through different ages and stages as families. Seasons help us understand our physical and emotional growth, and they guide us into a deeper understanding of our relationship with God.

Seasonal structure plays an essential role in the Christian calendar as well. The church calendar (also known as the liturgical year) helps believers journey through a cycle of seasons that reflect on the life of Jesus, such as His birth (Advent/Christmas), death (Lent/Holy Week), and resurrection (Easter). As we walk through these holy days, we discover "who we are as followers of Christ and beloved children of God."[1] Whether or not you grew up in a tradition that follows the church calendar and whether or not you attend one now, keeping these rhythms in our families helps us stay rooted in God's unchanging goodness throughout all seasons of life (and all stages of parenting).

In the overwhelm and constant demands of family life, it may be difficult to feel present in the season God has you in right now. (It often feels like I need every ounce of energy just to make it through the day.) But even on the days we drag ourselves to bedtime, it's not out of reach to be awake to ourselves and to the kids who have been entrusted to us.

We must slow down enough to be awake to the glory right in front of us.

According to author and minister Jan Richardson, the liturgical year "is itself a circle that draws us into the ongoing story of God with us. Season by season, the Christian year invites us to travel through the stories, traditions, rituals, and memories that help us know who we are as the people of God." When we are in tune with these rhythms, we are able to "enter into time with intention and mindfulness, rather than letting events propel us along."[2] Amid the push and pull of life's demands, the pages of this book offer an invitation to embrace a thoughtful spirituality—an opportunity to enter into reflection and explore where God is in all seasons of your life.

We don't get awarded honorary theological degrees when we become parents. And yet, suddenly, we have this child to nurture, protect, and guide as they have their own wonderings about the life of faith. Most of us don't have the privilege of embarking on yearlong pilgrimages to hear God. (It feels like a silent retreat when I can run to the post office alone.) So how do overwhelmed parents like us nourish our souls in order to help our families live out a flourishing faith?

In Matthew 11, Jesus tells people to get away with Him so they can learn to live freely and lightly. He shares that if they follow Him this way, He will teach them "unforced rhythms of grace" (Matthew 11:28, MSG). That opportunity is still available to us today.

This book is not another item to check off on your to-do list—it's an invitation into unforced rhythms. It's permission to release that breath you've been holding. As you parent your children and explore your questions together, may God reveal sacred moments to you—in each season of your life.

"We, as parents, must envision who our children can become in God's story, then be that ourselves."

MARK AND JAN FOREMAN, *NEVER SAY NO*

How to Use This Book

This collection of spiritual reflections, prayers, and prompts is split into four seasons:

- ▸ fall
- ▸ winter
- ▸ spring
- ▸ summer

Each section is broken into thirteen weekly chapters, one for every week of the year. You are welcome to read them in order or jump around in whatever way works for you.

At the beginning of each section, you'll find a reflection and a prayer for the season. You can return to this whenever you find yourself wanting to feel rooted in the deep love God has for you—and your family. These prayers include themes from liturgical seasons and holy days on the Christian calendar to accompany you in your spiritual formation. (For example, in "Winter," you'll discover Advent and Christmas reflections and prayers; in "Spring," you'll find meditations on Lent and Easter.)

The explorations in each season cover a wide range of what makes up your days. In "Fall," you'll find themes such as fresh beginnings, letting go, and embracing mystery; in "Winter," topics include fostering generosity, working through loneliness, and making memories; in "Spring," you'll reflect on learning to play, becoming new, and choosing to forgive; in "Summer," we'll cover embracing boredom, redefining freedom, and growing despite distractions.

Each short chapter includes two parts: one for you to read alone and one to share with your family. The weekly reflections are intended specifically for you—musings for your parenting journey as you reclaim your identity as a beloved child of God. This section is followed by spiritual conversation prompts and communal prayers, which are meant to be shared with your family.

WHAT YOU'LL FIND EACH WEEK

REFLECTION

As a parent, you must tend to your own soul to nurture your family's faith effectively. You'll find a reflection for you to read and think about each week of the year. My hope is that these words will speak to your real life and the world we live in. They're meant to invite you into a story that holds a mirror to your experiences and moves you to reflect on the story God is writing in your life and the life of your family.

Along with exploring Scripture, I share bits of my life as a child and as a parent, and I borrow wisdom from writers, theologians, artists, and leaders who have much to teach us as we journey through this life together. Give yourself time to read the reflection before embarking on the rest of the chapter. (If you're short on time, it's okay to read it in fits and starts.) The reflection is for you, the parent—no need to read it at the table with everyone. (Unless you want to. It's your book, after all.)

Pop in and out as you're able. An index in the back offers a list of themes and topics so you can find what you need for a particular season. Keep in mind that even if you've been through a season before, you may find *yourself* changed. "As we journey again and again through each season, our path is never precisely the same. The seasons change us. With each one, we move ever further into the circle that encompasses us and into the grace we find there."[3] You'll see there are no specific dates in this book—it's meant to be kept at your bedside for years to come. Jot down notes or dates, return to them a year later, and see how your conversations and questions have changed and how the reflections hit differently, season after season, year after year.

SCRIPTURE

Each weekly reflection includes an invitation into Scripture. Ruth Haley Barton says it best: "The sad truth is that many of us approach the Scriptures more like a textbook than like a love letter."[4] This book is not a Bible study, but the passages are connected to the readings and provide a way to get into the best Story of all.

I recommend having a Bible you can turn to in a translation that's easy to understand. I suggest *The Message* paraphrase for read-alouds and the New Living Translation (NLT) or New International Version (NIV) for personal reading. I often turn to the New Revised Standard Version (NRSV) for deeper explorations, and I have found myself moved by the First Nations Translation (FNT) of the New Testament. I also turn to Bible apps such as YouVersion and online tools such as BibleGateway. com so I can quickly read a variety of translations.

Audio versions are also fantastic, accessible options for kids and grown-ups alike. I recommend streaming or downloading the work

"Parenting reshapes the core of your being to help you love more like God loves."

RONALD ROLHEISER, *DOMESTIC MONASTERY*

of Streetlights, which shakes the dust off whatever old-fashioned ideas you (or your kids) might have about listening to the Bible.

"God's Word is to be heard by everyone in his own way and according to the measure of his understanding," wrote Dietrich Bonhoeffer. "A child hears and learns the Bible for the first time in family worship; the adult Christian learns it repeatedly and better, and he will never finish acquiring knowledge of its story."[5] In other words, the Bible isn't only for you, and it's not just for your kids; God speaks through it to all of us.

BREATH PRAYER

Breath prayers are short meditations to help you focus your body and your mind on the One who gives each breath. Christians have used this contemplative practice of praying as you inhale and exhale for generations as a way to be still and know that God is God (see Psalm 46:10).

These simple prayers can act as an anchor, tethering you to contemplation and reflection throughout the week. Ask God to help you become mindful of your breath and your body as you breathe in and out. In our overwhelming daily realities, it's easy to become disconnected from who God has created us to be—fully human, with a connected heart, soul, mind, and body. If parenting is a continual undoing, these breath prayers act as a tangible invitation to let God piece us back together, breath by breath.

"The value of a deep breath is something we must continue to learn and relearn on the path to peace," writes poet and artist Morgan Harper Nichols. In doing so, we exchange "quick, shallow breaths for a cycle of breath that represents the fullness of how we were meant to breathe—mindfully, wholly."[6] You can say these prayers silently or repeat the words aloud. Whether you're rocking a baby, helping with homework, or stuck in traffic, you can integrate these mindful moments into the rhythms of your day.

PROMPTS

Each week includes prompts for spiritual conversations with your family to help you notice and name your experiences of God in your real, messy, holy lives. This is low pressure—no concrete answers or theological degrees are necessary to tackle these questions.

You don't need to do one ounce of prep, though you may find

> "The breath prayer is the prayer of the beggar and carries with it the intimacy of asking for what we need."
>
> **RUTH HALEY BARTON,**
> *SACRED RHYTHMS*

yourself ruminating over the questions or personally journaling through the prompts after you read the weekly reflection and before you share them with your family.

Just come with an open spirit for a faithful conversation with the kids in your life. You know your children best, so choose which questions work best for their developmental ages and stages—ask one question, or ask them all. You can also put them into your own words, if you'd like. Even if your children are young, they might surprise you with the depth of their answers and additional questions. There's an opportunity to read a portion of Scripture together, too, but if you don't have the margin to do so, don't let that stop you from discussing the questions.

The questions are yours—fit them into a time that works best for your family. Talk about them on the way to school, around the dinner table, or before you say goodnight. This will look different depending on the season your family is in, but the purpose remains the same: for your family to grow in Christ and show up in the world with love.

If getting your kids to talk feels like pulling teeth, just get them to ask more questions! Spend any time with a preschooler, and you're bound to hear, "Why?" Spend any time with a teenager, and you're bound to hear, "Why not?" We can learn a lot from the curious nature of the youngest among us. In Jesus' parables, we see that the way He answered questions welcomed His disciples into a posture of learning. His sacred approach to curiosity shifted paradigms and broke up black-and-white thinking, inviting His followers into a more vibrant tapestry of life together.

As Dr. Traci Baxley says, "Our role as adults is to guide our children at all ages as they navigate their natural inquisitiveness and curiosity in ways that expand their knowledge and their love for others."[7] In journalism school, I quickly learned the five *w*s (and one *h*!) to fuel my questions:

Who?
What?
When?
Where?
Why?
How?

I discovered that if I was going to get a decent quote for an article, I needed to ditch all yes-or-no questions. Most of all, I needed to work on my listening skills—something I'm still, shall I say, refining. When we're willing to sit in the messy middle with our kids and resist the urge to tie up faith conversations with a bow, we permit our families to be in process.

Approach these open-ended questions and authentic conversations with nurture and nuance. You don't have to have all the answers—and if we're honest, many answers aren't ours to have. This is faith: holding on to the promise of what we cannot see, like constellations only revealed at the coordinates. Hebrews 11:1 reminds us that "faith shows the reality of what we hope for; it is the evidence of things we cannot see." My kids teach me more about the nature of God than many a theological treatise. The beauty of having a living God is that we have the Spirit to guide us, even when we feel alone in our parenting.

If your child is a processor by nature or is more introverted, they may prefer to write their answers in a notebook, and younger ones might like to draw a picture instead. Some children may need some time before they're ready to verbally process, so you may want to check back in after your time together. The questions you discuss will likely build upon one another and swirl around in their hearts and minds (and yours, too) long after your initial conversation.

PRAYER

Pray these weekly prayers together as a family. There are certainly times to pray *for* the children in your life, but the prayers nestled into these pages are meant to be shared. As Dietrich Bonhoeffer said, "It is in fact the most normal thing in the common Christian life to pray together."[8]

Each week, you'll find two prayer options. The first is more conversational and uses more straightforward language. It may connect better with younger readers. The second is longer and more poetic, and it may be a fit for older children. Pick what works for your family.

If you can, get into a rhythm each season. Read it on Monday morning as a commissioning before you head your separate ways or on Sunday evening before you go to bed. Pray the prayers together at mealtime. Maybe you can devote one weeknight meal to going through the questions and praying together. Perhaps you can set aside one evening to talk about the questions and pray together before bed. You may want to split the prompts and prayers into different days or times of the day. Give yourself (and your kids) grace when things don't go according to plan.

"Have we Christians forgotten the transforming value of a question? When we extinguish questions from our lives . . . we block ourselves from new truths and possibilities."

SUE MONK KIDD,
WHEN THE HEART WAITS

The words are crafted to connect you and your children to deeper communion with God. Mark them up. Cross out what doesn't fit. Add to them. These prayers are yours. Even if your family isn't used to reading prayers aloud, I believe you'll find great comfort in this time together. As you pray, I hope you're reminded in new ways that you're not alone. A great cloud of witnesses goes before you.

This Book Is Yours

This book is for you whether you grew up attending church or have barely stepped foot in a sanctuary. If you're simply curious to find out if faith holds any water so you can pass it on to your kids, this book is for you, too. It's for all of us—the faithful and the doubtful (though I'd say we're one and the same). This collection is for those who sense that, despite the deep inequities and injustices in our world, we sit under the stars of a loving God who doesn't leave us or forsake us, whose great mystery we may not understand but can feel in the cheek of a newborn or embrace of a child who is suddenly taller than we are.

I want to note here that God will not love you more or give your family an extra dollop of blessings if you read every week's reflection, work through every prompt, and pray every prayer with your child. God is so much more gracious than that. *The love already exists.* There's nothing you could do to remove the merciful, gracious love that flows from God. The work of Christ has already been done (see John 17:4).

Most parents I know (myself included) are exhausted. Excuse yourself right now from the pressure to use this book in a certain way. Pop in and out as you're able. If you miss a week—or a month—it doesn't mean you've failed. It means you're human. God made you human. Just take a breath and jump back in.

My prayer is that over the next year (and in the years to come), you will open your eyes to see in a new way where the divine has been present in every season of your life. I also pray that when you are reminded of that truth, the love of Christ will propel you to raise your family to do justice, love mercy, and walk humbly with your God (see Micah 6:8).

May what awaits you on the pages ahead be a guide for your journey through seasons of rest, renewal, growth, and new experiences.

A BLESSING AS YOU BEGIN

May what awaits you on these pages
be a guide for the changing seasons of
your faith and your family life.

May you experience the transformational love
of Christ in the seemingly ordinary moments.

May you move through parenting with intention
and imagination, presence and purpose.

May your family be filled with
holy curiosity, divine wonder, and sacred delight.

May your time of personal contemplation spur you on
to live out your faith in just, actionable ways.

May you release what is not yours to hold as God forms
your soul along with the souls of your family members.

May you grow spiritually alongside your children.

May you feel deep in your bones the glorious truth that
Christ dwells not only in you but also in your children
and in your neighbor, too.

May these words be an invitation into sacred rest for
your stretched-thin mind, heart, body, and soul.

And may all your life—your fantastic, dirty, messy, holy life—be a prayer.

Kayla Craig,
Ordinary Time, Fall 2023

FALL

Introduction

OUR HOUSE IS FLANKED by mighty maples that seem to shed their summer skin all at once, shaking off their leaves. Nearby oak trees scatter acorns in all directions. I fold school polos and look out the window, watching the trees' limbs sway in the autumn breeze. I marvel that just as our trees are in transition, so is our family, scattered in all directions in the fall months. I whisper a prayer as I gather backpacks, sharpen pencils, and coordinate schedules that have shifted with the seasons, balancing appointments, practices, work events, and school performances.

Our formerly green lawn is blanketed in fields of gold and red leaves. The ground that once welcomed bare feet and water balloon fights is now preparing for the first freeze. We box up summer sandals and replace them with sturdy sneakers, which will be exchanged for snow boots in a few short months. I send the kids out with rakes in hand, knowing that as soon as they make a pile, they'll be jumping in—scattering the leaves into the wind, riding off to their next adventure.

We lug pumpkins to our front steps, carving sloping grins to greet our neighbors. I light candles in the evening, a simple offering of autumnal warmth—a small way to bring light to the blanket of darkness that comes ever earlier. A pot of chili simmers on the stove, and a loaf of bread rises in the oven. All around my neighborhood, families of all shapes and sizes gather around weeknight dinner tables, sometimes lingering over homecooked meals and sometimes stopping by drive-thrus so they can pass the peace before soccer practice and school plays.

Fall invites us inward, beckoning us to notice God's peace and divine presence, not just around us but deep inside us too.

As you read these weekly reflections, I hope you can, as Morgan Harper Nichols so aptly writes, "turn to the sun rising above your head or the leaves of the deciduous trees falling to the ground and think, '*In the same way there is a rhythm to nature, I have rhythms too.*'"[1]

Throughout these selections, you'll find invitations to see the rhythms of your faith and your family life in a new way, drawing closer to the One who is making all things new, even in this transitional season. As you read, you'll be encouraged to throw open the windows and let the fresh autumn air fill your lungs so you can breathe in new possibilities deep within your soul. You'll also find invitations to explore the God-breathed longings you hold in your heart—and permission to sit in the darkness of mystery and untangle your deepest hauntings.

Throughout September, October, and November (a block of ordinary time in the liturgical calendar between Advent and Lent that invites us to reflect on the life of Christ), you'll find points of connection, beckoning you to listen to the One who breathes all seasons into existence. As you do, you'll embrace new ways of listening to and journeying with your children. You'll also find reflections connected to nature's seasonal changes, and to autumn's holidays and holy days.

In the months ahead, you'll be challenged to pursue peace in your parenting. And by the grace of God, you'll be comforted by Christ, who is ever present not just in your joys and celebrations but in your fears and failures too.

You'll be invited to create rhythms of gratitude within your family, and you'll be nudged to shed a scarcity mentality so you can stop your striving and rest in the arms of a loving God. As autumn wraps you in its embrace, you'll have opportunities to engage in creative hospitality and consider how Jesus defines abundance and blessing. The readings will welcome you to create spaces of belonging and encourage you to care for your soul as you look to the care and keeping of your children.

These devotions have been prayed over and pored over, but only you know what God might be whispering in your soul as you read and reflect. Release any pressure to read through everything in one day. You can set aside bits and pieces of your weekly schedule to contemplate the Christ-centered meditations, breath prayers, family discussion questions, and communal prayers.

Whether you're in the school pickup line or on your commute to work, take time to enter into personal contemplation before you invite your family to explore each week's questions and close your time in prayer. End your week by considering what action your family can take to be more present, faithful, and just in your home and your community.

May the honest words and hopeful prayers that follow welcome you and your family into rhythms of grace this fall.

A Prayer for Fall

O God, Creator of all seasons,
We thank You for the gift of fall's
    embrace.
Be near as our family embarks on
    autumn's adventures
And new ages and stages of life.

God, we breathe the crisp, fresh air
And ask You to guide us
In this ever-changing world.
Be our compass as winds change.
Direct us as we sit in the dusk
And marvel at Your mystery.

As twigs snap and leaves crunch
Under our weight,
We, too, give the weight
Of all we've been carrying
    to You,
For we know You care for us.

In the demands of domestic life,
Help us rest in You.
Soothe our discontent
And stoke the fires of our hearts
So we may be a soft place
For our children to return to
When the day grows dark.
May our children know now
And forevermore
That no matter what the day
    brings,

Our arms are always ready
    to embrace them
And welcome them home.

As the air around us grows cooler,
Help us to create dwelling places
That are warm and welcoming
So that our neighbors, as well as
    our children,
Will know that their presence is
    wanted.

As fall stretches out and blankets
    us in fields of gold,
Grow in us a sense of belonging
    in You, O Lord,
So that we might extend that
    warmth to others.
Help us be quick to listen—
    really listen—
To the children in our lives.

O God of harvest moons
And campfire tales,
O God of leaf piles for jumping
And apple cider for sipping,
O God of pumpkin pies with
    dollops of cream
And the swirl of steam that rises
    from
A cup of hot coffee in the cool
    morning,
Be near.

Let us hear You in the bird's song
As it hops from colorful leaf to
    colorful leaf,
Rustling a fiery blaze of motion
    in the trees
That stand rooted even as
    seasons change.
Help us to be a family that
    notices
The seemingly small
So we might be better attuned
To receive the big changes You
    have for us too.

O Christ who moved in
    empathy,
Move us in empathy too,

And clothe us in compassion
Like a warm and worn hand-me-
    down sweater
Pulled over our shoulders
And passed down over the years.

As the day grows darker earlier,
Help us get quiet
So that we might sit in the
    darkness
And dwell in the mystery
Of who You are.
Soothe our fears
And remind us that in every
Transitional moment
And time of change,
You are near.

Noticing

I'M PUSHING THE STROLLER around the corner when the podcast I'm streaming cuts out. I frown and glance at my phone. Out of battery. I've just promised my older kids thirty more minutes of park time with friends while I walk the nearby sidewalks. What am I supposed to do with no podcasts, music, or texting? I'm tempted to call them over and tell them it's time to go.

What will I do with thirty minutes of silence? With no one to listen to or talk with?

With a life full of loud children, I dream of silence often. But now that I'm forced to be in the silence and stillness of the day, I don't love it.

I take a breath and keep walking, determined to live up to the challenge. As I walk, my daughter giggles. I realize she's been giggling all along, but I was too distracted by my phone's speakers to notice the beautiful melody right in front of me. A few more minutes in, I start to hear the birds chirping as they keep watch from their perches in the canopy of trees overhead. The more I walk without manufactured noise, the more I notice: a symphony of hooting owls, the crunching of leaves, and creaking park swings.

My awakened senses bring me more into the present. With each step on the pavement, I add to the rhythm of the song that has been humming all along. As I walk, I ask God to help me awaken to what is happening right in front of me, to the beauty I've been too distracted to notice.

I feel the snap of the twigs as I push the stroller down the boulevard. I feel the embrace of the afternoon as little wisps of a cool breeze come and go. I breathe in the fresh air, the last vestiges of summer giving way to the beginnings of fall. A squirrel with a bushy plume of a tail gathers acorns, skittering across lawns, planning for the cooler days to come.

I look up to the two mighty oaks that line the boulevards and wonder when their leaves started to spin into golden hues. I eye the playground, where an elderly neighbor is picking up bits of trash and the neighborhood kids have joined in, making up a multigenerational litter brigade.

Would I have even noticed the ordinary grace right in front of me if I had planned ahead and charged my phone?

Our lives are loud. Even when we think we're clearing our minds, we often fill them with something else. Being awake to our lives feels almost unnatural. Disconnecting from technology so we can be present to where we are and who we're with isn't easy. Sometimes there are situations or emotions we'd prefer to escape or avoid. While I'm all for using technology in healthy ways, I'm aware of my propensity to scroll in an attempt to distract or numb myself, and then I'll tell my friends how I "just can't find space to think."

I often wonder what I'm missing out on—what we are collectively missing out on—when we default to zoning out on our phones. What delightful interactions pass us by in the waiting room because we're too engrossed in a Twitter thread? What glimpse of humanity do we miss because we're checking emails while waiting in line at the grocery store? As Morgan Harper Nichols writes, "After decades of an ever-increasing, ever-loudening pulse of mass communication, we have all been dealt the task of trying to navigate a global, growing machine that none of us ever asked for."[2] When my four children were young, my husband went out of town on a work trip. I was frazzled from parenting two toddlers, a preschooler, and an elementary schooler—by myself. I didn't have any energy to make dinner, so I ordered a pizza. I herded all the kids into the minivan (an Olympian feat) and finally made it to the pizzeria.

I unbuckled them, and with a toddler on each hip, I stood in line while my other children bounced around like they were in a pinball machine. When it was finally our turn to check out, I grabbed the diaper bag for my wallet. It . . . wasn't there. The thought of getting everyone back into the vehicle and doing this all over again felt like too high of a hill to climb. But the woman standing in line behind me was paying attention—not scrolling her phone—and generously offered to cover our bill.

Ordinary grace.

Jesus paid attention to people, often those who were unseen. When a woman in the crush of a large crowd touched the hem of His clothes, Jesus *knew*. He was awake to the place He was in and to the people around Him, along with their needs. He was paying attention.

Much ink has been spilled over our children's generation and the implications of so much technology at their fingertips. Navigating online spaces is complicated and overwhelming, to be sure. But I wonder how much starts with us as parents. We have to contend with our own habits and how our unhealthy patterns with technology form us—and our souls.

How can we hope to form the souls of our families when we're drinking from a firehose of information, entertainment, and connectivity twenty-four hours a day?

Andy Crouch, author of *The Tech-Wise Family*, writes, "We are made to live and learn in a physical world. And no human beings are more exuberantly and fundamentally rooted in the body than children. As children, our bodies are full of energy and primed for physical learning. We are designed to explore our world and learn through all our senses."[3] The youngest among us have much to teach us about paying attention. My six-year-old constantly stops on a walk, marveling at the shell of a fallen walnut or the wing of a butterfly.

With God's help, we can set our beeping and buzzing distractions aside, becoming like children as we awaken our senses to the glory that is unfurling all around us. When we partake in this holy work of noticing, we become aware of where we may extend ordinary grace—and where we're receiving, again and again, the grace that God lavishly pours into the nooks and crannies of our seemingly ordinary lives. We can pay attention to our inner worlds *and* to what's going on all around us. In this sacred noticing, we're given the ability to see not just the beauty springing up around us on a fall day but also the divine gift of seeing and serving Jesus in those often unseen.

In Matthew 25, Jesus tells His followers that people who consider themselves faithful will come to Him, but Jesus won't know them because they never noticed Him. He'll tell them, "I was hungry and you gave me nothing to eat, I was thirsty and you gave me nothing to drink, I was a stranger and you did not invite me in, I needed clothes and you did not clothe me, I was sick and in prison and you did not look after me" (Matthew 25:42-43, niv).

Jesus says that people will be taken aback: "What are you talking about? We never saw you and ignored you!" And Jesus will reply, "Truly I tell you, whatever you did not do for one of the least of these, you did not do for me" (Matthew 25:45, niv).

May we not get so busy that we miss Jesus in the people in front of us.

A practice I've been trying to incorporate to help me pay attention is praying the Examen, a reflection developed by Ignatius Loyola in the sixteenth century that has been used by the church for centuries (see appendix 2). As I prayerfully reflect on several questions each evening, I have an opportunity to examine and reflect on God's presence throughout the beautiful and challenging moments of my day.

When the lights are low and all the creatures of my home are asleep, I plug in my phone, silence it, and grab a book from my bedside table. When it's time to turn off the light, I begin to play back my day.

Where did I see God in the morning, afternoon, evening, and night?
What brought me joy?
What challenged me?
What disappointed me?

This prayer practice helps me stay rooted in the love of Christ that dwells within and around us (see Ephesians 3:17). When I pray the Examen, I look back and talk to God, not just recounting what happened or how I felt but also asking for help in exploring the deeper *why* within the contours of my day. Some people journal their Examen prayers, but I prefer the freedom of letting my mind wander through them.

When I pray this way, I feel like a child hashing out the day with a parent who is delighted to be in the presence of their beloved child. With the help of the Holy Spirit, I sometimes find myself convicted and other times comforted in this reflective examination of the soul.

I can tell when I've mainlined news and mindlessly doomscrolled, because I have a difficult time recalling the day. But no matter what my day was like, I am reminded of the presence of God with me through all of it—the joys, the sorrows, and all the mundane parts in between.

As theologian Wendy Wright says, "The fundamental art of the spiritual life is the art of paying attention. By this, I do not mean simply being aware of what is going on around you; I mean a contemplative attentiveness that is alive to both the outer and inner dimensions of life and especially alive to the deep ground of silence that undergirds all that is, an attentiveness that can discern, amid all the noise and confusion, the still, small voice of God."[4] In appendix 2 at the back of this book, you'll find a guide to help you and your family pray through the Examen. You can also revisit these reflective prayer prompts at the end of a season too.

SCRIPTURE
Matthew 9:20-22; Ephesians 3:17; Matthew 25

BREATH PRAYER

Inhale: Help me see You
Exhale: In and around me.

FAMILY DISCUSSION QUESTIONS

Read Matthew 25:31-46 together.

▸ What makes you feel most noticed? When did someone pay attention to you when you needed it?

▸ What distracts you from what's happening in the moment? What outside influences have been clamoring for your attention lately?

▸ When did you notice God's presence today?

▸ How did Jesus give us an example of paying attention?

▸ What happens when we don't pay attention to those around us who are hurting?

▸ What do you think Jesus meant when He said that what we do for the least of these we do for Him?

▸ Why do you think people spend so much time looking at their phones? How often do you look at a screen when you are waiting somewhere?

▸ What is one habit you can try to help you pay more attention to your life and the ways God shows up in it?

FAMILY PRAYER

younger

Dear God, we live in a noisy world. Distractions are all around us, and it feels like everything is shouting for our attention. We need your help to focus on what You have for us.

Help us to pay attention to the places we're in and the people around us, because what we do for the hurting, we do for You. Help us to pay attention to our feelings because our emotions have a lot to teach us.

Help us to get quiet so we can be noticers—in our family, our neighborhood, and our world. Amen.

older

O God of presence, we come to You and confess that we've been distracted, tangled up in our own thoughts and in the work of our own hands.

In a world that clamors for our attention, help us to be still so we remember that You are with us. In a world that is hurting and crying out, help us to notice so we may better love our neighbors. Release us from the grip of technology, and help us look up so we may truly live.

Jesus, thank You for leading us as we work to be a family of noticers. Amen.

PUT IT INTO PRACTICE

If you're feeling distracted or having a hard time turning off the noise, try a grounding exercise. This practice will help you become aware of your five senses. It can be used by kids and grown-ups alike. As you breathe in and out, naming what you're noticing, ask God to be with you in the moment.

Sit quietly. Take in your surroundings and use your senses to start noticing

5 things you can see (your hands, the sky, a potted plant)

4 things you can physically feel (your feet on the ground, a ball, your friend's hand)

3 things you can hear (the wind blowing, children's laughter, your breath)

2 things you can smell (fallen leaves, coffee, soap)

1 thing you can taste (a mint, gum, fresh air)

MAYO CLINIC,
"5, 4, 3, 2, 1: Countdown to Make Anxiety Blast Off"

Peace

THEY SCREAM WITH TEARS in their eyes as they wrestle and fight. "MO-OMMM!" they shout, beckoning me to referee yet another match of brother vs. brother.

I sigh and sit on their bedroom rug, motioning for them to take a seat next to me. Arms crossed and brows furrowed, two tearful, sweaty boys begrudgingly join me.

I look into Abram's eyes, the ones that hold the big blue waves. "Abram, the truest thing about you is that you are a beloved child of God."

I look into Asher's eyes, chocolate with a honey glaze. "Asher, the truest thing about you is that you are a beloved child of God."

"What is true for you is true for your brother," I say. "The words you said, the ways you chose to hurt and harm? Those aren't the truest things about you. And your brother's words, the ways he chose to hurt and harm? Those aren't the truest things about him, either."

I ask them to look into the eyes of their brother and affirm this truth: "The truest thing about you is that you are a beloved child of God."

All too often, we have spiritual amnesia. We're prone to forget who we are—and the One who calls us beloved. This leads us down paths far from the peace God holds out for us. Instead of being people who heal, we're overwhelmed by the violence of our world, clamoring over ourselves, choosing to harm ourselves and others.

How can we raise peacemakers when our own hearts are bruised and battered? If we want our children to choose paths of peace, we must also keep choosing these paths for ourselves.

To follow Jesus is to embark on a lifetime path of healing and wholeness. Jesus *is* peace. All His ways are peace. But this path is often at odds with a world that's not only saturated with violence but even celebrates conflict, aggression, and acts of war.

My sons can't walk down the toy aisle without being bombarded with violence. Plastic weapons meant for play come packaged in all shapes and sizes, marketed to the youngest among us. Plot lines of video games and movies glorify violence, forgoing creative problem-solving or collaboration when a gun, sword, or blaster will do. Children as young as toddlers are sold the lie that peace is weak or passive, that justice comes through vengeance.

But Jesus taught a different way.

Jesus gave us His teaching—and, indeed, His very life—so we can be free from vindictive violence. As theologian Miroslav Volf wrote, Jesus "broke the vicious cycle of violence by absorbing it, taking it upon himself."[5]

Thousands of years ago—long before Jesus broke into the world and ushered in a new understanding of peace—the prophet Isaiah foresaw a world brimming with peace that would be ushered in by the Messiah, one where violence wouldn't have the final say: "He will judge between the nations and will settle disputes for many peoples. They will beat their swords into plowshares and their spears into pruning hooks. Nation will not take up sword against nation, nor will they train for war anymore" (Isaiah 2:4, NIV). Other versions say, "Neither shall they learn war anymore" (ESV) or "They won't play war" (MSG). As people who worship a God who was violently killed, our hearts should not be calloused when it comes to violence.

We are our children's first teachers. At a young age, they'll learn peace—or violence—from us by watching how we navigate conflict and how we mediate our anger. Through the rhythms of life at home, they'll see if we lean toward reconciliation—or retaliation. They'll watch how we treat others and see how we advocate for a more just and peaceful world for everyone.

To raise children who pursue peace, consider that roaring fires start with a simple spark (see James 3:5). Peace isn't something we just teach but something we live out, by the grace of God.

Let the fragrance of peace linger like your favorite fall candle in your home. Bring your family into conversations about why you choose rhythms of peace at home, at work, and in your neighborhood. Ask them questions. Look to faithful leaders who have followed Jesus and advocated for peace, often at a great cost, such as abolitionists and civil rights advocates.

I often find a sense of peace sifting through used-book sales. While on a writing retreat, I stumbled upon a stack of vintage books for fifty cents apiece. My eyes fell on a small pamphlet about peacemaking from the 1980s that stopped me in my tracks. On the first page, it said, "Nurturing the spiritual potential of our children is also essential for developing peacemakers. Peacemaking calls for risk taking and suffering. Whether it is finding the courage to reconcile oneself with another person, or challenging a government policy or policy maker, peacemakers must pay a price. But so did Jesus!"[6] In our parenting, it's important to remember that Jesus went first, inviting us into a true and abundant peace that is so much bigger than false unity or passive peacekeeping. When we truly pursue peace, we come alongside the marginalized and oppressed, just like Jesus did. We call out the belovedness we see in others. We seek to heal where others intend to hurt or harm. And like Jesus, we don't bow to the whims of the empire, of those in power. We worship God—and God alone. We realize that our words and actions may ruffle feathers, but in our peacemaking, we don't resign ourselves to false unity, saying, "Peace, peace when there is no peace," as the prophet Jeremiah warned about (see Jeremiah 6:14; 8:11).

If parenting for peace feels overwhelming, take heart. We are not in this alone. Begin to pass on peace to your child by reminding them of their belovedness. Show them that they can choose to live a life that flows from the peace of Christ—that we love because He first loved us (see 1 John 4:19).

Our children are not too young to follow Jesus into ways of peace. They can create peace at the playground. Not only can they choose not to bully, but they can defend the one who is being hurt. Peacemaking isn't passive—it's an active stance. This kind of peace is fueled by Christ's power and passion, and it creates spaces where everyone's belovedness is honored. As contemplative writer, mother, and peacemaker Osheta Moore says, "Peace is fierce—it has to be, because violence and discord won't go down without a fight. Those who wield peace in the face of the world's violence do it fiercely."[7] The prophet Jeremiah was daunted by the life God had for him. Jeremiah felt like he was too young to enter the work that God invited him into. But here's what he sensed the Lord telling him: "Do not say, 'I am too young.' You must go to everyone I send you to and say whatever I command you. Do not be afraid of them, for I am with you and will rescue you" (Jeremiah 1:7-8, NIV). We can point even our youngest children away from the hurt hurled by the world and toward a God who heals.

I ended up finding a couple of quarters to purchase the little booklet. As I walked through the trees, I read, "We need to teach our children about a healing God, who loves and forgives unconditionally. Without self-esteem and compassion, our children will never become peacemakers—the people who are willing to work for change, reach out to the suffering, and take a stand against injustice."[8]

Our culture doesn't make it easy for followers of Jesus to resist the violent trappings of this world. In the United States, the months leading up to Election Day are full of rhetorical violence. Politicians hurl verbal assaults and vitriolic accusations. Violent words (and sometimes deeds) can run rampant among those who are charged with leading our nation. People who stoke fearful fires and political platforms that harm the vulnerable often garner millions of votes. It's overwhelming and disheartening.

If this behavior sounds antithetical to the gospel, that's because it is. But you can cast your ballot for peace. You can take heart that we do not parent as people without hope. Jesus offered a blessing for those who make peace, saying that "they will be called the children of God" (see Matthew 5:9). This is good news! We are set free from culture's claims that we need to be vengeful, powerful, and dominant—that we have to hurt one another with our actions or words. Instead, we can follow Jesus, who rebuked Peter after he attacked someone, thinking he was defending Jesus with his act of violence. But Jesus told him to put his sword away (see John 18:10-11).

It's easy to be like Peter, thinking we're fighting the good fight by taking vengeance (and violence) into our own hands. But while our intentions may come from a good place, our potential to harm someone else is not God's best for us or them. Jesus tells us to put our weapons (literal and figurative) down. This means we don't berate others on social media, even if we're convinced we're right. We don't speak violent words to our children or spouse. We advocate for victims of violence and oppression. We get involved in community advocacy and dismantle systems that harm others.

Instead of being combative toward each other, we can choose compassion. Instead of fighting with each other, we can choose communal flourishing.

We are not alone in this journey of peaceful parenting. Paul wrote these words to believers: "My sacred family members, let your hearts be glad. Mend your ways, walk side by side with each other, sharing the same purpose and living in harmony with one another. In this way, the Great Spirit who gives love and peace will walk with you on the road of life" (2 Corinthians 13:11, FNV).

May you and your family remember your belovedness so you may welcome the peace of Christ all the days of your lives, choosing to walk in God's good ways each day (see 1 Peter 3:11). May this way of seeking true peace cover all aspects of your life: your vocation, your work, your friendships, your neighboring, and your parenting. As Jeremiah cast in his vision long ago, may you seek the peace and welfare of the place you live (see Jeremiah 29:7).

PRAYING THROUGH
THE FALL

Fall is full of days that invite us to pray for peace.

INTERNATIONAL DAY OF PEACE:
On September 21, people around the world observe
a day to reorient their hearts to the way of peace,
lay down their weapons, and commit to working
toward the flourishing of all people.

FEAST DAY OF SAINT FRANCIS OF ASSISI:
On October 4, many Christians honor Saint
Francis, who devoted himself to a life of prayer
and intentional poverty. He cared deeply about
honoring God's creation and pursuing peace.

ELECTION DAY:
Consider spending time praying for peace during
your country's election day as well. In the United States,
Election Day is typically on the first Tuesday of November.

SCRIPTURE
Luke 15:1-7; Isaiah 2:4; Jeremiah 6:14; 8:11; Matthew 5:9

BREATH PRAYER

Inhale: Lord, make me
Exhale: An instrument of peace.

FAMILY DISCUSSION QUESTIONS

Read Matthew 5:9 together.

▸ What do you think it means to be a peacemaker? Who in your life is a peacemaker?

▸ Who are some historical figures that led the way in peacemaking? (If your family is having trouble thinking of someone, you might want to investigate Saint Francis, Martin Luther King Jr., or Dorothy Day.)

▸ Do you know someone who is a victim of war or violence? What have you learned from their stories?

▸ How can our family get more involved in speaking against violence in our community?

▸ What talents and abilities has God given you to use as you work toward peace?

▸ How did Jesus approach violence? Why do you think Jesus is called the Prince of Peace?

▸ What toys, games, movies, or TV shows have you seen instill a sense of violence? How should you respond when you're confronted with something like this?

▸ How does our family work through conflict? Why is forgiveness better than retaliation?

THE PEACE PRAYER
OF ST. FRANCIS

Lord, make me an instrument of your peace:
where there is hatred, let me sow love;
where there is injury, pardon;
where there is doubt, faith;
where there is despair, hope;
where there is darkness, light;
where there is sadness, joy.

O divine Master, grant that I may not so much seek
to be consoled as to console,
to be understood as to understand,
to be loved as to love.
For it is in giving that we receive,
it is in pardoning that we are pardoned,
and it is in dying that we are born to eternal life.
Amen.

FAMILY PRAYER

Jesus, we know You are called the Prince of Peace. But our world is often scary. It can be hard to feel peaceful, especially when we're angry or upset. Forgive us for the ways we've hurt one another.

Help us to be gentle like You are. Help us to forgive as You forgive. Help us to ask for forgiveness when we hurt a sibling or a friend. Give us the bravery to speak up for what's right and to help people who need it.

God, we know that true power doesn't come through violence; it comes from the peace of Jesus. Help us remember that. Amen.

O Prince of Peace, we come to You, for our hearts don't feel peaceful, and our world doesn't either. All around us, chaos swirls. We want to follow You, even in times of upheaval . . . especially then.

We seek the peace of Your Kingdom, and we ask You to help us be makers of peace too—in our community, our world, our family, and our hearts.

O Lord, we know we have confused passive peacekeeping with active peacemaking. We have sought a false peace that doesn't ruffle feathers and avoids conflict instead of the true peace that comes from being under the shelter of Your wings. Help our family to choose Your paths of peace and renounce the allure of what our world says will bring peace, like wealth, prosperity, and prestige.

May we be peacemakers, walking humbly with You, O Lord. Amen.[9]

PRAYING THROUGH MUSIC

As a family, listen to the song "Instrument of Peace" by The Porter's Gate. It's a new song with lyrics inspired by Saint Francis's ancient prayer. Reflect on the nature sounds at the beginning and the end. Discuss what it means to be an "instrument of peace."

Remember Your Vows

PARENTING, LIKE MARRIAGE, IS A COMMITMENT—a covenant between us and God, creation and Creator. I have the deep privilege of being a parent to two of my four children through adoption. Adoption is a broken, beautiful binding of family, forged through fire. There can be healing, but there's also deep heartache. It's a both/and, marked by loss and a separation of family, even as a new one is formed.

When a parent adopts a child, legal proceedings take place in court. Parents make a public, on-the-record commitment. Friends and family bear witness.

"I do."

"We will."

With right hands raised, they commit to journeying through life together. There is a before; there is an after. Life is never the same.

In Romans 8, we see adoption language (verse 15) and childbirth language (verse 22) to describe God's parental love for us. As someone who came to motherhood through both giving birth and adoption, I wonder what it would have been like if my husband and I had welcomed our newborns into our care with the same binding commitment as in adoption.

What if all new parents made vows to their children right from the start?

Let the record show, as God is my witness: We will do this together. I will show up for you. I am here to raise, guide, and love you. To honor you and protect you. I will do my broken best. Our stories have converged, and now we write a new book, moment by moment, day by day. No matter what, we are together. Today, tomorrow, for all the days to come, with Christ alongside me and before me, I will love you to the end.

As parents, we must remember our vows, over and over again. When our preschooler throws a tantrum in the middle of the grocery store or our teenager breaks curfew (and our trust). When we wake up in the middle of the night to rock a colicky baby or when our child says, "Just leave me alone."

Some Christian traditions dedicate little ones, and other denominations celebrate infant baptism. Either way, as one body of believers in Christ, we agree that parenting is sacred.

Even in the everyday moments, parenting is sacramental—it's an invitation for Christ to show up in a new way, in our real lives. We are given glimpses of the holy in the midst of our humanity—in the math homework at the dining room table, in the worn nursery rocking chair.

When I watch a baptism, I remember my own. I feel the Spirit breathing into my lungs, setting my heart ablaze with the reminder that I, too, am a beloved child of God. I am part of one family, united in Christ. When I watch a couple commit to each other in a marriage ceremony, I see a replay in my heart of the commitment I made to my husband to partner together in all of life's sorrows and celebrations.

When I see a bleary-eyed new mother holding a tiny baby in her arms, I remember the feeling of a soft newborn being placed on my chest. When I attend our friends' adoption ceremony, I remember the texture of the court bench beneath me, the documents I held in my shaky hands as I entered a new reality of motherhood.

Romans 8:14 says, "Those who are led by the Spirit of God are the children of God" (NIV). That means that God cares for us with a divine parental love that changes us from the inside out. "The grace-filled love of God, uniquely manifested in Jesus, gives us a new identity, purpose, and mission," writes Dominique Gilliard. "Through it, we become children of God, colaborers with Christ, and ambassadors of reconciliation."[10] Romans 8:17 says, "Since we are his children, we are his heirs. In fact, together with Christ we are heirs of God's glory. But if we are to share his glory, we must also share his suffering."

Every broken and beautiful moment in our parenting is a sacred invitation to remember our commitment to our children, to raise them in light of all that is true and just and beautiful in the woven-together family of God.

I do. I will. Even if. Even when.

May it be so.

SCRIPTURE
Romans 8:14-27

> Every broken and beautiful moment in our parenting is a sacred invitation to remember our commitment to our children, to raise them in light of all that is true and just and beautiful in the woven-together family of God.

BREATH PRAYER

Inhale: Spirit, lead me.
Exhale: I am Your child.

FAMILY DISCUSSION QUESTIONS

Read Romans 8:23-25 together.

▸ What does it mean to commit to something or someone?

▸ Why does God refer to us as children?

▸ When you know your identity, how does it affect the way you see yourself and other people?

▸ What was the last wedding, adoption ceremony, or baptism you attended? What stood out to you about the commitments that were made?

▸ When have you made a vow or a promise?

▸ Why is it important to remember our commitments to each other?

▸ What promises do we have as God's children?

FAMILY PRAYER

younger

God, You call us Your children. You love us with a big, deep love that doesn't give up or go away.

Thank You for giving us Your Spirit to guide us. Help us to remember our love for You as we love one another. Amen.

older

God of heaven and earth, we thank You for the ways You pursue us, for the ways You beckon us into Your loving arms and call us Your children.

Strengthen our commitments to You and to each other, especially in the moments when we groan under the weight of the world. You are our Sustainer and our Father. Help us live in the light of Your love. Amen.

REFLECTION 4

Listening

IN MIDDLE SCHOOL, I lived in the suburbs of Saint Paul, Minnesota. This was a thrilling place to be a thirteen-year-old girl in the early aughts—the Mall of America was practically next door. Every weekend, I'd beg my parents to bring my friends and me to our dream hangout location, where we'd inevitably land in the food court after a long day of browsing trendy tanks and tees we couldn't afford, giggling as we picked Auntie Anne's pretzel pieces from our braces.

As an adult, I have worked to unlearn the liturgy of consumerism, but as a tween, I was formed by mall culture—especially for back-to-school shopping. What I didn't realize while my dad was testing massage chairs at Brookstone was that perhaps bringing four middle-school girls to a sprawling, sensory-overloading shopping center—and staying there to provide occasional safety check-ins—was not his primary idea of a fun Friday night. It did not occur to me that my mom might not have desired to see boy bands perform in the mall atrium as much as I did.

I look back and realize that my parents made intentional choices to invest in spending time with me. I can only imagine the conversations my parents listened to as they navigated the minivan back and forth from the mall so many weekends in a row. They seemed so old then; now I realize they were the age I am now.

My mom laughs these days about how my father had difficulty wrapping his head around the middle-school "frenemy" drama that encircled my life. A friend who made me cry on Monday would likely invite me over for a pizza party on Friday. Another girl I vowed to never speak to again was soon the recipient of the other half of my BFF heart necklace.

"Wait, she's friends with Ashley now? Why would she want to go to her house? I thought Ashley was mean to her!"

He was listening.

Listening shape-shifts throughout parenting seasons. We learn to interpret what our newborn's different cries mean, translate our toddler's garbled requests that no one else can understand, and decipher our teen's eye rolls and door slams.

Listening—honest, humble, heartfelt listening—is a pivotal discipline. It plays a part in staying connected to our children—and staying connected to God, too.

"Just as we have to choose to hear what our children are truly saying, so we have to choose to hear those quiet whispers of divine love and guidance," Gary Thomas says. "The great challenge, of course, is that listening to our children and our God can be difficult. Sometimes we misunderstand our children, and sometimes we will mistake our own fears for the voice of God. But the fact that we aren't perfect hearers provides no excuse to throw out the discipline of listening."[11]

Maybe you're thinking the same thing I've wondered: *How do I get quiet enough to listen to God in the cacophony of my actual life? I'm a parent!*

Listening to God comes in many ways. Just as our natural seasons change, so do the ways we hear God. Of course, there is value in quieting ourselves in prayer and turning to Scripture, but maybe our extraordinary God is in the soundtrack of our ordinary lives too—the giggle of a daughter as she pops iridescent bubbles one by one, the triumphant shout of a son as he cheers on his teammates from the bench.

Maybe, when you're paying attention, you'll hear God in the fallen leaves crunching under your sneakers as you bring in groceries, or you'll catch a divine whisper in the *whoosh* of a cool wind bringing with it an autumn chill. And you'll become awake to the symphony of love surrounding you in the soft snore of a baby, the deep exhale of the school bus brakes letting you know the kids are home.

You'll listen to creation point back to the Creator in the crackle and pop of an autumn bonfire, the pitter-patter of rain hitting your roof, a chorus of geese honking and hollering as they get in formation to fly south. You'll hear the holy chatter of a squirrel, the drip of the first cup of coffee, the hiss of the tea kettle, and the thump and thrum of the heater kicking on for the first time.

When you practice a posture of listening to God in your daily comings and goings, what you hear might surprise you. God's still small voice (see 1 Kings 19:11-13) might not sound like what you expected—and may be exactly what you need.

And just as incredible, God listens to us too (see 1 John 5:14). Just like a caring, connected parent does.

SCRIPTURE
1 Kings 19:11-13; 1 John 5:14

BREATH PRAYER

Inhale: O God, help me hear
Exhale: Your still, small voice.

FAMILY DISCUSSION QUESTIONS

Read 1 Kings 19:11-13 together.

- ▸ What does God sound like?

- ▸ What would it look like to listen to God this week?

- ▸ What does it feel like if someone doesn't listen to you?

- ▸ Can you think of a time when you felt heard?

- ▸ How could you be a more active listener at work, at home, or at school?

- ▸ What distracts you from hearing God in your everyday life?

- ▸ How does it feel to know that God always hears your prayers?

- ▸ How could you widen your definition of what it means to hear God?

FAMILY PRAYER

younger

God of whispers and shouts, You are here in the quiet times and the loud times.

Help us to know that You are with us not just at church but also in our home, our neighborhood, and where we go to school.

Help us to show love to our friends and family through our listening. And help us to hear what You're whispering into our hearts too. Amen.

older

God of divine whispers, help us to hear You in the seemingly ordinary moments of our lives.

Open our hearts so we might hear You in the cry of a baby, the start of an ignition, the rustle of leaves. Help us to pay attention so we might love—and live—more fully.

May our listening be an honest, humble, heartfelt offering to all the human hearts You've given us to love. Amen.

SPIRITUAL LISTENING

Spiritual listening means moving beyond
what we physically hear, asking the Holy Spirit
to speak deep into our souls in a way that moves
beyond words or physical ability. We all have
access to hear God, whether or not we're
part of the hearing community.

Belonging

"JUST SEE IF YOU CAN MAKE ONE FRIEND," my mom tells me as I climb out of the car, backpack on, gazing at an unfamiliar school. "I know you can."

I take a deep breath and look at my new shoes. Entering middle school is a challenging time for anyone, let alone a student new to town, new to the whole state.

Questions fill my mind: *Will I forget my locker combination? Will I get lost trying to find my classes? Will I have enough time for a bathroom break?*

A second set of questions looms underneath: *Does everyone already know each other? Will I have anyone to sit with at lunch? Does one person even want to be my friend?*

I clutch the schedule my parents printed for me at home. I walk through the giant glass doors.

Inhale, exhale.

Let's go.

At the core of the worries we carry, both for ourselves and on behalf of our children, is the desire to belong.

Do I matter? Do they matter? Does anyone see us—really see us?

To be human is to know and be known. God, our Maker, understands our deep desire for belonging.

We see this in the way Jesus treated people on the margins of society: the poor, the young, the disenfranchised, and the unpopular. Jesus saw people—truly saw them.

He saw Zacchaeus, a man with a lot of money but not many friends. His profession as a tax collector was a despised one in his culture. Tax collectors took money from the people to support an oppressive empire, and it wasn't uncommon for collectors to skim off the top and take extra for themselves, too.

Yet Jesus made space for Zacchaeus. This was an unpopular man in a sea of faces, but Jesus knew him. He knew the inner struggles that were covered by bravado, and He saw who Zacchaeus really was—who he could really be, beyond the work identity he had assumed.

With Zacchaeus, Jesus extended an invitation into belonging. Of all the people in the crowd, Jesus chose to spend time with the short, unliked man who had climbed a tree to try to get a better view.

Jesus, who likely had never met Zacchaeus before, called him by name:

When Jesus got to the tree, he looked up and said, "Zacchaeus, hurry down. Today is my day to be a guest in your home." Zacchaeus scrambled out of the tree, hardly believing his good luck, delighted to take Jesus home with him. Everyone who saw the incident was indignant and grumped, "What business does he have getting cozy with this crook?"

LUKE 19:5-7, MSG

Jesus sees us. Jesus knows us. Jesus creates space. In Jesus, we have radical belonging.

If we dream of our children finding belonging beyond success or social status, we must shake off the dust and not find our identity in those qualifiers ourselves. When we embrace the promise that, in Christ, we are cherished and cared for, we can parent in ways that create safe, loving spaces for our children so they can believe that they belong too.

Belonging is not just a feel-good sentiment. It's a *need*. Dr. Traci Baxley, a mother of five and a professor of education who has spent thirty years teaching on belonging, says, "All children need to belong. When they don't feel this sense of belonging, it impacts the way they see themselves and their place in the world."[12] When we are secure in our attachment to God and believe deep in our bones that we belong, we can create rhythms and routines that remind our children they're beloved members of our family unit—and God's family too. Though the world's seas may toss them, they are safe. They already belong. And those who belong invite others into belonging.

Dr. Baxley made this finding: "When we create safe places of belonging in our home, our children will grow up to create spaces of belonging in the world. It is up to us to guide them so that standing up for others and speaking out against inequity are simply viewed as normal behavior—this is just *what we do*."[13] I did make one friend on that first day of school—likely an answer to my mom's many prayers. I shared a homeroom (and, it turned out, a whole schedule) with a girl named Aubrey, who tucked me under her wing and created a space of belonging. She didn't think about it; she just did it. We tried (and retried) our locker combinations together. Her friends were my friends at lunch. She saw me, learned my name, and offered me belonging. It made all the difference.

When Belonging called Zacchaeus's name, Zacchaeus was forever changed into a more compassionate and generous person. He was moved to give half of all he had to those who needed it, committing to honesty in his future work. *Belonging begets belonging.*

When our kids know what it means to belong, they live in a manner worthy of their calling (see Ephesians 4:1). They see those who aren't always seen. They advocate for and with the marginalized. They live into rhythms of generosity.

SCRIPTURE
Luke 19:1-10; 1 Corinthians 3:23; Ephesians 4:1

BREATH PRAYER

Inhale: In Christ,
Exhale: I belong.

FAMILY DISCUSSION QUESTIONS

Read Luke 19:1-10 together.

▸ How did Jesus offer belonging to Zacchaeus? What did Jesus risk when He decided to hang out with Zacchaeus?

▸ What does it mean to belong to Jesus?

▸ Where do you most feel like you belong?

▸ When have you felt like you didn't belong? How did that make you feel?

▸ How can grown-ups help kids feel like they belong?

▸ How can you make other people feel like they belong at your school? In our neighborhood?

▸ What risk do you take by sharing belonging with someone? What would you risk by sitting next to someone who's lonely at school?

FAMILY PRAYER

younger

Jesus, we belong in You.

You know our names. You can spot us in a crowd. When we're feeling lonely or like we don't belong, help us to remember that You care.

Help us to see others who feel different, alone, or left out, and help us to make space for them.

Help us to share belonging with others wherever we go this week. In You, Jesus, we are safe. Amen.

older

O Christ who knows our names, You draw us into a circle of belonging. In You, we are known and held.

Help us to form our identity not in what we do or what we have but in who we are as Your beloved. In the moments when we feel misunderstood, may we remember that You came to earth and made Yourself human.

In moments when we feel isolated or lonely, may we remember that You make spaces where we are wanted and loved. In moments when we feel excluded, may we remember that our belonging lies in You.

May we embrace our belonging so that we may extend it to others. Forgive us for the times we haven't shared this warmth with someone who needed it. Through Your Spirit, empower us to live in a way that shows others they truly belong.

You draw us into a circle of belonging. In You, we are known and held.

Just Checking

THE FIRST TIME I DROP HIM OFF at preschool, I peek inside his classroom from a picture window in the hall. He's sheepish as he makes his way to the blocks. He looks around and catches my eye. I blink back tears and, unsure what to do, give him a thumbs-up. Dimples appear on his round face as he flashes a grin, confidence filling his steps as he collects an armful of primary-colored blocks from the bin and begins to play with a little girl in pigtails.

A few years later, at the end-of-the-year elementary concert, he scans the crowd. He takes his place onstage and spots me. I give him a thumbs-up, a reminder that I'm here. I see his shoulders loosen, and he shares that same dimpled smile. Years inch forward and his cheeks get less round, but the wordless check-ins still happen—on the ball field, at the arcade for a friend's birthday party, at the fifth-grade science night.

My silly thumbs-up gesture whispers, *I'm here. I see you. I believe in you. You're doing great.*

He is now in a new season of life: middle school. Through his ages and stages, we continue to share tiny moments (more discreetly now) from afar.

Our check-ins may adapt and evolve, but the intentional connection points still punctuate our days. They're threads connecting us, parent to child, child to parent. All kids need connection points with safe, loving people. As parents, it's our honor, privilege, and joy to be that for our families.

One of my sons prefers sending me ridiculous emojis and funny messages from his tablet. *I see you.* Another's hand finds mine as the sky turns to dusk and we put away the last of the dinner dishes. *I believe in you.* My daughter, who is disabled and doesn't speak, brings her hand to my cheek. *You're doing great.*

These tiny moments of seeing and being seen are the ties that bind us together. As parents, we often feel pressure to perform on the big occasions and milestones, with lavish holiday celebrations or picture-perfect vacations. But relationship is sewn together in the tiny moments: the wave at the school pickup line, the unexpected hug in the kitchen, the nod before leaving with friends.

Just as we make space for these moments with our children in the bits and pieces of our real life, God makes space for us too. This is prayer: check-ins from child to Parent, connecting in the comings and goings of our lives.

It's easy to overcomplicate prayer. We often assume that prayer has to be done in large blocks of uninterrupted time, with just the right words, surrounded by candles and a Pinterest-worthy setting. But for most of us, especially during the busy years of parenting, the truth is that our prayers may often be small offerings given and received throughout the day.

In his wise and welcoming book *Learning to Pray*, James Martin writes that there is always a "lifting" in our prayers: "We lift our cares to the One who helps us," he says. "We lift our praise to the One who blesses us. We lift our very selves to the One who created us. We lift ourselves up to God."[14]

As a child checks in with a parent, I offer my messy, imperfect, slightly chaotic life to the One who knows my name. This usually takes the form of silent, short prayers.

In the morning, as I reach for my glasses (and before I reach for my phone): *This is the day the Lord has made; I will rejoice and be glad in it.*

In the afternoon, as I pick up discarded gym socks and run the washing machine: *God, be with me as I work.*

As I fill the gas tank with climbing prices: *Thank You for this privilege. Help me to share what I have.*

As I end up in the long line (again) at the grocery store: *Give me eyes to see You in the people around me.*

As I check my inbox and realize I missed a work deadline: *Jesus, help me remember I'm more than what I do.*

As I doomscroll while I sit in the waiting room, as I laugh, as I cry: *Be near.*

Our short, straightforward offerings amid our ordinary lives are check-ins with the One who calls us beloved children. Anne Lamott says her prayers boil down to three simple words: *help, thanks,* and *wow.*[15] Our seemingly simple check-in prayers fit the contours of our lives: begging for help, giving thanks, and embracing awe.

What a grace that God cares about the tiny parts of our days because God cares about the tiny parts that make up us. And what a grace that God not only hears but *listens*. "Prayer means that, in some

Prayer is a check-in from child to Parent, connecting in the comings and goings of our lives.

unique way, we believe we're invited into a relationship with someone who hears us when we speak in silence," Anne Lamott says.[16]

Just as you ache for your children to be able to bring their deepest aches to you, God wants to hear your concerns. God cares for you like a compassionate, caring parent who longs to lavish the deepest affection on their children. In 1 Peter 5:7, we're reminded that no worry or anxiety is too small (or too big) to share with the One who keeps careful watch over us.

As we check in with those we love, we secure our bonds and tighten our attachments. Martin writes, "The same practices that make for a good relationship with other people make for a good relationship with God."[17]

A friend is over when my phone buzzes.

"Grab it!" she says, refilling our kids' bowl of popcorn.

"Hey, Dad," I say, cradling the phone on my shoulder. I pull open the sliding door to the deck, and we chat for a few minutes, catching up on work drama and family news. I watch the first autumn leaves fall from their branches in the backyard.

Then I hear a child scream. My dad hears it too and laughs. I smile and tell him I'd better go, breathing in the fresh early fall air before sliding back inside.

"Is everything okay?" my friend asks.

"What?" I ask, popping a few kernels of the kids' afternoon snack into my mouth. "Oh, yeah, he just called to talk."

"Does he do that a lot?" she says.

"I guess so, yeah." I chuckle with a mouthful of popcorn.

"Wow," she responds. "He calls like that? Just to check in? That's pretty special. He must love you a lot."

Maybe we never grow out of needing those check-ins.

I see you. I believe in you. You're doing great.

SCRIPTURE

1 Peter 5:7; 1 John 5:14; 1 Thessalonians 5:16-18

BREATH PRAYER

Inhale: O God, You hear
Exhale: My every worry, my every prayer.

FAMILY DISCUSSION QUESTIONS

Read 1 Thessalonians 5:16-18 together.

▸ How do you stay connected with someone you love?

▸ Why is it important to check in with one another? What's at stake if we don't check in?

▸ When was the last time someone checked in on you, just because?

▸ Who could you check in on this week?

▸ How do we check in with each other as an immediate family and with extended family (family dinner, group texts, phone calls, letters, etc.)?

▸ What do you think of tiny prayers like *Help*, *Thanks*, and *Wow*?

▸ Is there one right way to pray? What are some surprising things you've discovered about prayer?

FAMILY PRAYER

younger

O God, You love to hear from us.

Help us to remember there's no perfect way to pray.

Thank You that we can pray silently or aloud. Thank You that we can pray whenever we want, wherever we are. Thank You for loving us with the biggest, widest, deepest love.

We feel safe when we remember that You watch over us and love us. Amen.

older

O God of connection, we thank You for Your deep care.

Forgive us for the ways we've gotten distracted and forgotten to check in with those we love—and with You, Lord. Thank You for hearing us even in our silence.

Help us to communicate love and compassion to all who cross our path. Amen.

Golden Hour

A TODDLER CLINGS TO my leg as I kneel at the last minute to change his sister's diaper. I hold a safety pin in my mouth (why didn't I remember that this dress doesn't fit quite right?) and grab the wipes as my older son protests the evening plans.

"I don't want to wear this scratchy shirt! I don't want to take family pictures!" he bellows from upstairs, where I've painstakingly laid out some clothes that aren't athletic gear on his bed. "And how am I supposed to wear these shoes? They squish my toes!"

I wipe the sweat off my brow, sure that the makeup I just tried to apply nicely has melted completely. I glance at the couch, where kid number four is playing a handheld video game and still hasn't combed his hair.

I inhale and step on a Lego.

"We're leaving in five minutes!" I shout into the domestic chaos surrounding me as I stand up, picking the lint off my dress. My husband, who has changed into a button-up shirt and real pants, chases a child decked out in only underwear. I glance at the front window, where the high afternoon sun is shedding the last of its brilliance, pouring rays against the tree, whose leaves have turned to amber.

Somewhere inside the house, a child screams.

I sling my camera bag over my shoulder and balance my daughter on my hip. I glance in the mirror and immediately regret it. I pat down my hair and repeat the mantra I've been saying all day: "One good picture."

If we get out of the house soon, we can make it to the trail in time for the golden hour, when a warm glow covers the earth, tucking a warm blanket over us, leaving little halos over our heads.

The leaves are turning from green to brown to gold. It's an unseasonably warm day, and when I walked the dog in the morning, I spied the perfect alcove of trees that had suddenly come alive in autumn hues. I borrowed a tripod from a friend and figured I knew enough about photography to set a timer and get *one good picture*. If everyone could just look at the camera. If everyone could smile at the same time. Just once.

We finally make it out of the front door. We're huffing and puffing, but we make it.

I check my watch. We'll have to make up some time on our walk along the trail. Jonny pushes the stroller. I hobble in my heels, pulling a wagon.

"I know none of you like taking photos." I sigh as we trek up the trail's incline. "That's why we're not doing a full professional session. We're just trying to take one good picture. One picture—can we do that?"

A child whines. Another pushes his brother.

Is it so wrong to want a Christmas card photo? To want a moment in time captured when I'm wearing real clothes and there isn't crusted oatmeal in my hair?

It shouldn't surprise you that my family portrait attempts resulted in complete chaos. I couldn't get the focus right. My daughter wouldn't look at the camera. We stirred up a spider that was residing in some of the fallen leaves. The light had already started to fade. Children were arguing.

I knew it was bad when a neighbor we'd never met came through her back door. "I can take a photo for you," she shouted across the trail.

How much chaos had she already witnessed?

"Oh, we're fine," I shouted over two wrestling children, one whining child, and one whimpering child.

Dear reader, we were not fine.

The warmth of the fall afternoon had turned into an evening chill. Our smiles were forced and frozen. I scrolled through the photo preview on the back of my camera.

Dark. Blinking eyes. Overexposed. Distracted by a bird. Not smiling.

The one photo where everyone was cooperating and smiling was out of focus. User error. My error. It was time to call it.

"Let's go home," I told my husband through gritted teeth.

One thing, I fumed, pushing the stroller home as leaves crunched under the weight of my fury. A spike of my high heel caught in the dip of the sidewalk, and my ankle wobbled. *I just wanted one nice thing.*

We arrived at our front door.

"Give me the keys," I told my husband, my voice eerily calm. I can't confirm this, but I'm pretty sure there was steam billowing from my ears.

"Everybody, let's go inside!" he said quickly, herding the kids to protect them from my impending wrath.

One child stopped whining about too-tight shoes long enough to ask, "Where's Mommy going?"

"Mom! Mom! Mom! Can I come?" another child piped up. "I want to come with you!"

I clenched my jaw and moved full steam ahead toward the minivan. I climbed into the driver's seat and slammed the door, hands shaking as I grabbed the steering wheel.

A friend further in her parenting journey once told me, "Sad looks like mad." I was very mad.

I had never dramatically left my family in the dust before, and I didn't have anywhere to go, so I pressed my high heel on the gas and went to the only place I could think of: the McDonald's drive-thru.

Why doesn't anything ever work out? Why can't we be a typical family like I see online, full of smiling faces? Why can't I make things work? Why is my house a mess? Why am I such a hot mess? Why am I such a bad mother? Why can't I have one nice thing?

I pulled up to the window, where a teenager was ready to hand me my one-dollar giant Diet Coke.

"How are you?" she asked as she returned my debit card.

I started crying.

"Good," I told her in between sobs, blowing my nose into a napkin.

As parents, we put so much pressure on ourselves. There are messages all around us that say, *Look like this; act like this.* We feel like we're the only ones struggling under the weight of all the spiritual, mental, physical, and emotional pressure. But who has it all together?

No one.

My failed attempt at a fall family photo was years ago, but I remember it like it was yesterday. My anger that night was a Band-Aid for other wounds I carried—sadness, overwhelm, loneliness, frustration, shame.

Recently, my husband flipped open his laptop. His wallpaper photo took my breath away. Shadows of two little boys are throwing not-quite-in-focus fistfuls of autumn leaves. Their profiles dance in front of a sunset, where deep oranges and pinks blend into bold purples and blues. The kids are smaller than I remembered, their faces rounder, their hands softer.

I'd forgotten that I grabbed the camera from the tripod and snapped that photo before admitting failure and heading home.

"I was going through an old flash drive and found these," Jonny said. "I loved this one so much I had to save it. Doesn't it look kind of magical?"

The night after the Family Photos of Doom, I'd uploaded hundreds of captures, looking for one that was salvageable. I didn't remember there being much of anything worth saving. I was so focused on chasing the golden hour that I hadn't paid attention to God's glory surrounding us in the form of a sunset, in the magic of little boys laughing and throwing fistfuls of crunchy leaves into the clear sky.

"Glory be to God for dappled things," poet Gerard Manley Hopkins wrote, "for skies of couple-colour as a brinded cow."[18]

When you're looking back, everything feels more in focus (and more glorious). I was parenting four kids under the age of seven. One was going through a significant medical diagnosis. I had just started a new position working from home. My husband was under a lot of pressure in his ministry.

I was hoping for a family photo because I wanted something nice, but underneath that was the desire for a memory I could hold in my hands—one I could return to when the world grew cold to remember the love shared between us.

We were all young, doing our best, figuring it out together. That's clearer to me now.

Much of parenting is a blur. We ache to see with clarity God's beauty in front of us but often see through a glass darkly (see 1 Corinthians 13:12). At the time, I was so intent on capturing memories in a certain way that I missed the sacred space of what *was*. Yes, God is with us in the golden hour—and in the swirls of the sunset too. (How often we look for the new mercies of the morning only to forget that Christ is with us in the darkest of nights as well!)

Every once in a while, we're given the gift of clarity. Of seeing the story behind the photo, the glory behind the story. We see glimpses of this truth: that every gift is from God, through God, and for God (see Romans 11:36). We're reminded that God has been there all along, speaking love into whining children, frazzled parents, and dappled sunsets.

After I drove around sipping my soda for a while, I returned to a quiet house. The lights were dim. My husband had put everyone to bed by himself—no small feat. I walked through the door, over a wayward Hot Wheels car, and into his welcoming arms.

"To be part of a family is to enter into the fullness of human life," writes Wendy Wright. "To find God present in all things is the thrust of the adventure. To explore the human face of love in family is to probe the contours of divine love itself."[19]

I don't remember what photo we printed on our Christmas cards that year. But I know that in the blur of family life, Love was there too.

SCRIPTURE
1 Corinthians 13:12; Romans 11:36

> How often we look for the new mercies of the morning only to forget that Christ is with us in the darkest of nights as well!

BREATH PRAYER

Inhale: O God, I am not alone.
Exhale: You've been there all along.

FAMILY DISCUSSION QUESTIONS

Read 1 Corinthians 13:12 together.

▶ When is a time your expectations weren't met? What did you learn from that?

▶ When have you been so focused on wanting something that you were distracted from the special things happening around you?

▶ Sometimes, the way we view a situation changes when we look back on it later. Tell about a time that happened to you. What changed?

▶ Where are some unexpected places you've encountered God lately?

▶ What does it mean to "see through a glass darkly"?

▶ When do you find it challenging to see God at work around you?

▶ Why is it so difficult to see God in our lives when we're feeling disappointed or upset?

FAMILY PRAYER

younger

God, You are the Maker of all things. We know everything beautiful and true comes from You alone.

When we're disappointed or upset, You welcome us to come to You. Thank You for being with us in the bright mornings and the dark nights.

Help our lives reflect Your light at all times, Jesus. Amen.

older

O God, all good things are in You, from You, and for You. We confess that we get so distracted by what could be that we miss out on what is. In our work and worship, we see through a glass darkly.

Help us to lay down our expectations so we can experience Your reflection in both the brightest mornings and the darkest nights. Amen.

Living the Mystery

ON AN EARLY SEPTEMBER MORNING, with the skies still deep in their slumber, my friend Jennie pulled into my driveway. I kissed my snoring husband on the forehead, tiptoed through the kitchen as I checked into my flight on my phone, and wheeled my suitcase outside. School was back in session, and I was heading to a writing conference. The fall air was thick with an early morning fog.

The mark of a good friend is someone who drives you to the airport. The mark of a best friend is someone who wakes up early and drives forty-five minutes of winding back roads to get you to the airport on time.

It was too early for conversation, so we were quiet during the drive, the two-lane road bending and shifting as the car carried us forward. Haze hung thick in the air, and the back roads seemed even quieter than usual. The far-stretching fields turned from green to gold. We could see only a slight stretch ahead of us.

The morning mist held a sense of mystery, inviting my mind to wander. *Will my kids be okay while I'm gone? Is it selfish to travel for work?* My unspoken anxieties hung in the autumn air as we continued on the sleepy roads. I wanted to see further ahead, to know everything was going to be okay.

No matter how much we want to see what will be, we live surrounded by mystery. We don't know what tomorrow will bring—we are but a vapor, our lives a mist (see James 4:14).

I wonder what it would be like if followers of Christ were known for our willingness to embrace the mystery rather than claiming to have always clear and concise answers. Because the truth is: a life of faith is mysterious.

"People who've had any genuine spiritual experience always know they *don't know.* They are utterly humbled before mystery," writes Father Richard Rohr. "They are in awe before the abyss of it all, in wonder at eternity and depth, and a Love, which is incomprehensible to the mind."²⁰ We believe in a God who breathed entire galaxies into existence and who, in love, sculpted us out of dust. We believe that this very same God, who is made up of three parts, left the heavens and broke into our world in the form of a human infant, born among the dirt. We believe that we're given the gift of God's very Spirit to dwell within us.

We live in mystery, believing there is truth in a swirl of now and not yet.

"Can you fathom the mysteries of God? Can you probe the limits of the Almighty?" (Job 11:7, NIV). It's a tale as old as time—we cannot fathom it. But we try. It's human nature to explain things away. To turn on the floodlights as we drive and say, "See, we know what's coming next." But we cannot escape the mystery of this life—and the mystery of the One who holds this life together.

Paul wrote in his letter to Timothy, "This Christian life is a great mystery, far exceeding our understanding" (1 Timothy 3:16, MSG). We don't have all the answers about the nature of suffering, the mystery of God, or even our own spiritual journey. We can't always answer our children's questions either.

I encourage parents to embrace a single word when it comes to these tough questions: mystery. "To say to children, 'We believe in mystery,' is a powerful thing," writes Traci Smith in her book *Faithful Families*. "It's important not to use mystery lightly with children. To teach mystery is to embrace the truth that we don't know everything, rather than run from it."²¹ But while we live in a vapor, we can trust that in the twists and turns of our journey, Christ is there.

Paul went on to write that, even in the mystery, "some things are clear enough. He appeared in a human body, was proved right by the invisible Spirit, was seen by angels. He was proclaimed among all kinds of peoples, believed in all over the world, taken up into heavenly glory" (1 Timothy 3:16).

This is what we hold on to—the mysterious truth that is *clear enough*. In our wondering minds and wandering spirits, we believe beyond what we can see, trusting that Christ will light our way just enough to keep going forward, even in the haze of the unknown.

The Spirit of God works like a mist rising up from the earth, surrounding us and filling our lungs. The psalmist wrote that "deep calls to deep" (Psalm 42:7, NIV). The vastness of our need can be met only with the deeper vastness of a God who covers us, shaping and forming our very souls.

We live in mystery, believing there is truth in a swirl of now and not yet.

"Perhaps one of the most basic things we need to understand about spiritual transformation is that it is full of mystery," Ruth Haley Barton writes. "We can be open to it, but we can't accomplish it for ourselves."[22]

Eventually, our drive through the dense fog ended. My friend pulled up to the departure line at the airport, and I opened the car door, the thick fog blanketing me.

Frederick Buechner said, "You do not solve the mystery, you live the mystery."[23] I didn't know what the future held, but at that moment, I knew that God held me.

SCRIPTURE
Psalm 42:7; 1 Timothy 3:16; Job 11:17; James 4:14

BREATH PRAYER

Inhale: This life is a mystery
Exhale: Beyond my understanding.

FAMILY DISCUSSION QUESTIONS

Read 1 Timothy 3:16 together.

- What parts of the mystery of faith has God revealed to us clearly enough?
- Do you find the mysteries of faith comforting or unsettling? Why?
- Why is there peace in knowing we can't fathom the mysteries of God?
- Have you ever felt guilty for having doubts about God?
- What does the phrase "deep calls to deep" mean to you (Psalm 42:7)?
- Why do you think people (especially adults) have such a hard time saying, "I don't know"?
- Have you ever shared your doubts and wonderings with God or with someone you trust? What happened?
- What can the fall season teach us about God's mysteries?
- What might it mean to "live the mystery," as Frederick Buechner says?

FAMILY PRAYER

younger

God, this world is big. There's so much we don't know—and so much we'll never know.

But we do know one thing: You are good. You are worthy of all our praise. Because You love us, we can trust You even when we are scared or doubtful or wondering. No question is too big for You, and no worry is too small.

Dear God, You are a beautiful mystery. We love you. Amen.

older

O God of mystery, hear our prayer.

Comfort us in our doubts. Give us peace when we don't know what comes next. We know our lives are but a vapor, but we also know that in the mist, You are there.

Help us to live into the mystery of a life of faith. Let us embrace the beauty in the unknowing. Give our family the courage to admit what we do not know and faith to trust You with our questions.

In our wondering and in our wandering, we believe in what we cannot see. Amen.

REFLECTION 9

Helicopters

"LOOK BOTH WAYS!" I shout to my almost twelve-year-old son as he runs out of the van for practice. My nine-year-old laughs in the background and says something snarky about my being an overprotective mother.

"It's a busy street! He's highly distractible!" I protest.

My husband doubles over in laughter.

I shoot him daggers.

"I mean . . ." he says, catching his breath. "He's not wrong. It's not like you *aren't* over-protective."

"I just want him to be safe!" I frown, not helping my cause.

They're right. I *am* overprotective. Have you seen [*gestures wildly*] all of this?

I admit I have a whole fleet of helicopter tendencies within myself. I'm working on it, but wow, it's complicated. My brain, prone to anxiety, tends to calculate about a million ways something could go wrong at any given time. I have four children. The mental math is exhausting.

I deeply value being awake to the world, as Jesus was. While this means I am more prone to notice the beauty in a candle's flicker or a sparrow's song, it also means I feel the weight of the world deep in my chest. I lament and grieve that so much suffering exists.

As a mother, I ache to protect my children from this pain.

As a follower of Christ, I know I must release my need for control.

I'm envious of parents who seem to trust the world more easily than I do. (I admit that sometimes I secretly judge these parents for not being protective enough of their children, but mostly I'm jealous. I'm just a basket of daisies, aren't I?)

Our urge to overparent can cause us to make decisions out of fear. And when fear is directing us, we tend to lose the thread, getting lost in our anxieties and forgetting our purpose.

Dr. Traci Baxley has worked with countless parents who want to raise their children in a more just and compassionate world. She writes, "In an overwhelming and primal effort to shield and protect our children, many parents have become hypervigilant and over-protective. No one *wants* to be a helicopter parent. . . . But our anxieties for our children—that they aren't hurt physically or emotionally, that they become successful, that they do as well as other children—can cause us to parent out of fear."[24] My desire to protect my cubs (and cover them with bubble wrap) flows out of love, but God is gently teaching me that sometimes the fiercest thing I can do is to be tender and trusting, to recognize that in my own weakness, I can trust the One who has written my children's names on the palm of His hand (see Isaiah 49:16).

"Radical love requires allowing the ones you love to experience hurt instead of trying to protect them from all hurt. In an age of helicopter parenting, we know that those who seek to overprotect and smother their children rob them of precious life experiences," writes theologian Phuc Luu. "Within reason, children need to experience hurt and to learn how to appropriately seek attention for their own wounds and the wounds of others. They need to know that their parents will be there for them, but do not need the constant protection from all possible sources of woundedness."[25] My immediate response to these words is "But . . ." and "What if . . . ?" He's right, though. If we want to raise empathetic and compassionate children, we must resist the urge to sanitize their lives. If we're going to raise children who live into the reality that Christ cares for the world with infinite grace, we have to allow them to see the world's pain and risk getting wounded too.

Courageous parenting means we allow our children to explore the world on their own (within reason), trusting that the One who created the most infinite galaxies and the tiniest atoms will be with them wherever they go.

After Moses died, God spoke to his assistant, Joshua: "Strength! Courage! Don't be timid; don't get discouraged. GOD, your God, is with you every step you take" (Joshua 1:9, MSG). In the moments we're courageous enough to release our grip on the control we *think* we wield, we let our parenting become a prayer, our loosened grasp an act of worship. The Holy Spirit dwells in us, and we know that while we cannot protect our children from hurt, we can teach them to know God as Healer.

When I was a new mom with one child, my toddler's playground confidence had me sweating bullets. He would lead with his round belly, waddling with purpose toward play structures that held infinite opportunities for injury. Every park playdate had me reverting to my lifeguarding days. I was on high alert, constantly scanning the playground. Someone with a few more years of parenting experience under her belt gently reminded me to take a breath.

"If he really needs you, he'll call out for you," she said. She encouraged me to replace my frantic "Be careful!" shouts as my son climbed the ladder with "What's the plan?" I didn't stop paying attention, but I gave him a wider berth to figure things out for himself. And miracle upon miracle, four kids in, we've yet to break a bone. (Though there have been a couple of close calls.)

As we see in 2 Timothy 1:7, "God has not given us a spirit of fear and timidity, but of power, love, and self-discipline." There are infinite ways to parent out of fear. I see it in myself, in parents with different political and religious views, and in parents with similar beliefs. None of us is immune to fear's clutches.

Fear can affect everything from our job choices to where we live to where we send our kids to school. It can impact what we teach (or don't teach) our children and how we respond to our children's questions and mistakes.

When we start to recognize where fear has crept in, we can invite Jesus into these places, asking the Holy Spirit to illuminate the dark, worry-riddled halls we dwell in. Jesus said, "I am the light of the world. Whoever follows me will never walk in darkness, but will have the light of life" (John 8:12, NIV).

With the light of life, we can take a different path in our parenting—one that is present but not pushy, caring but not suffocating. We can lead with love, which equips and empowers our children to experience all that God has written for them.

When fears for your children take hold of your heart, rest in Psalm 139:16, reflecting on how deeply God cares for your family:

You saw me before I was born.
　　Every day of my life was recorded in your book.
Every moment was laid out
　　before a single day had passed.

Fall often brings forth an air of new beginnings. School starts; schedules shift. Our children are surrounded by new invitations to independence, and we must accept that as much as we want control, it was never really ours in the first place.

We take photos of our backpack-wearing kids in their freshly laundered clothes (and secretly cry when our teens are over those first-day-of-school pictures). We feel our hearts beating out of our chests, full of worries and wonderings as they embark on new adventures.

But where we cannot go, God already is.

We cannot protect our children from the very real swirl of woundedness in this world. But we also cannot shield them from all that is true and beautiful that God has just for them.

SCRIPTURE
Isaiah 49:16; Joshua 1:9; 2 Timothy 1:7; Psalm 139:16

BREATH PRAYER

Inhale: When fear surrounds me,
Exhale: Help me trust in You.

FAMILY DISCUSSION QUESTIONS

Read Joshua 1:9 together.

- What's something you've been afraid of this week? How can you let God's love cover that fear?
- What does God say about our fear?
- What is your fear holding you (or those you love) back from?
- Does our family lean toward being overprotective or overpermissive?
- What are you having a difficult time releasing control over?
- How can you invite Jesus into your need for control?
- Why is it important for us to experience both pain and joy in our lives?
- How does it change your perspective if you know that wherever you go, God is already there?

THE HOLY TRINITY
OF PARENTING

Want to loosen your grip while still being
present in your children's lives? Focus on these
three values as you make parenting decisions.

AUTONOMY SUPPORT:
We foster intrinsic motivation and instill values
rather than simply obedience when we allow our
kids to feel a sense of choice, competence, and
understanding about their actions.

STRUCTURE:
We can set clear limits while helping our children grasp
the potential consequences of their choices.

INVOLVEMENT:
We can walk alongside our children, to the degree that
they need, so we can catch them when they fall and
teach them to stand up again on their own.

MOLLY BASKETTE AND ELLEN O'DONNELL,
*Bless This Mess: A Modern Guide to Faith
and Parenting in a Chaotic World*

FAMILY PRAYER

younger

Dear God, You are good. Thank you for caring for us, even when the world feels dark or scary.

When our family is apart, help us to remember that we are never alone. You are the Maker of all things, and You are with us always.

In all our adventures, help us to be brave, loving, and kind. Because You love us with the most immense love, we can share that love with others, too.

And when we're scared, help us to remember we can trust You. Amen.

older

O God, we know You are trustworthy, but so often we forget. Remind us that our family belongs to You and You alone.

When the day is done and the sun begins its slumber, and we return from our separate adventures, will You bring us back home? Cover our fears with the blanket of Your love. Loosen our controlling grip with Your gentle embrace. Help our family name our wounds so we may tend to the woundedness of others.

O loving and merciful God, You haven't given us a spirit of fear or timidity. Help us to remember this so we may more fully and boldly love those You've placed among us. Amen.

Take, Eat

"TA-DA!" My son grins as he pulls me into the dining room.

His older brother beckons my husband and me to sit.

"Bon appétit!" he says with a flourish, gesturing toward the table, where carefully arranged stoneware plates wait for us.

A crisp autumn breeze dances through the windows. Gone are the stretched-out days of summer. The sun sets at dinnertime now, its glow embracing an ever-earlier bedtime. The sky is streaked with ribbons of gold. The evening is nothing exceptional, an ordinary Thursday. But we've been invited into the extraordinary: the kids have made dinner—and set the table—*all on their own.*

We heard the clinks and clanks coming from the kitchen, praying that no fires would start and no child would be injured.

I take my seat and receive a folded piece of blue construction paper with *Menu* scribbled on it.

We'll be dining on waffles, fruit, and scrambled eggs. Beverage options include milk or root beer.

"Did you see your names?" our youngest son whispers. His brothers are the cooks, and he is our maître d', overseeing our dining experience. He points a chubby finger toward the table.

I look down and see slips of paper. He made place cards for each family member using his most delicate five-year-old print.

We are not just welcome; we are wanted.

"This is the best restaurant I've ever visited," I whisper back.

Before we eat, we thank God for our feast and for the ones who made it. Across the table, three boys beam with pride. I look at their school polos covered with splotches of waffle batter, and I'm overwhelmed with tenderness toward them.

As parents, my husband and I are the providers, often exhausted by the mundane domestic responsibilities of raising a family. But at this moment, the tables have turned.

We've been offered the hospitality of a homecooked meal by the ones who still ask us to pour their milk.

I look at our plates. The servings are small, the eggs are a bit burned, and the waffles have grown cold by the time we dig in.

It's a perfect meal. I savor every bite.

Life happens around the table. We pass bowls and clink glasses, chewing and telling stories and laughing all at once. We bump elbows, interrupt each other, and reach for seconds.

There's something so profoundly human about sharing a meal. It's the most essential thing in the world to eat and drink, and when we do it together, it fills our basic need for connection, too.

Perhaps this is why Jesus spent so much time eating with His disciples. There's more than just physical nourishment that takes place around the table—the Spirit of God is there too. When we gather as a body of believers, we take Communion, eating the bread (or wafer) and sipping the wine (or grape juice). We gather to take and eat in remembrance of Christ.

"To eat this particular meal together is to meet at the level of our most basic humanness, which involves our need not just for food but for each other," writes Frederick Buechner. "I need you to help fill my emptiness just as you need me to help fill yours. As for the emptiness that's still left over, well, we're in it together, or it in us. Maybe it's most of what makes us human and makes us brothers and sisters."[26]

My daughter, Eliza, is disabled and has difficulty chewing and swallowing. When my husband and I feed her, she can eat purees like applesauce or yogurt. But to get most of her calories, she uses a gastronomy tube (a tiny tube inserted through the belly that brings liquid nutrition to the stomach). Whenever she begins a new therapy or school program, we're asked about her mealtimes and locations.

I always reply with the same answer: "She eats breakfast, lunch, and dinner at the same time, at the same table, as her siblings."

The most common reaction we get is surprise. I'm surprised at their surprise! Eliza is a beloved part of our family. Why wouldn't she eat with us? When our kids made us dinner, Eliza's highchair had a handmade name card too.

This is what Jesus modeled when He brought people to the table and when He joined others' mealtimes (see Matthew 9:10-11). In God's family, we are kin. We all have the same need. No one is above another. And our kinship doesn't erase differences but honors them.

This is the radical reality of being siblings in Christ's love. We don't eat at staggered times. We humble ourselves and partake together in the ordinary act of breaking bread (see Romans 12:16). We do not have to shed any part of what makes us who we are. There is warmth and welcome at the table.

The table is also the place where memories are made and miracles are manifested. "It is our daily bread that we eat, not my own. We share our bread. Thus we are firmly bound to one another not only in the Spirit but in our whole physical being," wrote Dietrich Bonhoeffer in his classic book *Life Together*.[27]

Jesus was often a guest at other people's tables. This turns my traditional understanding of hospitality upside down. I would expect the God who created the universe to be the One doing the feeding, not the One being fed. But as my children taught me, it's a tender expression of humility and love to be the guest of another. To receive hospitality is to be like Christ.

Kat Armas, a second-generation Cuban American, credits much of her theological formation to her *abuelita* (grandmother), who fled Cuba during the height of political unrest and raised her children alone after her husband's death. In Armas's book *Abuelita Faith*, she writes that it's not enough for us to simply make space at the table. We must also join others' tables, especially those on the margins.

"An abuelita faith calls for the dominant culture to leave its own table and join the marginalized at theirs," Armas says. "The traditional notion of hospitality requires that we be hosts, but an abuelita theology requires that we be guests—regular guests at unfamiliar tables with only the motives of listening and learning."[28]

Phuc Luu is a theologian, a philosopher, and an artist whose family immigrated to the United States from Vietnam when he was young. In his book *Jesus of the East*, he says that sitting at the table not only with those who are unlike us but also with people we may not even like helps followers of Jesus truly live into His command to love our enemies (see Matthew 5:44).

"Sitting at the table with all people often means we will sit with those we do not like or care to know. We will sit at the table with perceived enemies or those foreign to us. We may be invited to dine with someone of a different ethnicity, cultural background, skin color, political affiliation, sexual orientation, or belief system," he writes. "To eat with each other reveals our deepest vulnerabilities: that we share the same hunger and thirst, that we are not exempt from needing others."[29] My husband lived in an ethnically diverse neighborhood as a child, and as long as he was back before dinner, he was allowed to spend his days at his neighbors' houses.

He'd usually return home stuffed to the brim from eating all day. A pot of refried beans was always on at his friend Josue's home, where Josue's Mexican mom ran the house from the kitchen, loading up the neighborhood kids with corn tortillas topped with fixings and a special soup called pozole, which still makes Jonny's mouth water, decades later. He also remembers his friend Ibrahim's parents keeping him in full supply of flaky Bosnian pastries and meat pies.

Jonny was the recipient of the admonition in Romans 12:13 to "always be eager to practice hospitality."

Life is rooted at the table. It's where, as children, we learn who we are and where we fit into our families and into the larger world. It's where families gather meal after meal, day after day. It's where little ones wearing bibs and spaghetti sauce on their cheeks somehow morph into broody teenagers who push food around on their plates. It's where neighbors get to know each other, passing the peace across their differences, serving and being served.

It's a gesture of love to say, "I made you a plate." And it's a gesture of love to receive it too. "Take, eat," Jesus said.

When our kids made us our waffle and egg dinner, they invited us to be childlike—to embrace our vulnerability and accept the care of another, including the spilled root beer and crayon-scribbled menu.

As we approach the Lord's table, we remember. We take. We eat. And, as Frederick Buechner concludes, "If it seems a childish thing to do, do it in remembrance that you are a child."[30]

SCRIPTURE
Matthew 5:44; Romans 12:13-16

BREATH PRAYER

Inhale: Give us this day
Exhale: Our daily bread.

FAMILY DISCUSSION QUESTIONS

Read Romans 12:13-16 together.

▸ What is hospitality? Why does the Bible say we should always be eager to practice it?

- Why is it important to share meals with loved ones?

- Why is it important to share meals with people who are different from us?

- When have you been invited to share a meal with someone different from you? What did you eat? What did you learn?

- Why do you think Jesus shared so many meals with His disciples?

- Why do you think the Lord's Prayer encourages us to thank God for *our* daily bread, not *my* daily bread?

- Why do you think so many celebrations (such as holidays, birthdays, and weddings) include a shared meal?

- How does our church observe Communion or the Eucharist? Why is this an important part of the Christian tradition?

- Who can you share a meal with this week?

FAMILY PRAYER

younger

Jesus, help us to be more like You. When we eat, help us to remember that You are near.

When we share meals with friends and family, help us to celebrate the ways we are alike and the ways we are different. Help us to be generous with others and to be grateful when others are generous with us.

Thank You for giving us what we need for each day. We love You, Jesus. Amen.

older

Jesus, help us to follow Your ways. You made space for people at the table, and You humbled Yourself to be a guest. You broke bread and drank wine with ordinary folks from ordinary places.

Help us to share what we have, breaking bread not only with our family but with those who think, look, or believe differently from us. Give us a spirit of listening and learning so we may love more like You.

Nourish us with Your presence, and help us to remember, in each meal we share, that we love because You first loved us. May all we say and all we do be in remembrance of You. Amen.

It is a powerful
thing to be able
to share with our
children the promise
that the scariest
elements of life do not
have the final say.

Our Hauntings

"I'M SCARED."

My kids are often brave about naming their vulnerability. They haven't yet learned the grown-up urge to brush fears aside and pretend they don't exist. The youngest among us wear fear like a badge of honor, even as they shut their eyes tight and cling to our sides. As parents, we must help them name what scares them and guide them through their fears.

When my son was on a computer at school, he stumbled on a website with horror movie characters. Though he wasn't familiar with the movies the characters came from, he couldn't shake the villainous visuals from his mind. He struggled with nightmares, his imaginative mind filling in the gaps and crafting sinister stories. I tried my best to tell him that what haunted him didn't exist, but the truth is, while the macabre monsters may have been fictitious, his fear was real.

We cannot shame our children out of fear. Instead, we have the opportunity to enter into their hauntings with gentleness and care, meeting them where they are, whispering that they are safe, known, and loved.

With the help of our family therapist, my son was able to work on visualizing a super-hero every time an image of a villain entered his brain. My son's hero of choice? A comic book character he modeled after himself.

For years, he's hand-drawn comics that follow this hero's adventures in a robust universe of his own creation. The desk in his room is loaded with sketched journeys of this character, who is bold and brave, kind and just. He works with his brothers and sister, leading them to foil sinister plots and help the vulnerable—all in time for supper.

"Children have an innate sense that there is an epic story behind the obvious world," write Mark and Jan Foreman. "They relish fantasy because they sense there is another reality, so much more than meets the eye. And they are right."[31] The truth is our world is scary. Evil exists in the seen and unseen parts of our lives. Children don't use logic to write off what even adults can't explain. They seem to sense that principalities and powers exist that are beyond our understanding. Their hearts are tender to the mysteries of heaven and earth, which means they're also tender to the glory and goodness of Christ in their lives.

It is a powerful thing to be able to share with our children the promise that the scariest elements of life do not have the final say. This does not mean we gloss over their legitimate worries; rather, we affirm that while our stories have scary parts, the scary parts will not win. The love of Christ has won already—and will always win.

In 2 Timothy 1:10, we see the truth that darkness will not—and cannot—win. "Since the appearance of our Savior, nothing could be plainer: death defeated, life vindicated in a steady blaze of light, all through the work of Jesus" (MSG).

As a child, I sat cross-legged at vacation Bible school one year, with Band-Aids and bug bites covering my bare legs. I picked at a scab as a leader shared that I could pray anywhere, anytime, and God would hear me. I believed it. Somehow, I had always believed it—I had never felt alone in the world.

"Children are naturally open to the supernatural," write the Foremans. "They are fresh spiritual beings, not yet dulled by adult sensibilities or matter-of-fact answers. They expect to be surprised and amazed. This means we can speak confidently about unseen realities to a child with great freedom."[32]

When I was told that Jesus loved me and would never leave me, I believed that, too. I didn't need to be a Bible scholar to believe the simple truth and glorious mystery of God's Spirit dwelling within me. I accepted the goodness in what I could not see. My imagination was active, and my heart was tender. I didn't have to have all the answers to know deep in my bones that God was with me.

I didn't separate this sacred truth from what grown-ups would call the secular world. I listened to read-aloud cassette tapes at night to help me drift off to sleep. But sometimes my mind wouldn't turn off when the stories ended. We lived on a busy street, and if a car blasting loud music drove by, the wooden floors of my bedroom would shake my metal bed frame. This rattled my little heart too, causing my brain and body to fill with anxiety. Bits of grown-up fears I'd overheard mixed together into a jumbled mess I couldn't quite piece together.

One autumn night, it felt like all my worries and fears were boiling over. Summer's bedtime glow had descended into fall's dusk, and darkness blanketed my pink Minnie Mouse bedroom. My twin bed rattled. The wind howled. I gripped my quilt and held my breath. It felt like the house was coming alive, the floors shaking beneath me. I couldn't find my voice to call for my parents. I couldn't move at all. With all the energy

I could muster, I remembered the truth I'd been reminded of that summer. I closed my eyes and prayed, full of childlike earnestness and blessed assurance that God would hear my prayer.

I don't know what I prayed, but an inexplicable peace filled me that I can remember to this day—a peace I believe came from the Holy Spirit, our Comforter (see John 14:16). The house became still. I fell asleep, full of contentment. I think that's the first time I remember being comforted in a way that didn't come from my mom or dad. Jesus was with me then, and I know He is with me now.

I want to pass on this peace to my children too. It doesn't mean scary, awful things won't happen. But when life seems bleakest, we have the Spirit of truth who will never leave us.

I was at a retreat once where the speaker asked, "What haunts you?"

That three-word question has stuck with me. It's a scary thing to explore what lurks in the shadows. Some of the most frightening and compelling storytelling in pop culture has been the exploration not of creepy crawly monsters but of our own ghosts. When I was a podcast producer, I worked at a nonprofit that supported Iraqis who had lived through the atrocities of war. I was surprised (and a bit horrified) when a colleague shared that families with young children often watched scary movies (the same ones that haunted my son with just a photo) *together*. They said that whatever the children saw on TV wasn't nearly as scary as what they'd lived through. At that moment, I realized that though I'd felt fear, my privilege had shielded me. There was so much I didn't know about other people's stories, whether abroad or next door. In a spiritual world, good and evil are constantly warring around us and within us. We are all haunted by something.

As people who follow the Light of the World, we are not immune to fear, but neither are we held captive by it. Because of this, we must not judge others for what haunts them. Instead, we can share our candles, illuminating the darkness together.

"I'm afraid of the dark—not afraid to go up the stairs in the physical darkness of night, but afraid of the shadows of another kind of dark, the darkness of nothingness, of hate, of evil," wrote Madeleine L'Engle.[33]

Where do you find comfort when you're facing the murky shadows cast by hate and evil? L'Engle said that the candles that lit her way were books, music, and friendship. But she also warned against candles that provide false comfort, like drinking too much alcohol or falling into toxic relationships.

Creativity and art in the form of comics provide comfort to my son. I, too, am comforted by the world of books (along with a hot cup of coffee shared with a friend or a neighborhood walk just as the sun begins to slumber). When I am most afraid, I turn to the simplest prayers.

Jesus, You are with me.
God, help me know You are here.
Jesus, You are Lord.
God, be near.

As a culture, perhaps we're attracted to carved jack-o'-lanterns and creepy Halloween costumes because it gives us one night a year to name our fears. As my coworker who had lived in Iraq said, the fake cobwebs and spooky movies could never be as scary as the hauntings of real life. Perhaps people flock to a day to be scared so we have a chance to be brave like children and say, "Yes, we're afraid." Because, yes, we're all haunted by something.

So what haunts you, really?

Take time to reflect on this difficult question. Maybe your hauntings have something to teach you. My podcasting friend Lindsy likes to ask guests, "What keeps you up at night?" to begin to unpack what a person is passionate about. As you explore what scares you, invite God into your processing. Remember that just as your grown-up anxieties are valid, so are your children's worries about the monsters under their beds.

And just as you want to comfort your scared child, remember that you don't have to hold your fears alone. Consider sharing with a trusted friend. (If complex traumas arise, reach out to a trained therapist to help you process and begin to heal.) And you can bring your fears to God, too.

If you're up for extra credit, ask yourself, *What candles do I light in the darkness? Which are healthy comforts, and which are causing more harm than good?*

Praise be to God, we are not alone in the shadows. The One who gives each breath cares for us and invites us to cast all our anxieties onto Him (see 1 Peter 5:7).

SCRIPTURE
1 Peter 5:7; 2 Timothy 1:10; John 14:26

BREATH PRAYER

Inhale: When I am afraid,
Exhale: You are with me.

HALLOWEEN AND THE CHURCH CALENDAR

Following Halloween (which used to be known as All Hallows' Eve) on October 31, many Christians around the world observe All Saints' Day on November 1 and All Souls' Day on November 2. These holy days beckon us to remember Christ followers who have died, honor those who have passed, and reflect on our own mortality—not in fear but in reverence to the Creator and Sustainer of life. Sometimes this stretch between October 31 and November 2 is referred to as *Allhallowtide*.

FAMILY DISCUSSION QUESTIONS

Read John 14:26 together.

▸ Why do you think the Holy Spirit is described as our Comforter? When have you experienced this comfort?

▸ Can you share about a time when you were scared? What happened?

▸ What helps you feel brave when you're facing something frightening?

▸ What "candles" do you light in the darkness?

▸ What haunts you? What do you think haunts the culture around you? How can you tell?

▸ What does it mean to cast our anxieties onto Jesus?

▸ What is a simple prayer you could say when you're afraid?

▸ Who is a trusted person you can share your fears with?

▸ Is it difficult or easy for you to name your fears? Why is it courageous to name your fears?

FAMILY PRAYER

younger

Jesus, You are the Light of the World. Your goodness has the final say.

While bad things exist in this world, the darkness will not win. You are bigger than anything that scares us. Even though we can't see You, we trust that You are with us.

Help us to choose courage when we're scared. Comfort us when we're afraid. Thank You for being there every time we pray. We love You. Amen.

older

O Light of the World, illuminate the darkness that haunts us. As we follow You, we know we are not immune to fear, but fear cannot hold us captive. Jesus, Your glory and goodness have the final say, extinguishing evil and defeating death in an unending blaze of light.

When evil creeps near and fear closes in, help us to remember that Your love has won and will always win. Help us to comfort one another, sharing our candles and bringing light to the darkness together. Amen.

A PRAYER FOR
ALLHALLOWTIDE

We pray that our sons and daughters would know
That no matter where life takes them,
They are never alone.
Your Spirit dwells within and among them,
And they have a great cloud of witnesses
That goes before them.

TO LIGHT THEIR WAY

Strivings Cease

I CHECK MY WATCH: two minutes until go time. I stand at the door, ensuring we have full backpacks and water bottles. I locate wayward jackets, hats, and scarves. I scribble my signature on last-minute permission slips. My husband grabs his keys and pushes out the door. Our sons follow suit like ducks in a row.

The moment the first one's sneakers leave the threshold of our home is the moment my heart tightens. They've been at this for a month now, but the weekday routine doesn't loosen the knot I feel in my chest every morning they embark on a new school day.

Leaves fall to a thousand little deaths, littering our lawn in a layered quilt of golds and reds. Parenting is mourning a thousand tiny funerals for the parent you were and the person your growing child will never be again, pulling further from you and journeying deeper into their own adventures. Yet parenting is a celebration of becoming—kicking off the covers and waking afresh to new hues and seasons of life.

"The child you see today will not be here tomorrow. The child arriving home from school, is different from the one who left from home this morning," poet William Martin writes, "Every moment is a death of all that has gone before, and a birth of all that is to come."[34] It's an ordinary Wednesday, and I repeat my usual: "Have a good day! I love you!" At the last minute, I add, "God loves you!" to my morning send-off. My youngest son turns his head as he turns the knob on the door.

"God loves you, too!" He smiles, and the door shuts behind him.

I hold my coffee and glance out the window. *I wonder if my perspective would change if I didn't see my children as little versions of myself but rather little reflections of God.* As steam rises from my mug, I watch the car pull out of the driveway, holding pieces of my heart as they embark on the day's adventure.

Our hundred-year-old house sighs. Without the symphony of children's voices and bodies filling the space, the house groans with the wind, shifting to accommodate the new emptiness.

It's hard to let them go. As my kids grow older, it doesn't seem to get any easier. They're not the babies I willingly let church nursery workers rock on Sunday mornings so I could have a minute to think. I know I have to loosen my grip, but I want to keep them home, safe under my wings.

I delight in who they're becoming but grieve for the way their hands no longer grasp mine like they did when they were smaller and their world seemed bigger. I think of how Jesus said He ached to keep the people of Israel protected under His wings like a mother hen (see Matthew 23:37-39).

I breathe in my coffee's bittersweet scent; I watch a sparrow that hasn't yet flown south dance over a puddle from last night's rain. I exhale and let my breath become a prayer—a prayer for my children to be safe and known, fully themselves and wholly loved. I pray they will make wise choices, be kind friends, and embrace curiosity as they learn new things. My breath is a prayer for all these things, though I can't quite put words to it. As I breathe, I let the Holy Spirit unfurl the tightness in my chest and unravel the prayers embedded in my soul.

In the quiet of the house, my thoughts get louder: *Am I living into this prayer myself? Am I letting the Holy Spirit shift my values from the world's ways to the ways of the Kingdom of God?*

We writers are often given the advice to "show; don't tell" in our work. Am I doing this in my parenting? I've told my kids I value empathy, curiosity, and compassion. But have I lived, as Ephesians 4:1 says, "in a manner worthy of the calling" (ESV)?

Harvard researchers surveyed ten thousand middle- and high-school students across the United States, interviewing and observing hundreds of kids, parents, and teachers over ten years. Here's what their findings indicated: "Most parents and teachers say that developing caring children is a top priority and rank it as more important than children's achievements. . . . But according to our data, youth aren't buying it. About 80% of the youth in our survey report that their parents are more concerned about achievement or happiness than caring for others."[35] This is a gut punch to parents who follow Jesus and want to raise children who reflect the Kingdom of God. The way we spend our time often communicates the unintentional message that what we accomplish is more important than how we treat others. This withering gospel of self could not be more antithetical to the flourishing gospel of Jesus. As Mark and Jan Foreman write, "Performance-based living, even in a culture of grace, is epidemic."[36] I want my children to try their best, but I also care deeply about their character.

We may tell our kids we value the fruits of the Spirit—love, joy, peace, patience, kindness, goodness, faithfulness, gentleness, and self-control (see Galatians 5:22-23)—but what if we're not bearing that fruit ourselves? As Jesus told His followers, each tree is known by its own fruit (see Luke 6:44).

"It seems our messages of 'get straight A's' or 'win this race' are drowning out messages like 'Make sure you help someone who needs it' or 'Share a smile today,'" observes Dr. Traci Baxley. "When you review your current parenting, which of these values do you actively and intentionally make the priority to set the foundation for your children's lives?"[37] As you reflect on the messages you might be giving your children, be gentle with yourself. Consider the messaging you were raised with. What did the adults in your life tell and show you about who you needed to be? How has that affected who you are today . . . and how you're raising your children?

It's not too late to course correct. It's not too late to choose a different path for yourself and your family, integrating new rhythms of Sabbath rest, choosing stillness, and letting striving fall to its place alongside the fallen leaves (see Psalm 46:10).

Our words reflect our hearts, just as our actions do. What is the last thing our kids hear from us as they leave for school? Will you tell them to get straight As? Or to be kind?

After Jesus told His disciples about bearing fruit, He used another example to get His message across: "Out of the abundance of the heart," he told them, the "mouth speaks" (Luke 6:45, ESV).

Fall often feels like a fresh start. Pencils are sharpened; planners are clear. The shift to autumn air holds the promise of new beginnings—an invitation to reflect on what was so you can become more of who God created you to be right now.

Fall offers an invitation to reflect on what was so you can become more of who God created you to be right now.

When my kids are at school, I bring myself to my desk, opening my computer. I consider the blank pages of my planner and push away its whispering lies that say, *You are what you accomplish*—that my work is my meaning. For I know I am more than my work, and more than my parenting mistakes too.

So are you.

Again, I let my breath become a prayer, asking God to bind up the broken parts of my heart—and my children's hearts too. I think back to the last-minute offering of "God loves you!" to my young son before he left and his automatic response to bless me back, reminding me that God loves me, too.

It's easy to feel a lot of pressure as parents. But as much as we want to impart encouragement and wisdom to our children, we get to be the recipients of God's love through them, too.

Even when we feel most lonely in our parenting, we are never alone.

SCRIPTURE
Matthew 23:37-39; Ephesians 4:1; Psalm 46:10; Luke 6:44-45

BREATH PRAYER

Inhale: Help me live in a manner
Exhale: Worthy of the calling.

FAMILY DISCUSSION QUESTIONS

Read Luke 6:44-45 together.

- ▶ What did Jesus mean when He said that the mouth speaks out of the abundance of the heart?

- ▶ What do you think is more important: caring for others or achieving goals? Why?

- ▶ Where do you feel pressure to achieve in your life? Does that pressure come from others or from God?

- ▶ What is the first thing most people share when they introduce themselves? Why do you think that is? When you think about Jesus' life, what did His actions and words show He valued?

- ▶ How does it make you feel if someone says one thing but does something else?

- ▶ How can resting help us reset our values? Why did God command people to observe the Sabbath?

FAMILY PRAYER

younger

God, help us to be a family that follows Jesus in what we say and do. Help us to live out the fruit of the Spirit: love, joy, peace, patience, kindness, goodness, faithfulness, gentleness, and self-control.

Help us to try our best, but also help us to remember that we are so much more than what we do.

You call us Your children and give us Your love without needing anything in return. You love us when we work and when we rest. Help us to receive Your mercy so we can be merciful to others too. Amen.

older

Living Christ, free us from self-centeredness so we may flourish in You.

Help us to grow toward Your light, bearing the fruit of Your Spirit. Let our hearts be nourished by Your life-giving mercy; let our speech be evidence of hearts changed by grace. May our family live into who You've called us to be in both word and deed.

Help us to remember that we don't have to toil, strive, or work for Your love—that You already call us beloved. Remind us that our identity is in You, not in how much we can accomplish. Amen.

REFLECTION 13

Idols

"AND THE WINNER IS . . ." She pauses for effect while glancing down at her hands.

The room goes silent. She announces my name.

I utter my most dramatic gasp as I throw off the blanket and run from the couch toward the brick fireplace in our family room, which has been acting as our makeshift stage.

My best friend hands me two TV remotes, one a stand-in for a microphone, the other a pretend Oscar statue. I clear my throat. "I'd like to start by thanking the Academy . . ."

I start rolling out a long list of all the people who helped me get to this distinguished (middle-school sleepover) honor. "And, of course, I want to thank God!"

With that, I take a bow, concluding my spiel.

My audience of slipper-clad, braces-wearing friends erupts into applause.

In Western culture, gratitude rarely goes beneath the surface. Our thankfulness tends to follow personal achievements or material accumulation. We earmark one holiday a year to list what we're thankful for and then spend the next month focusing on consumer culture.

Even Christian culture doesn't get healthy rhythms of gratitude toward God and others right. And what we thank God for often reveals what we've subconsciously turned into an idol, meaning anything we worship instead of God. Brimming bank accounts and physically healthy families are just a few shiny status symbols we easily value before God.

Matthew 6:21 says, "Where your treasure is, there your heart will be also" (NIV). If we're not careful, we can simply call our idols "gifts from God" and deem ourselves "blessed."

In a piece for the *New York Times* called "Death, the Prosperity Gospel, and Me," Kate Bowler writes, "*Blessed* is a loaded term because it blurs the distinction between two very different categories: gift and reward." She goes on to say, "It can be a term of pure gratitude. 'Thank you, God. I could not have secured this for myself.' But it can also imply that it was deserved. 'Thank you, me. For being the kind of person who gets it right.' It is a perfect word for an American society that says it believes the American dream is based on hard work."[38] As a parent, I want to raise humble, compassionate children who bear witness to the pain of this world while holding deep joy in Christ. One of the ways I can point them to gratitude is by modeling it myself. I don't want to be the person who only takes time to thank God (and others) when I feel I've gotten something or achieved something. I want to thank God in *all* seasons.

Our blessings come from having a compassionate, loving God who will never leave us and who gives us grace freely (see Romans 3:24).

One of the problems with having a "pull yourself up by the bootstraps" mentality infiltrate our Christian faith is that we mostly just thank ourselves . . . and tack God on at the end.

After being honored with a Hollywood Walk of Fame star, a popular artist devoted an entire thank you speech to *himself.*

"I want to thank me for believing in me," he said. "I want to thank me for doing all this hard work, I want to thank me for having no days off, I want to thank me for never quitting."[39] I don't want to take away from his perseverance and dedication or the real challenges he faced along the way. But his words are an illustration of how we (often unconsciously) overestimate our own role in what we've been given.

We hurt ourselves and others when we get trapped into a cycle of thinking, *I get what I have, I am where I am, and I am who I am because of my own effort.* This individualistic mindset is dangerous and confuses our understanding of who God is as Creator and who we are as creation.

That's not to say it's up to us to tell someone else to be more thankful; instead, we all need to examine our own hearts—what Jesus called the plank in our own eyes (see Matthew 7:5). Where have *we* gotten mixed up? Where have we lost the way?

We need to constantly reexamine how we've exchanged gratitude for self-aggrandizement, replacing the God of all creation with false gods of our own making.

When we give credit to ourselves alone (and only give praise to God when God's plans align with ours), we walk away from a life of worship and gratitude, trading it for confusion and strife. We take the people and privileges we've been given—and our very lives—for granted.

This is not the flourishing God has for us and our families. One of the consequences of self-congratulatory thinking is that we lose our pathways to empathy and compassion, becoming judgmental toward those we perceive haven't worked as hard.

If they just worked harder . . .

If they just prayed harder . . .

Jesus didn't speak like this, but for some reason it's easy for us to default to this dangerous way of thinking.

God loves the mom of three who works nights and weekends, never goes to church, and is barely scraping by as much as God loves the well-off married mom who leads a Bible study. He loves the woman who is dealing with family trauma as much as the woman who brings casseroles to the one in crisis.

Ephesians 2:7-9 says,

Now God has us where he wants us, with all the time in this world and the next to shower grace and kindness upon us in Christ Jesus. Saving is all his idea, and all his work. All we do is trust him enough to let him do it. It's God's gift from start to finish! We don't play the major role. If we did, we'd probably go around bragging that we'd done the whole thing! No, we neither make nor save ourselves. God does both the making and saving. He creates each of us by Christ Jesus to join him in the work he does, the good work he has gotten ready for us to do, work we had better be doing.

MSG

If we continue to toil for blessings (material or spiritual), we will miss out on God's real (and good) work for us and our families. In order to raise kids who aren't entitled, we have to be shaped by gratitude and generosity, giving thanks to the Giver of life in all circumstances (see 1 Thessalonians 5:16-18).

When we integrate gratitude into the rhythms of our lives, we can help our kids understand that God's favor cannot be earned by hard work, piety, or dedication. God's grace is freely given through Christ (see Romans 3:24). We give thanks out of an overflow of that love.

Jesus turns what our culture calls blessing upside down. Jesus invites us into humility and hope, into a Kingdom where the last will be first and the first will be last (see Matthew 20:16). Our rhythms of gratitude shape us to be more like Christ, who gave thanks to His Father in heaven and made himself a servant (see Philippians 2:6-11).

One of the most valuable gifts we can give our kids is to show them how to honor God by cultivating gratitude.

As humans, we're created to give thanks. Studies show that when people regularly take the time to reflect on and express what they're thankful for, their physical, mental, and emotional state improves. Psychology research shows that "gratitude is strongly and consistently associated with greater happiness."[40]

A Harvard Medical School article suggests that gratitude "is a way for people to appreciate what they have instead of always reaching for something new in the hopes it will make them happier or thinking they can't feel satisfied until every physical and material need is met. Gratitude helps people refocus on what they have instead of what they lack. And, although it may feel contrived at first, this mental state grows stronger with use and practice."[41]

Gratitude is so much bigger than a feel-good idea to embrace once a year as we pass the mashed potatoes and turkey.

May all the seasons of our lives be marked by thanksgiving. May we embody gratitude, consistently taking stock of what we're thankful for, who we're grateful for, and why. May our lives be an expression of our thanks, and may our children hear us thanking God and praising God in all facets of our lives.

SCRIPTURE
Matthew 6:21; Ephesians 2:7-9; Philippians 2:6-11; Psalm 69:30

BREATH PRAYER

Inhale: I will praise You
Exhale: And glorify You with thanksgiving.

FAMILY DISCUSSION QUESTIONS

Read Matthew 6:21 together.

- ▶ How can you tell if something is an idol and is competing for God's place in your heart? Is there something in your life that looks good from the outside but has become an idol?
- ▶ What is something you're thankful for? What people in your life are you thankful for?
- ▶ What do you think it means to be blessed? How is this different from the way the world views blessings?
- ▶ How can you incorporate gratitude into your daily routine?
- ▶ Why do you think Jesus gave thanks to the Father?
- ▶ How can you express your thankfulness to God?

INDIGENOUS PEOPLES' DAY

The second Monday of October is Indigenous
Peoples' Day, which honors and affirms the
dignity of Indigenous people who lived on
the land we now call the Americas long
before colonization.

As Christians, we lament the ways Native people
and cultures were forcibly assimilated, displaced,
and eradicated—and the ways they still experience
discrimination and mistreatment today.

▶ When you think of the successes you've had, who has helped you get there? What happens if we only give credit to ourselves when we experience a win?

▶ How does being thankful affect the way we view others?

FAMILY PRAYER

younger

God, we thank You today and every day. We know that we can't work to make You love us any more than You already do—Your love is that big!

Help us to take time to think about Your big love so we can give Your love to others.

Thank You for giving us Jesus, who taught us how to be more loving. We are so thankful for the people You've given us and the ways we see You in every season of our lives. Amen.

older

Dear God, we give thanks for all that is seen and unseen.

We lament the ways we have replaced Your goodness with idols, calling them blessings. Help us to remember that Your favor does not rest on our accomplishments.

Help us to receive Your love so we may live out of an overflow of gratitude. Help us to focus on what we have instead of what we lack. Give us a more robust understanding of what it means to be blessed in Your Kingdom.

O Giver of goodness and truth, help us to cultivate gratitude in all seasons. Free us from the bondage of self so we may live a more abundant life, not falling into the trappings of individualism but embracing the beauty of community.

Help us to remember that this life is a gift so we may enter into the good work You have for us. Amen.

FIRST NATIONS VERSION

This New Testament was translated by a team that included Indigenous North Americans from more than twenty-five different tribes. It's intended to provide an English Bible that connects, in a culturally relevant way, to the traditional heart languages of the more than six million English-speaking First Nations people of North America.

We can stand in a good way before the Great Spirit by trusting in Creator Sets Free (Jesus) the Chosen One and what he has done for us. This good standing is a gift to all who believe. It does not matter whether you are a Tribal Member [Jew] or from any other nation. We are all the same because all of us have followed our bad hearts and broken ways, but because of the gift of his great kindness all of us are put in good standing with the Great Spirit through what Creator Sets Free (Jesus) has done to set us free and make us whole.

ROMANS 3:22-24, FNV

WINTER

Introduction

WINTER AND I HAVE a love-hate relationship. As temperatures drop and days darken, December seems to crackle and pop with anticipation, like logs thrown on a fire. Little hands light Advent candles at the dinner table and hang handmade ornaments on evergreens. Sparkling snow covers the earth like powdered sugar sifted atop Grandma's cookies.

I delight in the way everything feels fresh and new. My sons search for the perfect carrot noses for their snowmen and take turns sledding before retreating inside. The home that has borne the brunt of so many winters welcomes us inside, softening our edges with borrowed books, worn blankets, and hand-me-down sweaters.

We make memories and mark the passing of time with snow boots pulled from storage that are now too small for growing feet. We host gatherings of friends and family we haven't seen in far too long, the entryway a stockpile of puffy coats and fuzzy hats. We watch with wonder as, before our very eyes, five-year-olds become the magi in Christmas plays. We listen to a tale as old as time about a star that guided the way and a God who took on flesh. We stoke the fires of our hearts as we tell and retell family stories over cups of hot cocoa. Home becomes a beacon of light, a place to escape the cold, shed our winter layers, and warm ourselves by the fire.

But the season has a shadow side too. Christ's birth becomes commodified. Kids pass around fevers and stuffy noses. Snow becomes slush. We cram calendars with overwhelming obligations and worry over our planners and pocketbooks, wondering how we'll ever get everything done. The holiday hustle and bustle lose their charm. Poverty, famine, and war do not pause for Christmas celebrations. Strained relationships don't suddenly heal as the countdown to Christmas begins. Among the Christmas carols and candy canes, many of us feel pangs of grief, too.

When January comes, we pack away the garland and the mistletoe, approaching the New Year with a flurry of pressure to do everything *right*. We (once again) resolve to become better parents—more patient, more faithful. We vow to make it to church more often, get more organized, make healthier dinners, and spend less time at work.

February sneaks in, bringing with it icy roads and dropping windchills. Loneliness settles in like a chest cold, and though fresh spring air is not far off, the shortest month of the year feels the longest. The final stretches of winter can feel, well, bleak.

If you hold tension as you approach winter, you're not alone. Katherine May's book *Wintering* invites us to embrace and learn from what this season has to teach us. "To get better at wintering," May writes, "we need to address our very notion of time. We tend to imagine that our lives are linear, but they are in fact cyclical."[1] In other words, winter is a part of a whole—a time to retreat and trust the rhythms of rest laid before us as we make way for spring's renewal.

Though we cannot fully fathom how endings and beginnings flow, we can trust that, time and again, God is with us in the winters of our lives. As Ecclesiastes 3:11 reminds us, God has made everything beautiful in its time.

"Some of the most beautiful and powerful blessings of the Christian tradition are those connected with the seasons and the turning of time, which is, in itself, a place of deep mystery," writes Jan Richardson.[2] Among these reflections about winter, you will find Advent readings that beckon you into time beyond time. (You can return to them year after year.) As you read these reflections, you'll explore the season's wonder by journeying toward the Light of the World. And you'll make space for grief in the darker, bleaker midwinter moments of life too.

These meditations explore darkness and light, invite you to take stock of what is spiritually forming you and your family, and welcome you into the life-changing, incarnational love of Christ. You'll find opportunities to prayerfully examine the year's end and a guide for helping your family name and lean into your values in the New Year. How might you live into rhythms of generosity long after Christmas? How might your family grow in compassion as Valentine's Day approaches? How might you help heal racism long after Black History Month is over?

Morgan Harper Nichols writes, "Even though every day is different, we go through cycles of life in the way we cycle through nature's seasons. Even though no two winters are exactly the same, we come to know winter every year."[3] As we grow older, we pass through phases of health and illness, optimism and deep doubt, freedom and limitation, says May. Winter reminds us of this push and pull. "There are times when everything seems easy, and times when it all seems impossibly hard. . . . Each time we endure the cycle . . . we learn from the last time around, and we do a few things better this time. . . . This is how progress is made."[4]

This winter, may you grow not only in wonder but in wisdom. James 3:17-18 says, "Real wisdom, God's wisdom, begins with a holy life and is characterized by getting along with others. It is gentle and reasonable, overflowing with mercy and blessings, not hot one day and cold the next, not two-faced. You can develop a healthy, robust community that lives right with God and enjoy its results *only* if you do the hard work of getting along with each other, treating each other with dignity and honor" (MSG).

This winter, may your family overflow with mercy as you learn how to treat yourselves and each other with dignity and honor. As the natural world lies dormant, remember that beyond what you can see, change and growth are happening under the surface.

Be with us in
our wintering,
And help
our hearts
prepare
You room
Over and
over again.

A Prayer for Winter

O God, Creator of all seasons,
We thank You for the wonder of
  winter.
As the earth is blanketed with
  soft snow,
Help us to feel the warmth
Of Your embrace.

As ice coats bare branches,
Glittering in the afternoon sun,
And Jack Frost nips at little
  noses,
Comfort us with Your love.

O Word who became flesh,
When the world is cold,
Ignite in us spirits of
  compassion.
Stoke the fires of generosity
Deep within our souls
So our family may reflect
Your light
To everyone we meet.

O Light of the World,
As we strike matches
And light Advent candles,
Spark in us—from the youngest
  to the oldest among us—
Childlike anticipation
For the arrival of the One
Who is with us in the darkness,

Illuminates a better way,
And changes everything.

God, we see You in frosted
  windowpanes
And feel You as snow crunches
Underneath our feet
On early morning walks
To the bus stop.

We thank You for bundled-up
  babies
And little children
In mismatched mittens,
For big kids
Who can never remember
To zip up their coats,
And for teens
who refuse to wear them at all.

Bless the bell ringers and coins
  tossed in buckets.
Protect us from the lies of
  consumerism,
And reorient our hearts
To follow the Light of the World
To the places and people
Most often unseen,
Pushed aside,
Or forgotten.

In all the expectations
And clanging cymbals

Of the holiday season,
Help our hearts get quiet.
May every Nativity scene
Help us remember
The Love that lies
In the manger.

We thank You for stockings
    hung with care,
Handmade ornaments for
    the tree,
And little hands covered in glue
That have crafted just the right
    Christmas gift.

We thank You for the "Here,
    let me take your coat"
And the sprigs of evergreen
In boutonnieres and corsages
For winter formal dances
With teens who used to be
    toddlers,
Now donning dresses and suits.

We thank You for snowmen with
    lopsided smiles,
Borrowed ice skates,
And neighborhood sledding hills,
For the sound of laughter
That echoes across town.

We thank You for the hand-me-
    down sweaters,

Sturdy boots, and wet socks
Drying by the heater.

In the cups of hot cocoa
Brimming with marshmallows
And topped with whipped
    cream,
We taste and see
That You, O Lord, are good.

We thank You for
The architects of gingerbread
    houses
Who adorn their holiday creations
With clumps of frosting
    and handfuls of sprinkles.
Give us patience for all the
    cleanup
That comes long after
They've lost interest.

As daylight falls into
The darkest nights of the year
And bedtimes get just a bit easier,
Help our family find deep rest
    in You.

Thank You for
The ones who shovel
The sidewalk of a neighbor
And, in doing so,
Extend an offering
Of kinship and kindness.

Thank You for New Year's
    countdowns,
Ill-fitting party hats,
And staying up past bedtime
To make memories
As laughter intermingles
With pops of confetti.

Thank You for the evergreen
    branches
Dusted in powdery snow,
And thank You for the wonder
That comes from
Watching our breath
Form in puffy clouds
As we watch the stars dazzle
And dance across the winter sky.

Bless the dark nights
And the wonderings
If winter will ever end.
Bless the lonely shadows
After the lights of the
    holidays
Have passed.

As we look at fresh calendars
And hold planners full of
    promise,
Help us to be intentional in
    how we spend our days
And where we invest our time.

We thank You for the magic
Of capturing snowflakes on our
    tongues
And tasting the promise
Of a fresh start to a New Year.

Help us to feel Your lovingkindness
In the extraordinary
And ordinary moments
Tucked away in this season.
Be near in every homemade
    valentine,
And help us know we are not
    alone
When the sniffles and fevers
    come
With another sick day at home.

Be with us in our wintering,
And help our hearts prepare
    You room
Over and over again.
Guide us as we enter fresh
    rhythms
And develop new routines
As a family.
Form us spiritually,
Mentally,
And emotionally
As we learn each day afresh
What it is to love You, O God,
And love our neighbor, too.

The Word

"ARE WE REALLY DOING THIS?"

My husband and I sat under a blanket, wiping tears as we looked out the window, watching white stretches of snow blanket our front yard. The thrum of the heater kept us company under the glow of white twinkle lights as our kids slept, visions of sugarplums dancing in their heads.

We had just decided to put an offer on a house back in our hometown. Now we were sitting in our living room, staring at our hand-me-down Christmas tree, panicking.

A global shutdown had shaken our family to the core, inviting us to reexamine our values, vocations, and vices. We asked hard questions: *What has become an idol in our lives? Do our beliefs align with our daily comings and goings? Are we just espousing good-sounding ideas, or are we living into them? Is how we fill our days a reflection of following Jesus or just a snapshot of our culture?*

We were home more than ever during that first year of the pandemic. Two of our children have compromised immune systems, so we stayed completely isolated—schooling and working from home—to keep them safe. We had a lot of time inside the four walls of our house to examine and reexamine our jobs and our neighborhood.

We finally had a minute to breathe and look into our lives—who we were and who we were becoming. *What do we want for our children? For ourselves? And do the little choices that make up our days and the big choices of where we live and work reflect those hopes?*

From the outside looking in, we were comfortable. My husband was pastoring a healthy, supportive church, and I had just finished my first manuscript. We had a cozy house in the suburbs.

But something was off. We only saw people who looked like us. Our neighbors never talked to each other. We ached for community—real, deep community. We wanted to be closer to family. We wanted to move to a city where our children would experience racial, cultural, and socioeconomic diversity.

The Holy Spirit may have been nudging us to examine our family's values for a while.

Still, it took a global pandemic for us to pay attention. *What if following Jesus and leaning into the values of God's upside-down Kingdom means something different from what we've always imagined? What if we're being called to do something that doesn't make much sense?*

The house we were ready to take the plunge on was a couple of hours away, in the town we grew up in. Due to redlining, a racist practice meant to keep cities segregated and prevent Black residents from owning homes, the town was effectively split into a Black side and a white side, an east side and a west side. I was raised to think of it as the "bad side" and the "good side," and it wasn't until I was an adult that I realized that framing was inherently racist and incredibly problematic.

The house I'd fallen head over heels for was on the "wrong" side of the literal train tracks. And yet everything about our potential new neighborhood seemed to reflect the values we believed Jesus was beckoning us to embody. Friends and family wondered aloud if we were making the wrong decision for our children. Would we decide to send them to *those* schools? Why would anyone buy a house there intentionally?

It's a privilege to be able to take a moment to examine the direction your life is heading. It's not inherently more spiritual to live in an urban area. But for us, we realized the comfort was making it easy to say we believed in God's vision for peaceful and just living while getting wrapped back into the fold of comfort, consumerism, and consumption.

Ripping off the bandage that has kept all your wounds covered is painful. It stings. It's uncomfortable to examine the choices you've made and why you've really made them. If you're like me, you're skilled at doing verbal gymnastics to justify what you've done and why.

As the winter sky got darker, my husband and I went back and forth, hashing out the pros and cons of moving across the state to a smaller working-class town, into a neighborhood our friends and family warned us was dangerous.

Was it dangerous? Or was it just different?

It wasn't enough for me to proclaim to be anti-racist. As a white mother to a Black son, I knew I needed to be more intentional about cultivating a life with racial mirrors for my child. For our family, divesting from white supremacy was a value worth moving over. Living in whitewashed tombs is toxic for all of us, across skin color. We realized that our family values were more cultural than Christlike, more comfort driven than community based.

When we made the offer, we were thick in the season of Advent. The pink and purple beeswax candles on our kitchen table were melting into stubby versions of their once tall, proud life. We had been thinking about anticipation and expectation, about the Word becoming flesh (see John 1:14) and changing the world in confounding and beautiful ways.

My friend Lindsy, who has intentionally chosen to raise her family alongside neighbors in marginalized communities, pushes me to consider whose stories we're centering and why we're centering them. The two of us were reflecting on the need for Advent in such a scary time, when hospitals were running out of space and hand sanitizer was hard to come by, and she mentioned that she loved reading John 1:14 in *The Message*:

> The Word became flesh and blood,
>   and moved into the neighborhood.
> We saw the glory with our own eyes,
>   the one-of-a-kind glory,
>   like Father, like Son,
> Generous inside and out,
>   true from start to finish.

"The God-with-us is a close God, a God whom we call our refuge, our stronghold, our wisdom, and even, more intimately, our helper, our shepherd, our love," writes Henri Nouwen. "We will never really know God as a compassionate God if we do not understand with our heart and mind that 'the Word became flesh and lived among us.'"[5] We have a God who moved into our neighborhood—not out of obligation but out of deep, abiding love. May we do the same.

SCRIPTURE
John 1:14; Matthew 1:22-23

BREATH PRAYER

Inhale: You are generous
Exhale: Inside and out.

FAMILY DISCUSSION QUESTIONS

Read John 1:14 together.

▸ What does it mean that "the Word became flesh"? Why is it important to remember that Jesus lived among us?

- Why do you think Jesus, who was fully God and fully human (and could have been born in any place, at any time), was born among the dirt and animals to a poor girl thousands of years ago?

- What do the circumstances of Christ's birth teach about God's compassion?

- What does it mean to care about people who are often overlooked? How did Jesus model this?

- Do you think where we live matters to Jesus? Why or why not?

- What's at stake if we don't get to know our neighbors?

- What do you know about the history of our city or state? How can we extend peace and work toward healing the historic hurts of our community?

- When have you made a difficult decision that you knew was the right thing to do?

- How can we be more thoughtful toward the people in our community this winter?

FAMILY PRAYER

younger

Before the beginning of everything, Jesus, You were there. We celebrate this beautiful mystery year after year, remembering Your birth that happened so many years ago. You are the King of Kings, and Your glory is over all things.

Help all we do, all we create, and all we say to honor You and show love to everyone we meet. Help us to be brave and to make choices that honor You, ourselves, and others. We love You, Jesus. Amen.

older

O Word that became flesh, thank You for making Your home among us and within us. We can hardly fathom the mystery and grace of Your presence. In this Advent season, invite us into rhythms of soulful reflection.

Help us to get quiet so we can hear who You are calling us to move toward. Bless the work of our hands and the doorposts of our home. Help us to journey with You, Jesus, as we anticipate Your arrival in a stable in Bethlehem so long ago. Amen.

RULE OF LIFE

Are you wondering if your family is living out
your values? Consider creating a Rule of Life,
a framework for helping you make big
(and small) decisions rooted in a love of Christ.
Learn more in appendix 1.

REFLECTION 2

Bearing Witness

I KNOW EXACTLY WHERE I was when I got the call: a magazine journalism class inside Meredith Hall. We had just split into groups to edit each other's final features. As upper-level college students, a fair amount of goofing off leaked out alongside our red-pen editing sessions toward the end of the winter semester. From our table, I could see campus streetlights highlight tiny flurries against the darkening sky.

My phone wouldn't stop buzzing inside my backpack. Annoyed, I unzipped the front pocket and glanced at the flip phone's screen. Two missed calls from my mom. That was weird—she knew I was taking this night class. Before I could throw it back in my bag, the phone started vibrating again.

The text said, "Call me."

I stayed at the table and mouthed, "One minute" to my friends.

"Hellooo?" I lightly spoke into the phone, eyeing the professor, unsure if it was okay to be on my phone during group worktime.

I waited.

"Honey, there's been an accident."

Time stops when you get a call like this, and then it splits. There's before; there's after. Senses are sharp, and memories are blurred.

I don't know what I said at that classroom table. Maybe I just left without saying anything at all.

Jonny and I got lost on our way to the hospital. We were college students away from home who didn't know where essential locations were. Our phones didn't have GPS. We didn't know how to navigate the real world—we'd never needed to.

We called a friend to ask for directions.

I unclicked my seatbelt, shifting in my seat as we rolled into the parking garage. It felt like we were late. *What is "on time" for something like this?*

We followed the fluorescent signs to the pediatric wing. I held my breath on the elevator ride up to the intensive care unit. The doors opened, and I saw groups of teenage girls in clusters, waiting.

I was one of the first of my family members to arrive. Someone enveloped me in a hug. I don't remember any words at all.

In times of unexpected crisis, we're reminded that control was never really ours. All we can do is sit on the crowded waiting room floor and bear witness.

My parents had left immediately from my hometown, two hours away. I wished for their steadiness as I was called back into the critical care room, where my cousin's bruised and beat-up body was lying on a hospital bed. Machines breathed for her. Blood was caked on her head, arms, and legs from the way the car crumpled as it crashed into a truck after skidding on black ice. I had never seen anything like this before.

I swallowed and pushed back my shoulders. My aunt sat in the corner, in shock. *I need to be strong for her,* I thought. *I need to be strong for myself.*

In the tiny family consultation room, doctors cautioned that collarbones could heal and bones could be set, but her brain injury was life-threatening. Neurologists called the damage *traumatic.*

I now understand that witnessing a life-threatening situation is a form of trauma too. My friend Aundi Kolber is a licensed professional counselor who specializes in trauma therapy. She defines trauma as "anything that overwhelms a person's nervous system and ability to cope."[6] How do we cope when the unimaginable happens? When we're in the middle of an overwhelming crisis, we often do what we can to stay breathing in the moment. The presence of another heart beating next to us can make all the difference as we try to metabolize the pain.

As the waiting room—decked out in a sad-looking miniature Christmas tree and tiny twinkle lights—filled with friends and family, I sat in a worn chair, my eyes rimmed in red.

We sat in silence. We whispered in confusion. We prayed in desperation.

I studied for finals under fluorescent lights, sitting on a hard plastic chair and balancing political science books on my lap.

A few days into sitting vigil in this thin space between life and death, I got a text from my friend Ashley. "I'm here—in the lobby."

While I focused on making space for my family, my friend made space for me.

We sat on a bench, huddled together. I don't remember what we prayed, but I remember how it felt to be sat with, prayed for, and cried with.

Lifetimes have passed since that winter. Over months in the hospital and inpatient rehabilitation, my cousin fought for her life. I bore witness not only to her suffering but also to the moment her eyes fluttered open after weeks in a coma. She is now a walking miracle, although she lives with the results of her injury. That night in December changed everything. She lives in the *after* every day.

I used to think I had to be strong in a crisis. Now I realize I just need to be human.

Jonny and I have sat with family and friends as they've absorbed the aftermath of the unfathomable. We've had people show up for us when we needed it too. When we don't know what else to do, we show up. (And in the Midwest, we do it with a casserole.)

It's in those life-altering moments, when the rug is ripped from beneath our feet, that we need the arms of another to catch us, to let their tears intermingle with ours. In Romans 12:15, Paul exhorts believers to "weep with those who weep" and "mourn with those who mourn" (NIV).

Jesus embodied this holy outpouring of humanity when He wept with Mary and Martha at the death of their dear brother, Lazarus. Though this was not the end of Lazarus's story, Jesus was fully present in His humanity, modeling what it looks like to bear witness, to show up, and to cry.

Winter holds the beautiful anticipation of Advent and the glorious wonder of Christmas, but for many of us, it also stirs up heavy emotions as our hearts hold grief and loss.

As we reflect on God breaking into the earth as a human to be with us, may we remember that incarnational love makes space for emotion. Jesus "is constantly pointing us to the truer story of our humanity. He is showing us how to move more deeply into our God-given humanness."[7] Colossians 2:9 says that the fullness of God existed in the human form of Jesus. When we come to Him, "that fullness comes together for [us], too" (MSG). With Jesus' help, we can embrace His example of being fully human as we parent our children.

We can start by being present to their hurts, affirming the dignity of their tears. We can sit with them in silence when they weep, even when we don't understand. We can replace "Don't cry" with "Tell me where it hurts." We can whisper, "I'm here" instead of "It's fine."

Like Jesus, we can hold space. And we can let our children see our tears too, knowing that God holds all of them in a bottle (see Psalm 56:8).

I used to think I had to be strong in a crisis. Now I realize I just need to be human.

SCRIPTURE

Romans 12:15; John 11:1-44; Psalm 56:8

BREATH PRAYER

Inhale: You hold
Exhale: All my tears.

FAMILY DISCUSSION QUESTIONS

Read John 11:33-44 together.

- ▸ Jesus wept when his friend Lazarus died. Why do you think it's important to remember that even God cries?

- ▸ When has someone sat with you when you were hurt, scared, or upset? How did their presence show that they cared for you?

- ▸ When have you shown up for someone when something difficult happened?

- ▸ How do you feel about crying in front of people?

- ▸ How does it feel when someone tells you to stop crying?

- ▸ How can you—without saying anything—show love to someone who is hurting?

- ▸ Psalm 56:8 says that God holds our tears. Why do you think our tears matter so much to God?

- ▸ Why might the Christmas season bring up sad feelings for people?

- ▸ How can we extend love to those who are sad at school, at church, at work, or in our neighborhood?

FAMILY PRAYER

younger

Jesus, help us to remember it's okay to cry. You are fully God, and You cried too. We don't have to hide our sad feelings from You.

Help us to sit with friends and family who are sad, knowing that when we share the weight of our pain, it feels a little less heavy.

Bless those who feel disappointed or lonely during the Advent season. Help our family to be loving to those who are hurting. And may we feel Your love around us always. Amen.

older

O God who wept, we give our tears to You as an offering.

And when the tears have been wiped away and our hearts begin to heal, grow us in empathy and move us in compassion so we may sit with the hurting, weep with the weeping, mourn with the mourning.

Thank You for calling us beloved and for making space for us to move through grief and pain. Christ, You are the fullness of God, and in You, we become more fully human.

We pray for those who hold the weight of grief and ask that You would move us to be agents of comfort in this Advent season. Amen.

Wake Up

MY DAUGHTER DIDN'T smile for six months of her life. As I scooped her up from her crib in the morning and as I rocked her to sleep at night, I prayed. I held her close to my chest and prayed she'd come back to me. I begged God to help our little girl awaken through the medicine's fog, to help her be with us again.

My prayers were desperate bargains and pleas.

This is how it began: At not even a year old, Eliza's brain was on fire. Pointing to the high peaks on her brain scans, the neurologist explained that her invisible seizures were like static from an old TV. "Infantile spasms," she said, adding the notation to Eliza's growing medical chart.

"This can be common for babies like Eliza," doctors told me. "You know, kids with Down syndrome. We need to try to get them under control."

After "irreparable damage," I think I stopped hearing their words.

I stayed up late by the glow of my laptop, researching medicines to consider, top doctors to visit, and new treatment options to try. Nothing worked. I wanted answers. Every time a top physician shared the refrain *There's so much we don't know*, I felt crushed under the weight of human fragility.

One of the last hopes for treatment was a specialized medicine we were trained to inject, twice a day, into her chubby thighs. We filled out the paperwork and waited for weeks to see if our financial aid application would be approved for the specialty drug, which cost $31,626 for a single vial.

She needed a vial every month.

After the pharmaceutical company deemed her case desperate enough, we received a box covered with warning labels and filled with dry ice. It contained a tiny glass bottle that held the hope it would stop the seizures from inflicting incurable brain damage.

I couldn't hold her soft body down without crying. My husband was brave, whispering soft songs for her as he slid the tiny needle into her flesh as quickly and gently as possible.

A month into the medicine, she stopped crying at the injections.

She stopped laughing, too.

She stopped doing much of anything.

I can't think about the pain we watched her hold without feeling ill myself. The steroid left her tiny body swollen and puffy. Her eyes lost their light. I believed she was still there, somewhere.

"Her smiles are asleep," I told our three-year-old and six-year-old sons. "Maybe someday soon they'll wake up."

She continued to experience seizures. The medicine didn't work. Her brain and body had been through enough. We decided to end the trial, to put a stop to this medical trauma. I rubbed lotion over her swollen, scar-marked thighs and whispered in her ear, "You are beautiful. You are loved. Come back to us."

Slowly, she did. The light in her eyes awakened. One afternoon, I buckled her into the car seat, and she flashed me a gummy smile, her almond eyes sparkling. It was one of the most beautiful sights in the world. I cried again—happy tears this time. I shouted to Jonny, "She smiled! She smiled!"

Today, our daughter is described as *joyful, happy,* and *smiley* in her school records. When my husband mentioned some of her early struggles to her first-grade teacher, she couldn't fathom that Eliza hadn't always been this way. *May I never forget that her laughter is the sound of a miracle.*

Now she's six years old instead of six months old. She continues to wake up to the world around her. I wish I could tell you that her seizures were cured and the brain damage was repaired. She works hard at physical, occupational, speech, and feeding therapy. We've learned to relearn our understanding of cognitive and developmental milestones. We are hearing her speak through assistive technology. We are seeing her use every extraordinary muscle to take her first steps with a walker.

Disability theologian Dr. Amy Kenny says, "The truth is that being disabled is hard, beautiful, heartbreaking, illuminating, full of loss, and full of life."[8] As we parent Eliza, we hold the heartbreak and celebrate every hard-won victory. Most of all, we rejoice that Eliza's smiles have shaken off their slumber. Because her smiles represent her joy, not what her body can or cannot do.

In Mark 5:35-43, we're invited into the story of a dying daughter, a parent's plea, and a good God who awakens us from our slumber.

The story starts with a man named Jairus, whose little girl is very sick. All the resources and treatments at his disposal won't make her better. He makes his way into the crowd, where a man named Jesus is teaching.

Jairus has heard that this teacher is unique—that this man isn't just a man. This man can perform miracles. Jairus is trying to make his way through the hordes of people when messengers from his house come, bearing the worst possible news.

"It's too late," they tell him breathlessly, staring at the ground as they struggle to look him in the eye, delivering an update no one wants to share. "Your daughter, the girl you used to hold as a baby, the little one you held on your shoulders, took her last breath. She's gone. Don't bother asking this man for help."

Through the crowd, Jesus hears what's happening. "Don't be afraid," He says to this man who has just received the worst news imaginable. "Just believe."

Jesus leaves the rush of people, allowing just a few friends to join Him, and walks with Jairus to his daughter. Maybe they journey in silence. Maybe they run until their sides ache, a parent's desperate return. As they get close, they can hear the weeping and wailing of everyone who loved her. Maybe Jairus's heart sank for the second time that day.

"Why are you crying?" Jesus asks the grieving friends and family who are gathered inside. "This child isn't dead—she's asleep."

The women and men who loved the little girl shake their heads and laugh bitterly, their eyes red and their noses running. *She's gone. It's honestly in poor taste to say she isn't,* they think.

Jesus clears the room, sending everyone outside. Then He gathers the little girl's father, mother, and the friends who have come with Him, and they return to where the daughter's lifeless body lies.

He holds her hand. Her parents take a breath.

"Talitha koum," He says, telling the little girl to wake up.

At the exact moment her parents exhale, the child opens her eyes. She sits up. She moves toward them. And for the first time that day, Jairus's heart soars.

They're "utterly astounded." Mark writes (5:42, CSB). What was asleep is now awake.

It seems like all creation sleeps in winter. Fall shifts to winter, as it always does, and as it does, the mighty oaks lose their laughter. Dark skies come early and stay late. Fields that once bore fruit grow stagnant. We call it "the dead of winter" for a reason. Limbs become bare and brittle, leaves sink into the soil, and animals hibernate, hiding in a deep sleep.

You will experience seasons of winter in your life; this is true. But winter will not stay forever.

In the winters of our lives, we wait. Sometimes we weep. And we wonder, *Will spring ever come? Will life return? Will we wake up? Will we ever see another smile?*

Just when we think our questions to Jesus are futile, the earth begins to awaken. Shoots of green grass push forward from the dirt. The warmth of the springtime sun greets us in the morning. And we begin to believe that, beyond all understanding, we will awaken with it.

We, too, will smile again. "Wake up, sleeper, rise from the dead, and Christ will shine on you" (Ephesians 5:14, NIV).

Scripture only describes the part about Jesus holding the girl's lifeless hand, telling her to wake up. We don't know what spring looked like for her after she awoke from her winter. Maybe she walked with a limp. Perhaps she didn't speak. Maybe she was disabled like my daughter, Eliza. Maybe not. We don't know what the next season of their family's life held.

But I have to think her mother held her in her arms and whispered that she was beautiful. I have to think her father never forgot that he bore witness to a miracle.

You will experience seasons of winter in your life; this is true. You likely already have, feeling the fragility of life as you ache for your children, yourself, and all of creation. But winter will not stay forever. Spring will come. It may not look the way you hoped, the way you thought it would. But it's there, holding your hand, inviting you to wake up. May you be present to the awakening.

As the cycle of the seasons repeats, may you bear witness to both the scars and the smiles. May you be utterly astounded.

SCRIPTURE
Mark 5:35-43; Ephesians 5:14

BREATH PRAYER

Inhale: Awaken me, Jesus.
Exhale: Astound me with Your presence.

FAMILY DISCUSSION QUESTIONS

Read Mark 5:35-43 together.

▶ What do you think Jairus was thinking and feeling in this story? What would you do if you were in his shoes?

- The people crying over the girl's death laughed when Jesus said she was sleeping. Why might others laugh or roll their eyes when they see our hope in Jesus?

- Why do you think winter comes before spring?

- Have you ever had a scar? What happened? What was the process of healing like?

- When have you felt like God didn't hear your prayer? What happened? How did you feel?

- What does it mean to stay awake to your feelings?

- What does it mean to stay awake to what's happening in our world?

- How can we stay awake to Jesus in our lives?

- It's said that Albert Einstein believed "there are only two ways to live your life. One is as though nothing is a miracle. The other is as though everything is a miracle." How do you define the word *miracle*?

- Have you ever witnessed a miracle?

FAMILY PRAYER

younger

Dear God, You are with us in every season. You are with us in the dark winter skies and in the sunshine of spring.

When we are sad, please comfort us. When we are scared, be near us.

Help us to believe You will never leave us, even when we feel sad or scared. Help us to believe You are the God who does miracles all around us, every day. We love You. Amen.

older

O God, awaken us from our slumber. Renew in us the ability to see the miracles surrounding us. Restore in us the trust that spring will come. Refresh in us the strength we need for the day as we hold out hope for tomorrow.

We give You every dark wondering we hold and ask that You would breathe new life into what is bare. Let us feel You in our scars.

Help us to remember that You are compassionate and that You are near. We believe, Jesus. Help us in our unbelief. Amen.

Time after Time

THE DAY AFTER CHRISTMAS, my local big-box store starts clearing the shelves, slashing prices on leftover sweaters and toys. Employees work diligently, torn from family gatherings, to make way for the next wave of seasonal sales, replacing candy canes with candy hearts.

In our culture's liturgy of consumerism, the seasons are marked by what sells and how much we can accumulate.

Pastel jelly beans and chocolate Easter eggs beckon us in February. Back-to-school supplies arrive on the shelves before the Fourth of July. How deep can our carts be filled with purchases? How wide can they stretch the shelf time of seasonal items?

"We live with a powerful cultural narrative that defines us first and foremost as consumers," says Wendy Wright. But she says that families and faith communities can be rooted in Christ, overcoming this commercial narrative.[9] As followers of Christ, we have the gift of marking our calendars with a different sort of time. We orient our year with the liturgical calendar, which walks us through the rhythms of Christ's life, death, and resurrection. We are no longer beholden to the marketplace, where we must consume our way into seasonal celebrations.

Christians across backgrounds, bloodlines, and borders enter this calendar with a larger understanding of God's time, rooted in Christ instead of in the shifting sands of constantly refreshed endcaps at our favorite stores. We incorporate yearly rituals and rhythms, welcoming God into our homes and hearts. As we enter this sacred circle of time, we worship and pray, celebrate and grieve. We read Scripture, practice traditions, and observe the work of Christ in us and around us. Year after year, we cycle through liturgical seasons, embarking on times of both contemplation and action.

The Christian year begins in Advent, and it's a natural time to begin to integrate liturgical rhythms into our families' days. In the midst of a busy, often stressful holiday season, observing Advent helps us to stay rooted in anticipation of Christ's arrival. It tethers us to something deeper so we don't float away like gifts on Santa's sleigh.

Advent invites us to be time travelers—to embark inside an ancient, sacred story of what *was* and somehow *is*, too.

Chronos, the Greek word for the chronological understanding of time, is not all there is. As children of God, we are also welcomed into *kairos*, a divine sense that time is a circle we live in and outside of. Kairos reminds us that as seasons shift and we raise our families, do our jobs, and live our seemingly ordinary lives, we experience extraordinary glimmers of something more. Though our feet are firmly planted on earth, kairos time allows us to catch a glimpse of heaven.

We cannot measure it, but sometimes this holy time beyond time can "enter, penetrate, break through chronos: the child at play, the painter at his easel . . . are in kairos. The saint at prayer, friends around the dinner table, the mother reaching out her arms for her newborn baby, are in kairos," wrote Madeleine L'Engle.[10]

My family started rolling beeswax candles for our Advent wreath a few years ago. (The kits make it easy—all you need is a blow dryer and about five minutes of patience.) Neither my husband nor I grew up with the tradition of lighting Advent wreaths in our homes, but it has become a beloved tradition for both grown-ups and kids in our family.

Over the four Sundays leading up to Christmas, we gather around our dining room table in anticipation. Our weeknight dinners of tacos and pizza feel more sacred as the candles flicker and wax pools below. Each Sunday, we light a new candle as we observe this family ritual. We reflect on the world's need for God to break in and usher in a new reality, and we pray simple prayers together. (Also, my sons *really* like setting things on fire, so lighting candles has a built-in level of excitement.)

Rituals like the lighting of the Advent wreath "are crucial to the well-being and identity of families. Too often, the word ritual connotes an occasion that is routinized, boring, or artificial. But in fact, ritual behavior is deeply human behavior."[11]

While holiday ads pop up on our phones and commercials crowd our TVs, inviting us into rituals of shopping until we drop, whispering that our identity lies in being a consumer, our little lighting-of-the-wreath ritual points us and our children toward something deeper: the knowledge that our truest identity is found in Christ.

"In historical time, Christmas happened over two thousand years ago in Bethlehem; in theological time, Christmas happens now, in the mystery of God choosing to dwell within humankind, a mystery that transcends all time."

VICKI K. BLACK,
WELCOME TO THE CHURCH YEAR

In the book of Ephesians, followers of Jesus are told to loosen their grip on the old ways, to leave the rhythms of the world for something more beautiful in Christ. *The Message* puts it this way: "Take on an entirely new way of life—a God-fashioned life, a life renewed from the inside and working itself into your conduct as God accurately reproduces his character in you" (4:24).

Advent is an invitation to reexamine how God has worked and will work in our lives as we wait for the light of Christ to illuminate every shadow. As we light more candles and journey further into the Advent season at the precipice of Jesus' birth, we become more in tune with the Light of the World (see John 8:12)—and what it means to wait for Immanuel, God with us (see Matthew 1:23).

May your family embrace the mystery of time this Advent season, remembering that your identity is in Christ alone.

SCRIPTURE
Ephesians 4:24; John 8:12; Matthew 1:23

BREATH PRAYER

Inhale: O Light of the World,
Exhale: My identity lies in You.

FAMILY DISCUSSION QUESTIONS

A PRAYER
FOR ADVENT

*O come,
    Emmanuel.
Ignite in us the awe
    of a child,
Looking into a
    manger scene
As we wait on the
    promise
Of the coming
    infant King
In a humble stable.*

TO LIGHT THEIR WAY

Read John 8:12 together.

▸ What do you think it means that Jesus is the Light of the World?

▸ Where do you see or hear advertisements throughout the day (TV, podcasts, YouTube, social media, radio, billboards, etc.)?

▸ Why do you think companies tell us we'll feel better if we buy more things?

▸ When have you desperately wanted an item only to be disappointed after you got it?

▶ How is God's time different from culture's time?

▶ Why is it important to follow God's time?

▶ How can we feel excited about the birth of Jesus if it already happened?

▶ How does Advent (waiting for the birth of Christ) invite us to be time travelers?

▶ What rituals does our family have during Advent and Christmas? Are there any rituals you'd like to add?

▶ How can traditions help us stay rooted in God's time?

FAMILY PRAYER

younger

God, You are the Creator of time. In You, all things are formed.

As we prepare to celebrate the birth of Jesus, help us to remember that there has never been a moment when You haven't gone behind us or before us. Thank You for the gift of Your presence yesterday, today, and tomorrow.

Christ, You are in all time, and You are all time.

Help us to remember that when You became a human, You could have come to Earth as a powerful king, but instead You came as a tiny baby who needed help. You know what it's like to be a child. Jesus, when You were born, it changed everything, and Your Spirit continues to work in our lives today.

Nothing we could ever buy—no present under the tree—could come close to You, Jesus. We love you. Amen.

older

O Christ, through You we enter a sacred circle of time.

As we anticipate the birth of Jesus, please orient our hearts so we might tune our days to You. As we journey through Advent, renew us from the inside out. Awaken us to a deeper sense of time that is both now and not yet.

In Your Incarnation, we hear echoes of eternity. May these sacred reverberations form our family as we journey deeper into knowing You. Fashion us to reflect Your character, O God who became a vulnerable baby, born in a barn.

As we approach Christmas, help us to subvert the empires of consumerism and consumption, living in the light of Your glorious love, time after time. Amen.

The Stories We Tell

"YOU CAN COME DOWN HERE," my grandma whispers, inviting me downstairs into her secret lair—the unfinished basement laundry room I'm not allowed to play in.

I follow her down the creaky stairs, a rush of cool air greeting me as I leave the warmth of the living room—full of sweater-clad cousins and platters piled high with sugar cookies—behind. I itch under the collar of my Christmas sweater and wonder if my mom knows I'm down here.

My grandma waves me over to the laundry area. "Look," she says, her eyes aglow.

She hands me a Tide detergent box she had spray-painted brown. "For the Nativity play."

She gives me a few other household items she had spray-painted gold. "For the wise men," she says with a wink.

I follow her up the stairs and smirk to myself. *This is my year,* I think.

For the past couple of years, the cousins have performed a haphazard living room performance of the Christmas story. My older cousin always gets to be the narrator, but I've claimed the angel role this year. I will be the one who stands above the manger scene, clearing my throat and projecting my voice to each grown-up sitting on the couch.

My grandma wraps me in a bolt of white fabric and places a halo crafted from a ring of starry wire garland on my head. I'm transformed into the star I was born to be. She wraps my cousin, ex-narrator, in a bolt of blue, preparing her to be Mary. We swaddle an old doll in a blanket, and I wrangle my little brother, directing him to his mark, where he'll have to act as all three kings since we don't have enough cousins to fill the cast.

My dad lifts a bulky video camcorder onto his shoulder. The performance is about to begin. Preshow jitters fill me with goosebumps. I can't wait to truly bless these audience members with my creative retelling of the birth of Jesus.

I'm about to start with, "In those days, a decree went out from Caesar Augustus that all the world should be registered . . ." when my cousin—playing *Mary*—starts narrating.

My eyes grow as big as the red bulbs adorning my grandma's Christmas tree.

This was *not* the plan.

Last year, when I was Mary, she told me Mary couldn't be the narrator because she was supposed to "sit still and be silent!"

Thirty-something years later, I have still to let this slight go. I've never been one for being silent.

When I think back on holidays past, I reflect on the stories we share. I feel a pang for what was and what never will be again, and at the same time feel a swell of gratitude for the gift of stories we can treasure time and again.

As families, we tell and retell stories, passing down bits of our history—reflections of our humanity—to the generations that come behind us. Our family stories make us who we are, helping us understand our place in the world. "Our stories tell us who we are and to whom we belong. So it is important that we tell stories—the small as well as the big stories," writes Wendy Wright.[12] Within my immediate family, my Nativity nightmare has become one of lore. Decades have passed, but every Christmas, the story of how I lost the narrator role—*again*—is somehow brought up. My mom can't stop laughing about the slight, and I can't overcome the indignity of it all.

As we observe Advent and approach Christmas, our families are filled with stories we can't help but share. As the family of Christ, we set aside time to tell one of the greatest stories of all time: the one where Love came down and God became flesh, entering the world in the form of a baby.

It's a riveting story: a cast of unexpected characters, a cosmic Incarnation, the culmination of a million smaller stories building until they burst into a night that changed history, its reverberations echoing into eternity.

When I first started dating my husband, he was taken aback by how my family shares stories when we get together, how we laugh at the same memories as we gather around the table, passing the peace in the form of memories. We trot out big stories about life events and vacations past, and we share little stories too, about seemingly mundane things that have been told and retold so many times that the telling itself has become funnier and more exciting than the original inspiration for the tale.

We've been married for fifteen years, and now Jonny knows all the tales by heart (he is the star in some stories of his own).

"When a story starts, you can see everyone in the room join into the common memory," Jonny told me once. "There's no hesitation or doubt about the details—the story has been honed; we all follow the

Our family stories make us who we are, helping us understand our place in the world.

beat together. No matter how often we tell the stories, they never seem boring or like old news. We become even closer knit as we remember together, enjoying the laughter and reflection of sharing family stories."

As we raise our kids, we create our own stories, passing them down at the dinner table as we pass the mashed potatoes. Wright says, "Family stories do more than cement us together in remembered intimacy. Our stories also point to the values we hold dear."[13] I look back to childhood Christmas celebrations at my grandparents' house and remember the intimacy of my grandmother's invitation into the laundry room, the way she made me feel special and seen as she placed a ring of garland on my head. I remember the value of being together, of finding my part in a bigger story.

When the terrifying and wonderful angels appeared above that field so long ago, telling the ordinary shepherds a story of splendor that seemed almost too good to be true, the shepherds were in awe. They had to see this Baby for themselves—they had to find their place in the story. And once they did, they couldn't help but tell and retell what happened, sharing with everyone the glory of the story they had a front-row seat to.

As for Mary, she rocked the fresh Baby, treasuring up all the tiny miracles that had culminated into the cosmic Grace she held in her arms. She held the greatest stories of all in her heart "and thought about them often" (Luke 2:19).

We hold our stories in the heartbeats of our days. We think about them often. We share them repeatedly, telling them to our children. As we do, we live into who we are and find beauty in who we're with.

As you approach Christmas, take time to marvel at the stories of Jesus' birth. Read Luke 2:1-20 aloud with your children. Listen to an audio retelling of the Gospel account. Attend a Nativity play.

And when you find at least a sliver of a silent night, ask Jesus—Immanuel, God with us—how your story fits into God's most extraordinary story.

SCRIPTURE
Luke 2:1-20; Matthew 1:18-25

BREATH PRAYER

Inhale: Immanuel,
Exhale: God with us.

FAMILY DISCUSSION QUESTIONS

Read Luke 2:1-20 together.

▶ Why do we tell the same story about Jesus' birth every year? How can we learn new things from listening to the same story over and over again?

▶ Why is the Christmas story one of the best stories of all?

▶ What is your favorite family story that we retell?

▶ What family story makes you laugh?

▶ What story reminds you that you belong?

▶ Why is it special to remember together?

▶ What is your favorite Christmas memory?

▶ Tell about a time you attended a Nativity play. What stood out to you about it?

▶ Who is a good storyteller you know? What makes someone a good storyteller?

FAMILY PRAYER

younger

God, You write the best stories. Thank You for letting us be part of them.

As we think about the birth of Jesus, we thank You for the many stories in Scripture—and in our lives—that reflect Your big love.

Help us to be storytellers who share the ways we see You, feel You, and hear You. Thank You for the special memories we've made over the years with friends and family. As we look forward to Christmas, help us to make space in our hearts for the story Jesus is writing in our lives. Amen.

older

O God, You are the Author of life itself. You whisper life in all its glory into existence and invite us to dwell on the pages of the best story of all.

In this season, we set aside the noise of the world to tell the truest tale—the one where Love came down and You became flesh, taking Your first breath among us and changing the course of history forever.

We marvel at Christ incarnate and give thanks for the invitation to enter the story of Jesus, now and forevermore. Amen.

God of Galaxies

I ADORED MY HIGH SCHOOL astronomy class—and not just because we got to take frequent field trips to the planetarium (my learner's permit allowed me to drive there *myself*).

Though I participated in my fair share of whispering and giggling with friends in class while we were supposed to be listening, I found myself growing increasingly interested in the swirl of space as I learned more about the vastness of our universe.

Our teacher would push an orange, square button on a beeping and buzzing machine (the planetarium was a relic from the 1960s space race), and the domed ceiling would shift to black, transporting us into the great unknown, where projected planets seemed just out of reach. I couldn't pretend to be too cool to be captivated. I spent afternoons with my nose in my textbook and nights gazing into the stars.

"You're into this?" my friend asked, popping her gum. "Is it, like, because of horoscopes?" Then she asked if she could copy my homework.

Teenagers tend to think they have everything figured out, and I was no exception. I spent most of my time convincing my parents—and myself—how grown up I was. But as my patient teacher invited us to consider the stars, I was pulled back to earth, reminded of just how much I didn't know. With my head tilted heavenward, I felt an overwhelming sense that I was—and would always be—a little child, hemmed into this world by the love of a Creator God.

We know that we are called children of God, but how often do we get so lost in the cold, harsh edges of the grown-up world that we forget the comfort of being small, climbing into the warm lap of a loving, protective Parent?

When the skies turn dark and the kids are asleep, I sometimes leave the roar of the fireplace and step out into the silent snow, watching my breath swirl into puffy clouds. I look to the stars, the ones still sparkling amid the glow of the streetlights, and think of Psalm 8:3-4: "When I look at the night sky and see the work of your fingers—the moon and the stars you set in place—what are mere mortals that you should think about them, human beings that you should care for them?"

When the James Webb Space Telescope released never-before-seen photographs of glittering distant galaxies in 2022, the world stopped shouting at each other and entered a communal sense of wonder and awe. The images captured mountains and valleys of cosmic dust, shedding new light on how stars are born and revealing "thousands of galaxies in a tiny sliver of vast universe."[14] People spanning all religious and political ideologies found themselves captivated, eager to put words to the unexplainable.

When I was a child, rocking crooked bangs and wire-rimmed glasses, I loved getting lost in stories. When my fifth-grade teacher pointed me toward a copy of *A Wrinkle in Time* by Madeleine L'Engle, a book about a seemingly ordinary girl who embarks into the great unknown of space to do extraordinary things, I gobbled it up.

In *A Circle of Quiet*, one of L'Engle's memoirs, she reflects, "Just as we are taught that our universe is constantly expanding out into space at enormous speeds, so too our imagination must expand as we search for the knowledge that will in its turn expand into wisdom, and from wisdom into truth."[15]

As I examined the space photos, I could hardly fathom that the captures were real. The colors seemed much too vivid, their depth too vast. They looked like paintings, each curve and contour crafted with precision, crafted with skill by the hand of a masterful artist. I was captivated.

The groundbreaking photos reveal much to scientists (who are brilliant in their own right) about the mysteries our galaxies hold. While we all grapple with uncovering the answers within the mysteries, part of me feels like the girl who read books and the teenager who studied the stars, comforted in my smallness in this universal unknowing, resting in the fact that the One who hung the stars and breathed entire galaxies into existence also knows every hair on my head (see Luke 12:7).

As L'Engle puts it, "If every hair of my head is counted, then in the very scheme of the cosmos I matter; I am created by a power who cares about the sparrow, and the rabbit in the snare, and the people on the crowded streets; who calls the stars by name. And you. And me."[16] Whatever exists, exists because of the One who whispered it into existence.

John 1:1 says, "In the beginning was the Word, and the Word was with God, and the Word was God" (NIV). This truth swirls around us like the stardust in the photos. We can barely fathom it, yet somehow we believe it, leaning into the wonder despite our wanderings. And that is enough (see Mark 9:24).

As we observe Advent, the four weeks leading to the incarnational birth of Jesus, we sit in this mysterious, magnificent truth: In the beginning, the Word was with God. The

Word *was* God. Despite the mess humans created, God, being the very essence of love, chose to enter our world and become one of us: "The Word became flesh and made his dwelling among us. We have seen his glory, the glory of the one and only Son, who came from the Father, full of grace and truth" (John 1:14, NIV).

Jesus, the One who became fully human, was born as a baby among the muck and the mire of this complicated world. He existed out of space and time, and existed entirely within it too: "Truly, truly, I say to you," Jesus declared, "before Abraham was, I am!" (John 8:58, ESV).

Even the stars rejoiced at His birth, breaking through in brilliant swathes of light, showing the way (see Matthew 2:9-10).

As you approach Christmas, rest in the wonder of our big God, and let it compel you to live in the light of infinite divine love, extending love and grace to yourself, your children, and your neighbors. As L'Engle writes, "To matter in the scheme of the cosmos: this is better theology than all our sociology. It is, in fact, all that God has promised to us: that we matter. That he cares. . . . If God cares about us, we have to care about each other."[17] May you rest in your smallness this week, letting the children among you remind you that the God of galaxies loves you so much that He became like you—born as a baby. Let your imagination ride the waves left by the trail of stardust; let your life be captured by the glorious, limitless love of Christ.

SCRIPTURE
Luke 12:7; John 1:1; Mark 9:24; John 1:14; Matthew 2:9-10

JAMES WEBB SPACE TELESCOPE IMAGES

If your family is interested in exploring our galaxy more, you can visit webb.nasa .gov to see the images.

BREATH PRAYER

Inhale: O God of every galaxy,
Exhale: Help me to rest in my smallness.

FAMILY DISCUSSION QUESTIONS

Read Matthew 2:9-10 together.

- ▸ Why do you think God used a star to guide people to Jesus?
- ▸ Why did God, who was so mighty and powerful that He created entire galaxies, come to earth to be born as a baby?

▶ Have you ever watched a solar or lunar eclipse? What happened?

▶ Why is pop culture so drawn to fictional universes in space?

▶ Why do you think so many people are curious about the moon and the stars?

▶ What can space teach us about God's character?

▶ Why is it important to use our imagination when we wonder about God?

▶ What do you imagine heaven is like?

FAMILY PRAYER

younger

Dear God, You made the heavens and the earth. Every shimmering star and spinning planet whispers Your name! The sun and the moon do too.

It's hard for us to understand just how good and loving You are.

Thank You for the gift of Jesus and for sending a star to point people to You. God, You are powerful, and Your love is perfect. Amen.

older

O God of space and time, You are the creator of the heavens and the earth.

With purpose and power, You sculpted shimmering stars and set planets in motion. The sun, moon, and stars whisper Your name, reflecting Your goodness and inviting us into glory we can barely begin to fathom.

We marvel at the mystery of Your compassion that stretches through eternity in Christ. We find comfort that You—the God of galaxies—love each of us with divine, perfect, and infinite love. You are the Artist who sculpts us out of dust and knows us down to every hair on our heads. We dwell in the mystery and delight in how deeply You care for us.

Help us to reflect Jesus this Advent, caring for those who feel unseen and cast into the shadows. May we cultivate peace for all people in this season and in the days to come. Amen.

Vulnerable God

MY PATENT LEATHER shoes don't reach the floor mats. I dangle my legs from the car seat, a lap belt hemming me in. My tights are itchy under my tartan dress, but for once I don't seem to mind. I exhale as the engine starts; my breath is a puffy cloud. I rub my eyes and rest my head on the cool window, trying to resist sleep.

Magic swirls around me as my dad pulls out of my grandpa's driveway, the snow crunching under the tires. Christmas lights strung across banisters and windows blur in bright streaks as we pull out of the neighborhood.

The streets are asleep, and everything feels anointed. My dad shuttles us from one set of grandparents' house to another, where we'll spend the night. If I weren't so exhausted from adventuring with my cousins, if my tummy weren't so full of pie, if my cheeks weren't so rosy from the waxy remnants of my great-grandmother's smooch, I'd consider asking my parents to retrieve my new purple Care Bear from the trunk, which they strategically packed full of freshly unwrapped presents, putting their Tetris skills to good parental use.

Instead, I lean toward the backseat speaker, listening to Nat King Cole offer a "simple phrase to kids from one to ninety-two." The music mingles with my parents' hushed tones as they rehash the holiday events. My baby brother is fast asleep. My eyelashes flutter, but I fight sleep. I'm a big girl. And I don't want the night to end.

The drive across town takes one hundred hours. At last we pull into the driveway.

"I think they're asleep," my dad whispers.

"We can carry them in," my mom offers.

I shut my eyes tight. She opens the sedan's backseat door. Crisp night air greets my cheeks. I squeeze my eyes together.

As Mom unbuckles me, I sneak a peek and assess her quickly. *Yep, she's totally buying it.*

I try to suppress my smirk. I keep my eyes mostly closed and make my legs, arms, and neck go limp for the full effect. My mom clears her throat and announces in a voice a bit louder than usual that *both* kids are fast asleep.

I let a smile escape as I rest my head on her shoulder. At five years old, my acting skills are through the roof. The air is cold. But in her arms, I'm warm. She positions my puffy coat over me like a blanket. Her musky perfume mixes with traces of a woodburning fireplace in the winter air as she carries me up the steps.

I fall asleep believing I've pulled a fast one on my parents. I also fall asleep knowing I am safe, understood, and loved.

I marvel at the mystery that the God of all—the mighty One full of power and wonder, worthy of every praise—entered our world not as a conquering king but as a vulnerable baby. He made himself vulnerable, fulfilling Isaiah's prophecy that "a little child will lead them all" (see Isaiah 11:6).

I have to wonder: Why would He have come in such a humble way? Maybe He wanted to know what it was like to be held by a mother, carried safely in her arms while the rest of the world was asleep. Perhaps He wanted to know what it felt like to be tucked in by a father, the shoes on His feet gently removed, the sweaty hair on his forehead pushed away for a good-night kiss.

"How can anyone even begin to have an incarnational view of the universe without an incredible leap of the imagination? That God cares for us, every single one of us, so deeply that all power is willing to come to us, to be with us, takes all the imagination with which we have been endowed," wrote Madeleine L'Engle.[18]

Jesus, our God-made-flesh, embraced humanity to the extent that He entered the most vulnerable human state: a newborn, just like the rest of us. Through extraordinary circumstances, Jesus was knit together in the womb of a mother, like you and me—fearfully and wonderfully made (see Psalm 139:13-16). He was a babe, tiny and vulnerable, swaddled and held close by his mother (see Luke 2:12).

In the glittering overwhelm of our culture's Christmas preparations, it's easy to lose the cord that binds our celebrations together—this beautiful, incarnational mystery of Christ. When we relegate this cosmic reordering to an oversimplified greeting-card scene, it's difficult to fathom a mighty God choosing to wear our human vulnerabilities.

What was it like for Jesus to breathe in the scent of his mother, finding comfort in her arms? Did He trip and fall as a wobbly toddler? Did He climb trees as a knobby-kneed child? Was He awkward, with facial breakouts, as a teen?

Artist-storyteller Scott Erickson used his visual illustration skills

"Vulnerability is not weakness; it's our greatest measure of courage."

BRENÉ BROWN,
ATLAS OF THE HEART

to create a compelling, contemplative Advent series that depicts fully human, fully divine scenes such as a laboring Mary, Jesus growing in the womb, and even the incarnate Christ getting a diaper change. The striking images shake us from the serene, sanitized storybook version of Christmas and invite us into a sacred posture of imagination. "Any real connection involves vulnerability because it takes the act of making oneself open to truly be known. God came to us floating in embryonic fluid. Slowly forming and taking shape," Erickson writes.[19] Jesus' birth is a tangible offering of connection through vulnerability—a divine, redemptive reauthoring in the story of who we are. Though the words are familiar, may we reclaim our sense of astonishment as we hear about this ancient dream that became a reality: "For to us a child is born, to us a son is given" (Isaiah 9:6, NIV).

As I unbuckle my half-asleep child from her five-point harness, I wonder, *Did Jesus hold close to those first tender childhood memories as He grew older? In His ministry, and as He held out His arms in death, did He remember what it was like to be held by a mother?*

My daughter's cheek rests on my shoulder as her older brothers run up the sidewalk to my parents' house, stretching their legs after a long car ride. I hold her in my arms, tiptoeing up the icy sidewalk under a canopy of stars. I breathe in the smell of woodsmoke and open the front door. We step into the warm living room, full of sweater-clad family members who are laughing and shouting and sharing stories on top of each other.

In many ways, I still feel like a child. The world is big and overwhelming. But at this moment, I know I am safe, understood, and loved.

This is the gospel message. This is Christ incarnated, again and again and again. The One who was born a baby calls me and you beloved.

What a mystery.

What a gift.

SCRIPTURE
Isaiah 11:6; Luke 2:12; Psalm 139:13-16; Isaiah 9:6

BREATH PRAYER

Inhale: O God incarnate,
Exhale: You understand.

FAMILY DISCUSSION QUESTIONS

Read Luke 2:12 together.

- ▶ Why do you think Jesus entered Earth as a baby? What do you imagine Jesus was like as a baby?

- ▶ What does it mean that Jesus was fully divine and fully human?

- ▶ What does it mean to be vulnerable?

- ▶ In what ways is a baby vulnerable? What do parents have to do to care for their babies?

- ▶ Have you ever pretended to be asleep so your parents would carry you? Why do you think kids do that?

- ▶ How does it feel to know that Jesus understands what it's like to be human and that He has experienced all the emotions we feel?

- ▶ When have you been vulnerable with a friend or family member? Why is it courageous to be vulnerable?

- ▶ How have you felt someone else's love or God's love after sharing a tender part of yourself?

- ▶ Can you tell about a time you felt safe, understood, and loved?

FAMILY PRAYER

younger

Jesus, You know what it feels like to be human.

You could have entered the world as a powerful king who shouted demands and ruled over all, but instead you came as a tiny baby, born in an unexpected place in an unexpected way. You chose to be a tiny baby who needed help, just like us. Your mom swaddled Your tiny body and rocked You to sleep.

Do You remember how that felt? We know that when we need help, we can turn to You. We don't have to pretend to be powerful or perfect or like we don't have problems. You understand. We can give our full, honest selves to You because You know exactly what it's like to be human.

Help us to use our imaginations as we approach Advent and celebrate Christmas. Amen.

older

O Christ who dwells in us and among us, help us to be people of courage and vulnerability.

Jesus, You went first, breaking through to our world as an infant, swaddled and held by a mother. We cannot begin to fathom the mystery of the Incarnation, but we delight in the awe of Your mystery. Your cosmic love transcends space and time, and You are worthy of every praise.

In this Advent season, ignite in us holy wonder and sacred imagination. May we stay awake to the divine offering of connection that You so generously give us. May we feel safe, known, and loved, never forgetting that You're always pursuing us and making a way where there is no way.

You know what it's like to be carried and to be the One who carries. May we take time to reflect on this beautiful mystery. Amen.

More Abundant

THE SOUND STARTLES ME from my slumber. I'm groggy. *What was that rustling noise?* I glance at the alarm clock: 6:03 a.m. It's still dark out. I push off the covers, the floor cold under my feet. My heel hits something. I grab my glasses and pull the oblong tote from underneath my bed. The lid is askew. Its contents have been rifled through.

Wrapping paper, gift bags, and tape are missing.

I catch the culprit out of the corner of my eye, a blur of bedhead and candy-cane pajamas. I hear the clink of LEGOs being dumped from their bins and wonder what my son the elf is up to.

It's too early to investigate. I grab my slippers and pad down the stairs, treading lightly so I won't wake anyone else. The wood floor bends and creaks, giving me away. I head into the kitchen and flick on the lights, making my way to the coffee maker. I glance at the kid-art calendar hanging on the wall and feel a pang of panic. The twenty-fifth is circled in red marker. I can hear the holiday commercial voice-over in my head: "Only nine shopping days left until Christmas!"

The wind howls from the window above the sink. Coffee percolates, pushing steam into the cold air. I hear footsteps above me, and for the second time that morning, I wonder what new mission my early riser has embarked upon.

I fill a mug and make my way back upstairs. I stand in his bedroom's doorway, waiting for him to notice.

After a few moments, he finally does. "Mom! Don't look!" he says. "I'm wrapping presents!" He's tangled in tape. *So much tape.* The wrinkled wrapping paper he pilfered carpets his room. I leave him to it.

One by one, gifts in odd-shaped packages arrive under the tree. In the evening, as we eat our macaroni and cheese, his excitement bubbles over. Throughout the day, he asks if I want to know which presents he's giving each of our family members. With my mouth full of noodles, I nod. He runs to the tree and comes back with a *Happy Birthday!* gift bag and a paper towel roll covered in seven layers of leftover Father's Day gift wrap.

He peels back the first layer so I can peek inside. There's a bouncy ball, some crayons, and one of his favorite LEGO mini figures, surrounded by wads of tissue paper.

He beams, outlining—in detail—why he picked each item for each recipient.

The gifts are accompanied by homemade cards adorned with custom drawings and lopsided hearts.

"I can't wait for them to open my presents! Why can't it be Christmas yet?"

His tender thoughtfulness and his willingness to give away some of his favorite toys grows my heart three sizes.

It's a convenient narrative to embrace: *kids are selfish.* But my children have taught me much more about generosity than most adults I know. We grown-ups get caught in a web of consumerism, plotting out Black Friday specials and falling over ourselves to buy the biggest and newest items, going into debt and working ourselves to the bone to pay off our layaways, believing a commercialized Christmas will bring us comfort and joy.

Kids seem to understand the joy of giving in ways adults tend to forget. They rifle through our recycling bins, grab Elmer's glue and handfuls of markers, and transform what we see as trash into handmade presents just for us. They go through their belongings and joyfully give them away. "God loves it when the giver delights in the giving," as it says in 2 Corinthians 9:7 (MSG).

Throughout the Old and New Testaments, we're told that God loves when we give. Because when we give out of an overflow of love, we reflect the heart of God.

I was taken aback by my son's gifts because they were some of his favorite toys. Yet he didn't bat an eye. He wanted to give what he could, even if it meant he would have less. Too often, as grown-ups, we overcomplicate giving. We think that only the ultrawealthy can make a difference, and we write off the seemingly small gifts from people who don't carry cultural clout (such as children or the poor) as well-meaning but simple and naive.

Is a wealthy person who signs extravagant checks while they winter in their beach house a better giver than a little child who wraps up a tiny toy in borrowed wrapping paper?

Jesus spoke directly to this question:

While Jesus was in the Temple, he watched the rich people dropping their gifts in the collection box. Then a poor widow came by and dropped in two small coins. "I tell you the truth," Jesus said, "this poor widow has given more than all the rest of them. For they have given a tiny part of their surplus, but she, poor as she is, has given everything she has."

LUKE 21:1-4

God broke into this earth as a baby born in a barn. When the magi heard of this miraculous birth, they had to see it for themselves. When they finally entered the house, road weary and exhausted, they looked up and saw the mother with her Son. Time seemed to stop.

It was a seemingly ordinary scene—just a mother and a baby. But when they saw Jesus in the arms of Mary, they just *knew*. This was different. They couldn't fully comprehend it, but they felt it deep in their bones: this incarnational mystery changed everything.

These powerful, educated kings were so overcome, they were moved to worship. Though they were used to giving orders, they fell to their knees, worshiping a little one who needed His nose wiped and His diaper changed. The men gave what they had out of pure joy and unabashed worship (see Matthew 2:11).

May your generosity reflect that of little children, poor widows, and humbled kings. May your giving be an act of worship to the King, who grew to spend his life inviting humanity to a more abundant way.

"Jesus' world was one of abundance. It was not one of wealth or prosperity, but of fulfillment and flourishing. Not extravagant, but enough, and even more than enough," writes Phuc Luu. "His kingdom consisted of showing the abundant nature of God's being, that there was more than enough to go around, that we can both have and share."[20] As your Advent calendar counts down to Christmas, may you have the heart of a child when it comes to giving. May your perspective be reoriented to reflect the King who left the glory He was due to be born in a humble barn.

SCRIPTURE
2 Corinthians 9:7; Luke 21:1-4; Matthew 2:11

BREATH PRAYER

Inhale: May all I give
Exhale: Be an act of worship.

FAMILY DISCUSSION QUESTIONS

Read Matthew 2:11 together.

- What's the most thoughtful gift you've received? What makes a gift special?

- ▸ When have you felt deep joy after giving someone a gift?

- ▸ When was the last time you created a homemade gift? What did you give?

- ▸ What do you think generosity means? How is God generous to us?

- ▸ How does it feel when someone extends generosity to you?

- ▸ How can generosity be an act of worship?

- ▸ What does our culture say about being wealthy? How is that different from Jesus' teaching about abundance (see John 10:10)?

- ▸ How can you be generous with your time?

- ▸ How can you give something you have more than enough of this week?

FAMILY PRAYER

younger

God, You are generous and kind. Thank You for giving us good gifts.

Your love is more than enough, but sometimes we forget that. Forgive us for the ways we haven't shared with others.

Help us to give out of what we have, like the widow with her coin or the kings who visited baby Jesus. Let our hearts make room for You by giving our time and talents without asking for anything in return. Help us to give with joyful hearts.

May all we make, all we say, and all we do be generous acts of worship to You. Amen.

older

O God of abundance, we come to You aware that even in light of Your lavish love, we hold within our hearts a propensity to store up our pennies, hoard our privileges, and clutch our power. Forgive us for the ways we've chosen greed over generosity, for in doing so we have worshiped at the altar of self instead of the manger of Jesus.

O Christ, as we reflect on Your humble beginnings, form a spirit of generosity in our family. May what we give and the spirit we give it in be acts of adoration and worship to You, our Servant King. Check our motives and move us forward in Your grace so we may live more abundant lives. May all we give—our time, our energy, and our resources—honor You, for all we have is Yours. May we be a family that finds our fulfillment in You so fully that our words and deeds are an overflow of Your peace for the flourishing of all people. Amen.

A PRAYER FOR
CHRISTMAS MORNING

As we watch our children,
Warm with last night's sleep,
We marvel that You,
Maker of heaven and earth,
Entered this world as one of us—
A cosmic King made vulnerable infant,
Swaddled in strips of cloth—
And You let us hold You in our arms.

TO LIGHT THEIR WAY

A Light Still Shines

MY SON'S ROOM GLOWS. A blue hue emanates from his lofted bed, rope lights casting a soft glow over LEGO creations, race cars, and stacks of comic books.

He loves his lights. I think they make his room look a bit like a bowling alley. It's a battle not worth fighting.

Beyond aesthetics, though, is the comfort—and courage—the lights give. He has his own room and is "way too old for nightlights," but he still keeps the lights on as he falls asleep. The glow pulses through the darkness, keeping bad dreams at bay.

Our world is often a dark place. Raising kids while navigating what lurks in the shadows can feel overwhelming and exhausting. But the Advent season, year after year, reminds us that when the darkness closes in, the Light of the World breaks forth.

I don't know about you, but I need the reminder that Jesus has, as Lisa Sharon Harper says, "transformed the world from a cesspool of overwhelming darkness, despair, sorrow, misery, destruction, and death into a world where darkness is limited by the light."[21] Having the Light of life doesn't mean we won't have to feel our way through dark times. It does mean that when we do, we aren't alone; we have Christ who will light the way. Jesus said, "I am the light of the world. Whoever follows me will never walk in darkness, but will have the light of life" (John 8:12).

In the first winter of the COVID-19 pandemic, a global shadow seemed to cover the world. We were all trying to feel our way out, but we weren't sure how. The physical world got darker sooner. Winds howled; snow fell. I wrapped lights around the tree much earlier than usual, kissing my kids on their heads as they decorated with glee. I watched the streetlights flicker on and clung to the hope that the Light of the World was with us—and breaking in again and again and again.

My husband and I couldn't shield our children from what was happening. Even our youngest, who was three years old, could sense the shadows that lingered over our life together. We ached to connect with others and missed the community we were used to having during the Advent season. I ordered extra boxes of lights, and as the temperatures descended, we climbed ladders (well, Jonny climbed ladders; I gave loving directions from below) and draped our home in a canopy of light. It served as a physical reminder that the Light of the World was with us, even then.

We came inside after stringing the lights, our noses red and our cheeks frozen, and we threw logs into the fireplace. Blanketing our home in sparkling lights hadn't solved anything, but it reminded us, and maybe a neighbor or two, that no matter what darkness lurks in the shadows of our lives, the Light still shines.

That Christmas Eve was different. Instead of joining a sanctuary full of kindred hearts, singing "Silent Night" as we passed the flame across wooden church pews, we worshiped from home in front of the glow of the living room computer. We didn't know what the future held. We were reminded in a deep way of our need for Christ's light.

During so much darkness, we held on to our belief that the Light of the World was a beautiful mystery who changed everything thousands of years ago—and is still illuminating the darkness. As headlines full of grief and loss tumbled in, the need for Christ's light felt all the more real. Søren Kierkegaard wrote, "Faith sees best in the dark."[22] In our darkest moments, faith is, as Hebrews 11:1 reminds us, being sure of what we hope for and certain of what we do not see.

I still shiver when I think of the dark unknowns of that pandemic winter. But I also know that God was with us all along, in the thick of the darkest night.

When my kids flick on their flashlights for a round of midnight tag, the light beams reveal what has been there all along. This kind of illumination reflects the nature of God, who "reveals the deep things of darkness and brings utter darkness into the light" (Job 12:22, NIV).

When we light a candle, or when the sun rises from its slumber, we witness in new ways the vivid colors all around us—colors that have existed all along, even in the shadows. When darkness closes in, it's easy to forget the wild kaleidoscope of hope and joy surrounding us too.

The seasons of Advent and Christmastide remind us that we are people of hope. Though our world is marked by despair, we also have delight. We have a God who didn't leave us in the darkness but made us to bear the light, reflecting and refracting into eternity.

As parents, we must guide our children through the very real pain and suffering in this world. It doesn't help to pretend the darkness doesn't exist. But as the anticipatory season of Advent reminds us, we also must invite them into the light. Madeleine L'Engle wrote,

THE TWELVE DAYS
OF CHRISTMAS

Your Christmas celebration doesn't have to end after December 25. Around the world, followers of Jesus observe the twelve days of Christmas, culminating in a holy day on January 6 (the twelfth day of Christmas), known as Epiphany. This day on the church calendar celebrates how a brilliant star led the faithful magi (or wise men) to visit Jesus after His birth.

"If we are not going to deny our children the darker side of life, we owe it to them to show them that there is also this wild brilliance, this light of the sun: although we cannot look at it directly, it is nevertheless by the light of the sun that we see."[23] As with my son's blue bedroom, lights offer comfort and courage against the backdrop of night. Advent is a season of hopeful waiting in a hurting world. As you anticipate the birth of Christ this winter, may you meet the Light of the World, right in the shadows.

SCRIPTURE

John 8:12; Hebrews 11; Job 12:22; Psalm 130:5

BREATH PRAYER

Inhale: Light of the World,
Exhale: You are with me.

FAMILY DISCUSSION QUESTIONS

Read John 8:12 together.

- ▸ Have you ever been somewhere that lost power? What happened when the lights went out? How did you feel?

- ▸ When a flashlight shines, it illuminates colors that have been there all along. What can this teach us about Christ?

- ▸ When has your world felt dark? What did it feel like to wait and hope for light to break through?

- ▸ What impact have dark seasons had on your faith?

- ▸ What helps you feel comforted or courageous in the dark?

- ▸ Why do you think Jesus calls himself the Light of the World?

- ▸ How can we add more light to our home and our community this Advent?

A PRAYER FOR EPIPHANY

Let this not be an end to Christmas joy But rather a beginning, Beckoning us toward the future, Toward a life of worshiping You.

TO LIGHT THEIR WAY

FAMILY PRAYER

younger

God, You are with us in the dark. When bad things happen, when we're lonely and afraid, when we wonder where You've gone, help us to remember that Your Spirit will never leave us.

Jesus, as we look forward to celebrating Your birth, we imagine the star that lit the way so long ago. When we think of You, we picture in our hearts a Light so full of love that it illuminates the whole world. Help us to remember Your love every time we see a twinkling star on a Christmas tree or the flicker of a candle's flame.

Give our family the faith to dance in the days to come. Amen.

older

O God, You are present in every dark night that surrounds us and every looming shadow that threatens to swallow us whole. When we wonder where the light has gone and we're feeling our way through the dark, unsure where You are, help us to sense Your Spirit.

Spark in us a holy hope, for You are Immanuel—You are with us. Light our way toward You.

Though we journey through despair at times, we are not alone in our cold, dark winter. You do not forsake us but call us to bear the light, reflecting and refracting Christ into eternity. Help us to dance in your wild brilliance. Amen.

"Our Christian wisdom is to name the darkness as darkness, and the Light as light, and to learn how to live and work in the Light so that the darkness does not overcome us."

RICHARD ROHR,
PREPARING FOR CHRISTMAS

Gathering the Stones

ONE OF THE MARVELOUS MYSTERIES about time is that we can't see it unfold. Logically, we know that our kids are growing older and that as time marches on, we grow older too. But we can't grasp the moment our toddler is no longer soft and round, our child ages out of wanting bedtime stories, or our teenager can suddenly fit into our shoes. We can't put our finger on the transitions that surround us. It takes a friend or family member who hasn't seen our kids in months to point out what we've been too close to see: *My, how they've grown!*

If you've captured digital snapshots of your family's life, you know the emotional roller coaster you ride when your photo app reminds you what happened on this day one, three, or six years ago. There are so many feelings wrapped in the swaddled blanket, so many emotions that woosh back from those birthday photos, the little faces aglow from the few candles ready to be wished upon.

As we look ahead to the dawning of a new year, we're also given the gift of reflecting on the past year—the millions of scattered moments that make up a life together, the countless memories that form us. Before we move ahead, we have to look behind at what was.

Parenting, like faith, is a constant remembering. We drop our kids off at school and remember what it felt like when we held them in our arms for the first time. We toss them the keys so they can make it to their new job and remember when we first removed their training wheels.

The demands of parenting and modern life are such that we rarely get to set aside space to intentionally remember. But throughout Scripture, God's people created physical monuments to memorialize God's movement in their lives.

After the people of Israel miraculously crossed the Jordan River into the Promised Land, God told Joshua to gather stones from "the very place where the priests are standing in the middle of the Jordan." They were to "carry them out and pile them up" where they were going to camp for the night (Joshua 4:2-3). The stones were gathered to create a physical reminder, a testament to the ways they'd experienced God's mysterious, miraculous love. There the rocks would stay, reminding generation after generation what God had done—and encouraging them to have faith in what God would do.

Since the beginning of time, God has told His people to share their memories. Remembering is not just an individual act; it's a communal one too. When we share our memories, we share our lives. Through remembering, we distill ourselves into the very essence of who we are and how we've experienced God's presence in our lives.

Old Testament theologian Walter Brueggemann says that time and again, God instructed the people of Israel to remember their lived experiences—and to share their stories of God's work in their lives for the sake of their children. When they focused on remembering, they'd be "prepared to answer the questions of children who inquire about the meaning."[24] Psalm 78:4-7 reminds us to share the wonders of God so that our children will also set their hope anew on God:

> We will not hide these truths from our children;
>   we will tell the next generation
> about the glorious deeds of the LORD,
>   about his power and his mighty wonders.
> For he issued his laws to Jacob;
>   he gave his instructions to Israel.
> He commanded our ancestors
>   to teach them to their children,
> so the next generation might know them—
>   even the children not yet born—
>   and they in turn will teach their own children.
> So each generation should set its hope anew on God,
>   not forgetting his glorious miracles
>   and obeying his commands.

As you approach the new year, set aside time to reflect by yourself on the past year, and then enter into a time of remembrance with your family. What wonders has God worked in your life this year, maybe even through times of trials? What surprises has God worked in your family? Your stories are meant to be shared and passed on to the children entrusted

Parenting, like faith, is a constant remembering.

134

to your care. As Bishop Michael Curry says, "Our stories are the song of the soul sung in the language of life."[25]

If you're unsure where to begin when reflecting on the past year, turn to appendix 2 for Examen questions to get started. (You can pray the Examen yearly, seasonally, and daily.)

At the end of the year, my husband and I get out a piece of paper and write down each month from the past year. Then we spend time filling in little moments or memories for each one. You are invited to try something similar as the year winds to a close. Let your bullet points act as stones of remembrance—tiny memorials to the work of God in your life.

SCRIPTURE
Joshua 4:2-3; Psalm 78:4-7

BREATH PRAYER

Inhale: You were with me then;
Exhale: You are with me now.

FAMILY DISCUSSION QUESTIONS

Read Psalm 78:4-7 together.

- What happened this year that surprised you?
- What happened that left you disappointed?
- Where did you go that was interesting or different?
- Who is someone new you met this year?
- What is something you felt proud of?
- When did you have fun this year? What brought you joy?
- Where did you see God at home? At work? At school?
- What scared you?
- What was the best compliment you received?
- What did you find energizing about your days? What felt draining?
- What did you learn about Jesus this year?

- How did you help someone else this past year? How did someone help you?

- What is something you'd like to improve for next year?

- What happened in the news that left you confused, curious, or concerned?

FAMILY PRAYER

younger

God, You have been with us all year long. When we were scared and when we felt safe, when we were lonely and when we felt loved—You were always with us.

Help us to remember that You never leave us. Help us to learn from the good moments, and the tough ones too. Bless all the places we went and all the people we met. We know that our stories are important, so help us to share with others the way we've seen You at work this year. All along, You've been with us. Thank You. Amen.

older

O God of the past and the present, we thank You for writing the best stories. You were with us in the times of deepest grief and in times of jubilant celebration.

Thank You for Your constant presence in our comings and goings this year. Please bless the stories we hold—all our victories, all our defeats, and all we learned. Imprint in us a spiritual memory of Your goodness and Your grace.

Help us to gather stones so we do not forget Your faithfulness in the coming year. All along, God, You have been there. We remember. Help us in our remembering. Amen.

Formed

"I HAVE SOMETHING FOR YOU, but I can't tell you what it is," my son whispers. He shifts his weight in excitement, his surprise on the precipice of bursting forth.

"It's a present! For you!" he says, his eyes wide.

He gestures to a small bag under the tree. The gift bag is stapled shut, as though his art teacher knows his kindergarteners are prone to revealing their crafts before it's time for their loved ones to open their gifts.

"I'll give you a hint!" he declares, brimming with pride. "I made it! With clay!"

He's not whispering anymore. His wide smile makes his face even rounder and sweeter than usual.

"That is so special," I tell him. "But maybe you shouldn't give me any more clues if you want to keep it a surprise."

He nods in agreement, taking his role as creator and gift giver seriously. He takes a beat.

"I'll just show you one last hint," he says, unable to contain his excitement.

He snaps his mouth shut to prevent himself from letting any more words escape, and instead of speaking, he uses exaggerated pinching motions, moving his pointer fingers and thumbs together. He looks like a little lobster.

I pull him close and kiss his soft cheek. "I can't wait to open it."

Like generations of parents before me (and all who will come after me), I've been the recipient of quite a few handmade pinch pots. These small ceramic creations adorn office bookshelves, kitchen windowsills, and bedroom nightstands. Some are large enough to hold about one earring post; others can hold tiny trinkets. They come in a kaleidoscope of colors and shapes, formed with care by little hands, their fingerprints caught in a moment in time. My collection may never end up at a Sotheby's auction, but whenever I add another pot to the others I've acquired, I feel like the world's winningest fine-art connoisseur.

When it's time to unwrap my gift, my son beams with pride, outlining the steps it took to form his clay creations. His elementary pottery illustrates a spiritual truth: we're created beings.

We're constantly being formed, each of our experiences leaving fingerprints all over us, shaping who we become. As we approach the new year, I wonder what it would be like to take some time to consider what's forming us. Where have we spent our time? Who have we been with? What have we consumed? Where have we gone? What have we done?

Sometimes we don't like to take the time to ask ourselves questions because we aren't sure if we want to sit with the answers. But we ask questions like these because it helps us take stock of what and who is forming us.

I'm aware of my propensity to let myself be spiritually formed by the whims of whatever is trending. Lisa Sharon Harper calls this "thin faith," which she says "creates its own collection of Instagram memes that serve as life principles."[26] My husband and I watched a reality dating series where contestants gazed into the camera, spilling their deepest hopes and dreams. As they shared their confessions, I realized they were all repeating the same inspirational phrases, motivational lines, and misattributed quotes.

I cringed and turned to my husband. "It seems like an algorithm mashed together random memes and wrote everyone a script," I said, unable to turn away.

While it's easy to laugh and feel a little judgmental about the empty clichés the contestants shared with such conviction, I couldn't help but wonder how my own consumption has formed me. As we continued to eat popcorn and chuckle at the cheesy dating show, questions peppered my mind: *Am I a regurgitation of what I've mindlessly allowed into my life? Is my faith an accumulation of thoughtfulness and nuance, or am I a collection of empty clichés and snarky hot takes?*

Many people have walked away from institutional Christianity not because they don't love Jesus but because all they've experienced from people proclaiming to be Christians is a regurgitation of manufactured church culture. The cheap formation rings hollow at best and incredibly problematic at worst.

As people of Christ, we should be formed by the ways of Jesus. But all too often, we've allowed ourselves to be formed by the wrong things. Whatever forms us leaves its fingerprints not only on us but on our families, our neighbors, and our coworkers. We're all vulnerable to being shaped by self-serving influences, whether they're motivational memes disguised as spiritual truth or dangerous ideologies packaged as religious fervor.

Spiritual formation isn't something that happens to a transcendent few—it happens to all of us, all the time. Perhaps that's why the Bible includes dozens of references to people being like clay. It's up to us whether we'll be formed by God's hand (see Isaiah 64:8).

"To live in God's Kingdom, in the way of shalom, requires that we discard our thin understanding of the gospel," Harper writes.[27] Thin faith is hollow, leaving us constantly hungry for more. We'll never be satisfied if we let emptiness fill us and if we allow ourselves to be formed by influences that speak to the most untrue parts of us. A robust understanding of God's ways—full of justice, mercy, and humility (see Micah 6:8)—makes us people of profound peace. When we're marked by the liberating way of Jesus, we are set free from thin faith.

In his book *The Deeply Formed Life*, Rich Villodas explores how being rooted in Christ can help us to live more robust lives, formed by God. "Whether we know it or not, see it or not, or understand it or not, we are always at risk of being shallowly formed," he warns. "We are formed by our false selves, our families of origin, the highly manipulated presentations of social media, and the value system of a world that determines worth based on accomplishments, possessions, efficiency, intellectual acumen, and gifts. So we need to be regularly called back to the essence of our lives in God."[28] We reflect on our spiritual formation not to shame ourselves but to be discerning and to ultimately remember that we are creations held in the loving hands of our Creator. As we become more deeply formed in goodness and truth, we learn from our mistakes. If our children make their clay pots with care, how much more does our God desire to develop us in lovingkindness?

SCRIPTURE
Jeremiah 18:1-17; Isaiah 64:8; Micah 6:8

BREATH PRAYER

Inhale: Form me
Exhale: Into Your image.

FAMILY DISCUSSION QUESTIONS

Read Isaiah 64:8 together.

▸ Tell about a time you made something out of clay. What does it feel like to mold something like that?

▸ How is God like a potter?

▸ How does it make you feel when you think about being created by God?

A PRAYER FOR
A NEW YEAR

O God, You
hold all
eternity in
Your hands.
Thank You for
songs to
sing
And moments
of quiet too.
May we reflect
on the year
behind us
As we look
ahead to
the year in
front of us.

*TO LIGHT
THEIR WAY*

- ▶ Do you agree that everything that forms you leaves fingerprints? Why or why not?
- ▶ How are you being formed by the people around you?
- ▶ How can social media form us spiritually?
- ▶ What happens when people are formed by politics instead of by Christ?
- ▶ What happens when people are formed by church culture instead of by Christ?

FAMILY PRAYER

younger

God, You are the Maker of all things, and You have created us. Help us to be formed in goodness and truth, not in the world's lies.

You care deeply for our family and for families everywhere. Help us to be mindful with the lives You have given us.

Help us to be thoughtful about the screens we watch and how we spend our time. You have given us so much freedom. Please grant us wisdom to make choices that honor You, ourselves, and others. Amen.

older

Creator God, You breathed us into being out of dirt and dust. You are not done with the forming and fashioning of who we are and who we are becoming. In You, each of us is invited into infinite possibilities for who we might become. Protect us from influences that whisper lies, distorting the divine shape of our hearts and minds, bodies and souls. God, we know You are forever speaking into the contours and crevices of our lives. Carve mirrors into our hearts so we might examine and reflect on who and what we have allowed to form our days and our lives.

O God, You are full of mercy, not manipulation. You are a God of order, not chaos. In your generosity, You give us the freedom to be formed. You do not micromanage, exploit, or control our lives with divine algorithms. When we have allowed our false selves to become hardened in the fires of life, call us back so we may return to being formed by love, joy, peace, patience, kindness, goodness, faithfulness, gentleness, and self-control. Soften our harsh edges, and form us into Your image, through Christ alone. Amen.

Moving Toward

IF YOU'RE LIKE ME, you want your kids to know deep love—a divine kind of love that goes beyond candy hearts and boxes of chocolates. We want to teach our children about God's love. But what if kids have more to teach *us* about the compassionate nature of Christ than we realize?

By the age of three, children begin to show genuine compassion and empathy. This means that little ones just starting preschool can differentiate their feelings and experiences from those around them.[29] No matter how old your children are, it's not too early or too late to nurture their natural inclination to embrace compassion.

As time ticks by and years wash over us, our culture implicitly (and sometimes explicitly) teaches that generosity is childish, that unconditional love is foolish, and that empathy is a weakness. But children have not yet unlearned compassion toward one another. Their acts of kindness reflect Jesus, going against the grain of a world that tells us to take care of only ourselves.

When we were playing outside one snowy afternoon, a little neighbor friend tripped and ended up with scrapes on her hands. My young son gave up his turn to play on the sled and rushed inside to find a bandage. With great intention, he picked a bandage that matched his friend's skin color, and then he burst outside to give it to her. He knew what that pain felt like. He would have wanted tenderness and gentleness himself, so that's what he offered to her.

He wasn't bitter about losing his turn—he felt better knowing she was okay.

Compassion keeps us tender to our own humanity and the humanity of our neighbor. "Compassion is the sometimes fatal capacity for feeling what it's like to live inside somebody else's skin," writes Frederick Buechner. "It is the knowledge that there can never really be any peace and joy for me until there is peace and joy finally for you too."[30]

Our world is breaking under the weight of inequity and oppression. What if we embraced this mutuality, this way God has formed us for connection? I think our world would be full of more empathetic, compassionate people. As Christians, we're not just welcomed into compassion. We're *called* to it.

"In everything, do to others what you would have them do to you," Jesus taught, saying this command summed up all of what the prophets of old taught—and all that God's law required (Matthew 7:12). In other words, if we have all the right knowledge and do all the right things but lack love, we're just banging a useless gong (see 1 Corinthians 13).

Every day we're given opportunities to move toward others in love or to retreat into our selfish desires. What we forget is that when we move toward others in compassion, we care for ourselves at the same time we're caring for them.

"In companionship with Jesus Christ, we are called to be compassionate as our loving God is compassionate. In and through him, it becomes possible to be effective witnesses to God's compassion and to be signs of hope in the midst of a despairing world."[31] I look around at the suffering and inequity baked into the world our kids are inheriting. I wonder what it would look like if the adults who are set on choosing harm had been raised in families and communities where healing was prioritized. How would their actions be different if they'd learned to give and receive the empathetic, compassionate love that Jesus embodied?

With God's help, we must wear compassion like a worn scarf knit together with intention and shared with whoever is cold. Throughout His life, Jesus showed that compassion is a "way of living together," as Henri Nouwen writes.[32] Compassion is not just how we love. It's who we become. As Dr. Traci Baxley says, "Compassion is something that is nurtured and modeled through your love and care."[33]

To raise compassionate kids who become compassionate adults, we ourselves must live out Jesus' command to care for others as we wish to be cared for. Our children are watching what we say and how we say it. They absorb how we interact with an unpleasant neighbor. They hear how we talk to our spouse. They watch how we react to the news, spend our money and time, and treat those around us (including the youngest in our care).

Kindness—a fruit of the Spirit (see Galatians 5:22-23)—is "compassion in action," according to Baxley. She says that living out compassion "can be a powerful tool in overcoming society's greatest challenges. Amid the many challenging issues that plague our country and the world—poverty, homelessness, climate change, immigration, gender inequality, civil rights, and racial discrimination—we need kindness now more than ever."[34] I see my son Asher embody compassionate kindness when he cares for his sister, Eliza. Eliza has a vibrant personality and adores her older brother. She also has Down syndrome and a long list of physical and developmental disabilities. She doesn't speak or walk, which means there are moments when her brothers run out of a room for one reason or another and she accidentally gets left behind.

Time after time, Asher runs back and picks up his sister so she can come along. He includes her in the show he's watching or the book he's reading. He's patient when she tugs on his hair. And when he thinks no one is watching, he tests out a variety of silly voices and goofy faces just to get her to smile.

No one has asked him to do any of this—he is moved by compassion, his actions reflecting the Lord's lovingkindness (see Psalm 36:7). When Asher cares for his sister, he sees a beloved child of God who is often unseen by others. He embodies Jesus' admonition to care for her as he wants to be cared for.

Love moves *toward*. Over and over again, Jesus modeled this kind of compassion. He made space for the Samaritan woman at the well (see John 4:4-26). He humbled himself and washed His disciples' feet (see John 13:1-17).

When we act out of compassion,

we become Christ, showing an uncanny interest in the poor, the excluded, the despised, and the least. We find ourselves sitting by a Samaritan well, more interested in breaking down barriers than in religious do's and don'ts. We wrap a towel around our waist and wash the dirtiest feet around, proclaiming the preposterous message that there are no more lords and servants, no more ranks and hierarchies, but that we're all equal friends, serving one another.[35]

A life knit together with compassion embraces the truth that, as Paul wrote to the Galatians, we "are all one in Christ Jesus" (Galatians 3:28, NIV). We love because God first loved us (see 1 John 4:19).

Because of God's love, we can soften the shards of our hearts and reflect the loving-kindness of God in our parenting and our neighboring. We can raise children who pay attention to their emotions so they can tend to the hearts of others. We can be families that live with compassion, keeping our hearts tender and free from the world's hierarchies.

It sounds audacious—and maybe a little naive. But this is no sappy valentine: with

God's help, we can be families who embody compassion, move toward others, and change the world in love.

SCRIPTURE

1 Corinthians 13; Psalm 36:7; Matthew 7:12; John 13:1-17

BREATH PRAYER

Inhale: Compassionate Christ,
Exhale: Help me to move toward love.

FAMILY DISCUSSION QUESTIONS

Read Matthew 7:12 together.

> ▸ What does it mean to do to others what you'd have them do to you?
>> ▸ What does God's love feel like? How is God's love different from romantic love?
>> ▸ What are some clues that God has shaped you for connection?
>> ▸ When have you seen kindness in action this week?
>> ▸ When was the last time you offered an act of healing to someone who's hurting?
>> ▸ In what ways was Jesus compassionate? How do we know that we're called to be compassionate?
>> ▸ What does it feel like to receive compassion?
>> ▸ How can we as a family pay more attention to those who are hurting?

A PRAYER FOR
ST. VALENTINE'S
DAY

Help us to love
    bravely
And to model
    what it is
    to keep
    choosing love,
Even when it's
    not easy—
Especially then.
May our children
    know the gift
Of loving another
And being loved
    fully in return.

*TO LIGHT
THEIR WAY*

FAMILY PRAYER

younger

Jesus, the way You lived in love shows us how to live in love too. Thank You for showing us how Your lovingkindness changes everything.

Help us to more fully receive that love so we can give it to others. Protect us from the lie that we should care only for ourselves or those who are like us. Help us to move in love toward our neighbors and those who look, think, or act differently from us.

Help us to treat others as we want to be treated, for we are all connected. Help us to move toward others in love. Keep our hearts tender and our motives pure. Amen.

older

Compassionate Christ, we thank You for opening the chasm between our hurting hearts and God's lovingkindness. In all we say, all we do, and all we are, help our family to be bathed in Your light so we might reflect Your love.

Protect us from the hierarchies of the world that tell us to care only for ourselves or those with power and popularity. Keep our hearts tender so we may move toward our neighbors, extending care and pouring out the compassion we would want to receive.

Thank You for the ways the youngest among us embody Your mercy and show us how to live out Your love. Help us to see how interconnected humanity is by growing in us an understanding of kinship. Move us toward a future of mutuality, where compassion is freely given and received, where justice flows like a river. In the light of Your divine love, may our family grow in compassion. Amen.

REFLECTION 13

Learning and Unlearning

AS MY HUSBAND AND I weaved through the school cafeteria to find our children's classrooms for parent-teacher conferences, a bulletin board decked out in bright construction paper caught my eye. It posed a single question: *Can we love God while hating others?*

Students and teachers had turned the hallways into historical reflections and cultural celebrations to honor Martin Luther King Jr. in January and to recognize Black History Month in February. Elementary explorations of what Dr. King's dream might mean today were taped on classroom doors; cardboard cutouts of Black creators, artists, and inventors decorated lockers.

Most of the students in the school are Black and brown. Their displays showed an understanding of past and present racial inequity that stretched well beyond one designated time of the year. It was unlike anything I'd seen in our kids' previous school, which was in a majority-white suburb.

After we finished the conferences, I found my way to the bulletin board. I wanted to know what had compelled my son's public-school classmates to ponder these questions.

As I moved closer, I saw that third-grade students had posted biographical information about Audrey Faye Hendricks, who at nine years old became the youngest known Civil Rights demonstrator to be arrested in the 1960s. I have seen the racist anti-desegregation signs that picketing white Christians shared at that time, and it's a gut-punch to see even young children holding such hateful words. (It is easy for white Christians like me to denounce historical sins, but are we doing the same thing today when we don't speak out when our Black and brown siblings are in pain?)

I can only imagine what it would have felt like for kids like Audrey to see grown adults acting hateful, spiteful, and evil—and sometimes in the name of Jesus! But the truth is we don't have to look far from the headlines to see that discrimination and racism are still happening today. We only have to watch cable news or scroll social media to see it in real time.

In 1 John 4:20, we find an answer to the bulletin board's question: "Whoever claims to love God yet hates a brother or sister is a liar. For whoever does not love their brother and sister, whom they have seen, cannot love God, whom they have not seen" (NIV).

Despite all the pain of the world (sometimes inflicted by those who claim to be Christians), we believe that Jesus really is the Way, the Truth, and the Life (see John 14:6). As parents who hold to this promise, we are called to grow in Christ as our children grow.

God's love pulls us out of a passive stance toward suffering and propels us into a better way of living. In the United States, we are hurting under the weight of hundreds of years of systemic and individualized racism. Racism did not end in the 1960s, nor is it delegated to shaved heads or white hoods today.

Raising children where such ugly legacies exist can feel overwhelming and terrifying. But Jesus offers us hope and extends an invitation to align our families' comings and goings with the incarnational life of Christ, which doesn't ignore the pain but, instead, enters into it.

As we do our best to live into rhythms of loving our neighbors as ourselves, stand in solidarity with the marginalized, resist the trappings of evil, push against the lure of power, and pursue peace for all, we proclaim the Good News with our lives. When we do so, resisting hatred and clinging to Christ, we help our kids learn about the world, the One who made it, and their place in it.

"Christianity is not about internal morality or rigorously keeping a list of commandments," writes Dominique Gilliard. "It is about becoming more like Jesus. As we grow in Christlikeness, our lives will become more reflective of the love, mercy, and justice of Jesus."[36]

As a white mother who loves God—and who wants to share that love with my kids by living in step with Christ—I have to do the deep work of disentangling myself from the often invisible clutches of white supremacy's grasp. I must wrestle with my privilege, name and repent of my racism, and follow Jesus beyond colorblindness and feel-good clichés.

My kids are watching and listening to what is happening in the world—and to what I say or don't say, what I do or don't do.

Yours are too. And that can feel heavy.

"Racism is a reality of the world our kids live in—and it affects them, whether their parents talk about it or not," writes Dr. Traci Baxley. "There is no magic wand to wave, no foolproof way of discussing the complexities of race, no single conversation that will resolve the issue for any family. The conversation is ongoing, and it may be messy at times. And while it's never too late, the goal is to start talking about it when our kids are young."[37]

If you're part of the dominant culture, you might be afraid to talk about racism with your kids because it's awkward and you aren't sure what to say. Or maybe you're worried you might say the wrong thing. But BIPOC (Black, Indigenous, and People of Color) parents and children don't have a choice; they have to talk about it.

> What a burden that any Black child has to carry in a world that is covered with the smog of the generalized racism felt by those around us, and the systemic racism of built-in inequalities of work, education, incarceration, maternal mortality rates, police shootings, and so much more. This is the lived experiences of Black moms, and it doesn't go away when the headlines fade and the protestors have gone home.[38]

Dr. Jemar Tisby is a historian who studies race, religion, and social movements. His faith in Jesus roots him in his anti-racism work. He's also a father who adapted his bestselling book *How to Fight Racism* into a young reader's edition for his kids. He says, "When talking to kids about race it is often necessary to push through your fears. . . . Bumbling through a conversation about race is often better than not having a conversation at all."[39]

One of the best ways parents can start to reject passivity and raise children who are part of the solution is to educate themselves. Raising compassionate, caring children who work for the flourishing of all people means we have to follow Jesus into living it out.

Proverbs 22:6 tells us to train up children in the way they should go. The foundation we give our kids matters. "The stakes are high as we train up our children to value everyone and treat people with dignity," Tisby writes.[40]

It can feel overwhelming. Where do we even begin? "The first step in teaching kids about race is teaching yourself," Tisby writes. "You cannot appropriately respond to someone else's questions about race if you have not asked and attempted to answer your own."[41]

I confess that I didn't know the history of Audrey Faye Hendricks before that night at school. My son and his classmates taught me. And I have so much more to learn. By the grace of God, I will continue learning humility and lamenting the ways I've gotten it wrong so the Author of justice and truth will do a new thing in me, even in the wilderness (see Isaiah 43:19).

There are thousands more like Audrey in the Black community who, with courage, pushed against racial injustice—often at high personal cost. It's not too late to learn and to be transformed by the renewing of our minds (see Romans 12:2). As we untangle the deep roots of racism in the world and in our hearts, and as we learn from history, both biblical and current, we can be agents of change and healing.

Your children are never too young—or too old—to talk with about the inequities and evils of this world. We are fortunate to have the deep work of believers in the BIPOC community to learn from and be changed by so we can fight racism. As followers of Christ, we don't parent as those without hope. May we invite Christ to illuminate the ways we may have been proclaiming the love of God while living in a way that hurt others.

Can we love God while hating others? It's an excellent question to ask and keep asking as we grapple with the many racial inequities (both obvious and hidden) in our neighborhoods, our country, and our world.

May the beginning of this year also mark a new beginning for doing justice, loving mercy, and walking humbly with God (see Micah 6:8). Let's keep learning and living it out. Let's create a better world for our children, *with* our children.

SCRIPTURE
Proverbs 22:6; Isaiah 43:19; Romans 12:2; Micah 6:8; 1 John 4:20

BREATH PRAYER

Inhale: O Lord, Your ways are just;
Exhale: Your gospel is peace.

FAMILY DISCUSSION QUESTIONS

Read 1 John 4:20 together.

▸ What does the Bible say about loving God but hating others?

▸ Do you feel comfortable talking about race and racism in our home? Why or why not?

▸ How have you seen racism in your school, workplace, or neighborhood?

▸ What are some things you can say when you hear a classmate or teacher saying something racist?

▸ What choices can our family make to be anti-racist and reflect the love of Jesus in how we live?

RECOMMENDED BOOKS ABOUT RACIAL AWARENESS

▸ *Subversive Witness: Scripture's Call to Leverage Privilege* by Dominique Dubois Gilliard

▸ *How to Fight Racism: Courageous Christianity and the Journey toward Racial Justice* by Jemar Tisby

▸ *Be the Bridge: Pursuing God's Heart for Racial Reconciliation* by Latasha Morrison

▸ *Teaching for Justice and Belonging: A Journey for Educators and Parents* by Tehia Starker Glass, PhD, and Lucretia Carter Berry, PhD

▸ *Faithful Anti-Racism: Moving Past Talk to Systemic Change* by Christina Barland Edmondson and Chad Brennan

▸ *Social Justice Parenting: How to Raise Compassionate, Anti-Racist, Justice-Minded Kids in an Unjust World* by Dr. Traci Baxley

▸ Throughout Scripture, God tells us that our past affects our present. Learn alongside your kids as you read *The Youngest Marcher: The Story of Audrey Faye Hendricks, a Young Civil Rights Activist* by Cynthia Levinson together. It's a picture book for kids ages five to twelve that explores the 1963 Children's March in Birmingham, Alabama.

- How old does someone need to be to do what's right?
- Share a time you stood up for yourself or someone else. What happened?
- How can our family be more intentional in confronting hate?

FAMILY PRAYER

younger

Lord, racism is not of You. Help us to yank the weeds of racism from our hearts by the root.

Help us to remember that while speaking up against racism and working for justice may cost us something, it will never cost our souls. We know the fight against racism starts at home.

Help our family to live boldly in love, knowing that nobody is free until we are all free. When given a choice, may we choose community. May we choose the love of neighbor, which flows out of the love of God—a love that overcomes.[42]

older

O compassionate and merciful Christ, be with us as we learn about racism and talk about it as a family. Help us to name it for what it is, and keep us from minimizing its legacy.

O Comforter who weeps, help us to sit in a spirit of peace as we wade into these conversations, but help us not to resist our own deep emotions.

Help us to embrace our humanity and, in turn, be a family that believes it's right and righteous for all of us to be upset about injustice.

Help us to repent of and lament any harm we may have caused, and heal us from the ways we may have benefited from or been hurt by oppressive systems that are not of You.

O reconciling Christ, who calls us to be peacemakers, we pray for true unity, rooted in Your justice. And in all things, help our family to turn from the worn-out ways of the world to the life-giving ways of Your Kingdom, now and forevermore. Amen.[43]

Introduction

I'D HOPED TO HELP MY FAMILY shake off winter's final doldrums with a library trip. I grabbed the worn *Frog and Toad Are Friends* picture book from the library stacks in dreams of passing on my delight in Frog and Toad's friendship to my children. My mom had read it as a child and passed it on to me, and now I was doing the same with my family.

In these short early reader stories, the two amphibians embark on shenanigans and meander through the seasons together: sledding in the winter and sharing ice cream cones in the summer. In the story "Spring," Frog runs to Toad's house, thrilled to announce that spring has arrived. He pounds on the door, shouting, "The sun is shining! The snow is melting! Wake up!"

But Toad is wintering—he is struggling to emerge from his slumber. At the moment, he'd rather stay in the dark and go back to bed. Frog tries to convince his pal to shake off those winter blues.

"What you see is the clear warm light of April. And it means that we can begin a whole new year together, Toad. Think of it," says Frog. "We will skip through the meadows and run through the woods and swim in the river. In the evenings we will sit right here on this front porch and count the stars."[1] Frog flips through Toad's calendar, tearing off the winter months one by one. Finally, Toad is convinced that a newness has come. He realizes he doesn't need to hibernate anymore. The story ends with Toad and Frog running outside "to see how the world was looking in the spring."[2]

Perhaps no other season so clearly highlights the cyclical, transitional nature of the created world and our spiritual lives. Like God's Kingdom, it's both now and not quite yet. Spring's beginnings are messy here in the Midwest: snow melts into slush and then morphs into mud puddles. Daytime stretches longer, but we still send the kids to school with snow boots and gloves.

The church calendar also reflects this messiness, inviting us to enter into a time of reflection and repentance as we observe Lent (the forty days leading up to Jesus' death and burial) and—finally!—His resurrection. The tough part about spring is that we don't get to skip the mess and go straight to the celebration of Easter.

Just as the daffodils and tulips and cherry blossoms take time to burst forth, we, too, have to take time to sit in the messy, muddy middle space.

When my husband and I were teens, we were in an improv acting group together. One of the key rules of improv is to reply, "Yes, and . . ." to your fellow actors. Spring is an offering of *yes, and*. Yes, we can shed our winter layers and spend more time outside—*and* our kids will track muddy footprints inside right after we've mopped the floor. *Yes*, the tiny buds are bursting forth into glorious blooms—*and* we're sneezing from pollen allergies. *Yes*, more daylight is emerging—*and* sometimes it seems like the gray skies will never leave.

Amid a backdrop of muddy boots and rain puddles, spring unfolds and pastel blossoms unfurl, reminding us that, in Christ, we are invited to be new creations too. In Jesus, God brings "all creation into harmony once again" (2 Corinthians 5:18, FNV).

We can journey through the fasts and feasts of spring with hope, holding tight to this promise: "The Great Spirit has chosen us to represent him in the sacred task of helping others find and walk this path of peacemaking and healing—turning enemies into friends." (2 Corinthians 5:18, FNV). Together with our children, we are being changed, from the inside out.

God is with us in the tension of wondering if winter will ever fully leave and if summer will ever fully arrive. During Lent, we're invited to tend to the soil of our inner lives so we may have growth and new life.

In the weeks ahead, you'll find reflections that connect to holy days such as Ash Wednesday, Palm Sunday, Good Friday, and Easter. You'll find connection points to help you walk through the world's weariness with your children, as well as invitations to look for the tiny resurrections you experience together.

John O'Donohue, an Irish teacher and poet, reminds us:

Beneath the surface of winter, the miracle of spring is already in preparation; the cold is relenting; seeds are wakening up. Colors are beginning to imagine how they will return. Then, imperceptibly, somewhere one bud opens and the symphony of renewal is no longer reversible. From the black heart of winter a miraculous, breathing plentitude of color emerges.[3]

As you cultivate a spirit of both contemplation and action this spring, I pray that God will meet you on these pages and in the conversations with your family.

As you emerge from winter's hibernation, I hope you'll be like Toad, ready to emerge outside again. I hope you'll marvel at everyday wonders with your kids and tend to God's creation together. (And I hope you'll embark on some dance parties.)

As you begin to crack open the windows and inhale the fresh air that comes after a spring rain, may these reflections, invitations, and prayers be a resource for you and your family to experience in new ways the "God of green hope" (Romans 15:13, MSG).

May the *yes, and* of spring remind you that God really is, as Isaiah 43:19 says, making all things new.

A Prayer for Spring

O God of all seasons,
We thank You for the hope
Ushered in by spring.

After a long winter,
We ache for the newness of life.
We give thanks for the firstfruits
Of a new season—
The sprouts of green
Pushing through the earth,
Reminding us
You were working all along,
Even when things felt dark—
Perhaps even dead.

We thank You for the daylight
    returning
And, with it, a renewed promise
That we are never alone.

Thank You for the return of robins
That hop and frolic,
Inviting us into playful
Rhythms of grace.

We see You in the spring showers
And the mud puddles
Made for tiny feet to jump in.

We hear You in the trill of the
    bird's song
And the fragrant blooms of lilacs
That seem to emerge overnight.

After the austerity of winter
Comes the jubilation of spring—
Help us to remember that
    You care for the lily
And the sparrow,
And the depths of Your compassion
Stretch deep around our family,
    too.

Thank You for the invitation
To quiet our souls during
The season of Lent.
Reveal in us
Where we have lost our way
So we may return every part
Of our bodies and souls
To You.

Help us to enter into reflection
So we may see the face of Christ
More fully in the round,
    rosy cheeks
Of a sleeping baby,
The missing-tooth grin
Of a mischievous child,
The tousled bed head
Of a moody teen.

Help us to remember that spring
    always comes
And that we do not parent
As people without hope.

As we approach Holy Week,
May we meet You
In a new way.

As you form the robin's egg
And the sparrow's nest,
Form us in Your love.
Create us in Your image
Again and again and again.

As winter thaws,
So do we.
Soften our hearts
And reveal all the parts of
    ourselves
We keep hardened and cold
And tucked away.
Help us to clear away the brush.
Help us to grow in You.
And create in each of us
Clean hearts, O Lord.
Renew a right spirit
Within us.
With Your resurrection power,
Breathe new life
Into weary bones.

In our spring cleaning,
Rifling through closets
And finding which clothes
Still fit and which ones
Can be given away,

We ask for You to clear away
The cobwebs of our hearts.

O God of pastel eggs
Hidden in the park,
Bless the chubby hands
That clutch Easter baskets,
Ready to find a treasure.

As the natural world awakens,
Returning to life year after year,
We praise You that
Winter's chill
Does not have the final say.

Thank You for the ways
You whisper millions
Of tiny resurrections
Into our lives
Every day.

Help us to live as an Easter people,
Delighting in Your creation
And the newness of life.

Awaken us from our cocoons,
And transform us
Through all the transitions
Of life together.

We see you in the downy
    covering of the chick
And the knobby knees of
    the lamb;

In the parent-teacher conferences
And early morning soccer games
    on a dewy field.

We see you in the dance of the
    daffodils
And in the bouquets of dandelions
Lovingly picked by the youngest
    among us.

Thank You, God, for this season
Of repentance . . .
Into renewal . . .
Into rejoicing!

Turn our mourning into
    dancing.
Breathe in us new hope

So we may offer that hope
To the hurting people
And places around us.

Turn our grief into celebration.
Help us to shed our winter
    skin
And live into the newness
    of life
You've called us to.

As we plunge our hands into
    fresh dirt,
We plant our summer hopes
And know that You turn
Seeds of faith
Into something beautiful.

REFLECTION 1

Mourning into Dancing

COLD WEATHER STRETCHES well into spring in the upper Midwest, and the cabin fever that comes along with it is real.

When our kids were energetic toddlers and preschoolers, the early spring months felt particularly restless in our home. Our children were itching to get outside, but the temperatures were still too cold for their little red noses to stay out for very long. Listless myself, I'd look out our picture window at the barren trees and muddy yard and pray for better days.

I felt depleted in the demanding parenting season and the dark natural season. My kids were young, antsy, and pent up. We lived in a small town with not much to do.

Sometimes I wondered if the grass would ever be green again.

The stretch between January and April tends to be challenging for me. Seasonal depression, also known as seasonal affective disorder (unofficially referred to as the winter blues), occurs around the same time every year, typically when the seasons change, and most often in the winter months.[4] For me, the sadness lingered into the spring, despite what the calendar said—especially when the slush lay gray and heavy on the ground.

I kept in contact with my doctor about ways to take care of myself (some folks take medication; others use a light lamp). As time brought us closer to warmer months, I felt a sliver of hope that the days would soon be getting brighter, and I'd feel lighter too.

As we waited out the long winter, we found, through trial and error, an antidote to our family's cabin fever: good old-fashioned dance parties. We'd crank the music to an obnoxiously loud level, gather in the living room, and let loose—grown-ups included. When Jonny and I danced, we didn't think about the stress of domestic life. We let go of the worries of every news headline that was lodged in our hearts.

There's a time to sit with the pain and let our tears tumble out, and there's also a time to kick the LEGOs and laundry piles to the side and dance (see Ecclesiastes 3:4).

I recently found an old video on my phone that captured our slick moves in slow motion. It gets funnier with every rewatch: my tall, thin husband's limbs bend and bob

159

as if they're made of putty, and my kids look like blurry tornados. I watch their carefree spins and dips that lack the self-consciousness we put on as we get older. When kids (and my husband, apparently) dance, they're free.

Throughout Scripture, we see God turns "mourning into dancing" (Psalm 30:11, esv). As followers of Christ, we're not immune to suffering and pain. Depression, anxiety, and mental health struggles are real. While we do not want to minimize or overspiritualize the real pain we hold, we, too, have hope that God will turn tears into laughter, seasonal sadness into unabashed living room dance-offs—if not now, then in eternity.

Years ago, I interviewed pastor Mandy Smith on a podcast.[5] She shared her experience of feeling like, amid her lament, God was calling her to quite literally "dance for the healing to come."[6] It's a phrase that I've carried in my heart ever since.

"We dance for what is to come," she shared during our interview. "We dance for what we believe God is doing, even if we can't see it. And somehow, that actually helps to make it possible."

I was later delighted to see she wrote about this experience in her book *Unfettered*, in which she writes, "We dance not to avoid or numb but to heal our own hearts. We dance as an act of faith that there are things at work beyond our seeing and understanding. We dance as testimony to each other and to the world."[7]

At the time, our family dance parties seemed more like acts of survival and less like divine invitations. But now I see that the Holy Spirit was with us in our whirls and twirls. My heart needed the dance parties as much as my kids needed to get their wiggles out.

We often overcomplicate sharing spiritual truths with our children. But what if, as Mark and Jan Foreman write, we can "communicate more theology through a family dance party . . . than sitting stiffly for an hour"?[8] Just as we cycle through seasons, so we cycle through times of sorrow and joy, mourning and dancing.

Here's how *The Message* paraphrases Psalm 30:11-12:

We, too, have hope that God will turn tears into laughter, seasonal sadness into unabashed living room dance-offs.

You did it: you changed wild lament
into whirling dance;
You ripped off my black mourning band
and decked me with wildflowers.
I'm about to burst with song;
I can't keep quiet about you.
God, my God,
I can't thank you enough.

Perhaps you're in a dry season in your parenting, and being decked out in wildflowers seems very far away. But what if you could embrace joy even before seeing the first signs of spring? What if you could throw caution to the wind, turn up some tunes, and dance for the healing to come?

SCRIPTURE

Jeremiah 31:13; Psalm 30:11-12; Ecclesiastes 3:4

BREATH PRAYER

Inhale: Change my wild lament
Exhale: Into whirling dance.

FAMILY DISCUSSION QUESTIONS

Read Psalm 30:11-12 together.

- ▸ How has God turned your mourning into dancing?
- ▸ Do you like to dance? Why or why not? What kind of music do you like to dance to?
- ▸ When was the last time you danced with others? What was it like?
- ▸ Why do you think times of celebration (such as weddings) often feature dancing?
- ▸ What can we learn about God through family dance parties?
- ▸ What makes you feel better when you are feeling sad?
- ▸ What might it look like to praise God when things aren't working out the way you'd hoped?
- ▸ Cultures approach dancing differently. What can we learn as we respect and appreciate different cultural dances?
- ▸ How can the way we move our bodies in dance be an act of praise or worship?
- ▸ Why might God want us to dance?

FAMILY PRAYER

younger

God, You are with us in deep belly laughs and in tears full of sadness.

Help us to remember we can always tell You how we feel. You understand all of our emotions—we never have to hide from You.

Be with us in our family dance parties, and may all we do—what we say, what we sing, and even how we dance—show our love for You, Jesus. Amen.

older

O God, You hold our tears of joy and grief in Your hands.

Help us to reach out to You, letting go of what is not ours to hold so we might dance as freely as children running barefoot through a field. Be near to us in life's sacred, ongoing dance of mourning and celebration. Turn our wild lament into whirling dance.

Rip off our mourning clothes and adorn us with wildflowers. We know that hard times won't last forever. In good times and bad, help us to sing a new song, proclaiming our thankfulness to You. Amen.

HEALTH BENEFITS TO COMMUNAL SINGING

Many worship services include singing together. But did you know that when groups of people sing together, their hearts begin to beat in unison? As reported in *Frontiers in Psychology*, a Swedish study at the University of Gothenburg found that when we sing with others, our hearts quickly become synchronized. Singing is also a form of guided breathing (similar to breath prayers) that has a calming effect on the heart.

Circle of Life

THE PASTORS DIP INTO the ash and oil, smudging the shape of the cross. "Remember that you are dust, and to dust, you shall return."

The children trot down the aisle, waving their palm branches. "Hosanna! Hosanna in the highest!"

The Christian life is one of death unto life, life unto death. When we observe holy days such as Ash Wednesday and Palm Sunday, we're reminded year after year of the circular rhythms of life in Christ.

A number of Christian denominations collect the palm fronds waved by little ones on Palm Sunday (the Sunday before Easter, which observes the Triumphal Entry of Jesus into Jerusalem) and burn them down to dirt and dust for the following year's observation of Ash Wednesday (an introspective holy day that begins the season of Lent, inviting believers to reflect on their mortality and their need for Christ).

The circle repeats, moving us through a loop of life unto death, death unto life.

Lush green leaves that once danced in the breeze become gritty gray ashes—a tangible picture of Jesus' sacrificial, life-giving love for us. This love flips our understanding of mortality upside down.

We lose our lives to gain them (see Matthew 16:25).

Jesus died so we may live (see John 10:10).

Lent invites us into a time of pulling weeds and pruning the wilted parts of our lives so we may grow more into the people God created us to be. We let parts of ourselves die so we can have a more abundant life.

I never gave a second thought to inviting my children to grab a palm frond, their light-up sneakers adding to the joyful procession as they paraded down the church aisle on Palm Sunday. But the thought of bringing my kids to a family Ash Wednesday service made me shudder.

They're too young for that somberness, I thought.

But are they?

Palm Sunday is a bittersweet day of remembrance. Yes, we celebrate the way Jesus subverted His culture's notions of power and prestige, riding into town on a donkey as the true God of the people. These were the same people who laid palm branches on the road before him in an act of welcome, blessing the One who came in the name of the Lord, shouting "Hosanna!" (see Matthew 21:8-9).

It's a beautiful picture. But this is only part of the sacred circle of the Christian life. At the Palm Sunday service, after the palm procession, the tone changes. It goes from a "joyful celebration of Jesus' triumphal entry to the sorrowful remembrance of His passion."[9] The cycle repeats: life unto death, death unto life.

Children are intuitive. They may not have the words for it (or the nuanced understanding of mortality that we grown-ups *think* we have), but kids understand that life has a cycle. They know that no creature, big or small, is made to live forever here on earth.

Our family once lived in a home with a wood-burning fireplace. From the first freeze in September to the last snow in March, we'd throw logs into the fire and watch the flames dance, illuminating the hearth and warming our home. Because we were tired parents of young children and loved keeping it classy, an old shoebox held the fireplace's ashes for two weeks. There, the ashes accumulated, abandoned and ignored, as we watched the TV above the mantel.

Surrounded by children and blankets, we sang along to *The Lion King* (who can resist a sing-along to "Circle of Life"?) one night. Then we got to the harrowing scene when Mufasa, the kind leader of the pack and the father of beloved lion cub Simba, dies.

I could feel the air change around us as my children processed the gravity of what they had just watched. They inched closer to me, little limbs finding their way across the sofa. With a child on each arm (and two more on my lap), we found ourselves in a call-and-response.

Children: "He died, Mom."
Me: "Yes, he did."

Children: "Someday, will you die?"
Me: "Yes, I will."

Children: "Someday, will I die?"
Me: "Yes, someday."

A soft hand found mine, and I pulled my son close, tucking him under my arm. I thought back to the day my five-year-old bounded through the door with ashes on his head. He smiled, and I cried. Death is a part of life—but a part I want to ignore.

I want to look ahead, to pretend not to see the ashes below the TV.

Before Mufasa dies, he tells his son, "Just as the sun rises from the night, and winter becomes the spring, so life arises from death."

As I sat on that couch, sinking under the weight of heavy little hearts, I found myself praying that I would be awake to the circular nature of celebration and grief, of life and of death.

When we acknowledge our finite time here in this beautiful, broken world—in our beautiful, broken bodies—we can be assured that God will never leave us in our scariest fears and deepest wounds. Even in this reflective, repentant season of Lent, God is whispering that we are beloved. God is making us whole.

Ash Wednesday invites us to receive a stark truth that we often seek to avoid: from dust we are formed, and to dust we will return (see Ecclesiastes 3:20). As people of God, we normally celebrate life and resurrection, but during Lent, we become fully aware of the weight of being human. It's only when we embrace our humanity and our need for Christ that we can prepare for Easter morning.

There is no life apart from death. There is no resurrection without the tomb.

"There are some hard and frightening themes in Holy Week: betrayal, abandonment, torture, and death. But these days are also an opportunity to have powerful conversations with your kids about power and privilege, jealousy, friendships that have soured, death and what's beyond it, and many other topics that feel taboo or hard to bring up."[10] We don't have to have "right" answers or use euphemisms to bubble-wrap the hard edges of death. None of us have all (any?) of the answers, but our genuine offerings of humility and honesty go a long way.

The ancient sign of a cross, smudged with the very ashes of celebrations past, speaks to the frailty and uncertainty of what it is to be human. This is a reality I need to reflect on year after year. I also need to remember that I am not alone in this spiraling journey of death unto life and life unto death.

"As we journey again and again through each season, our path is never precisely the same," writes Jan Richardson. "The seasons change us. With each one, we move ever further into the circle that encompasses us and into the grace we find there."[11] Lent is a time of reflection. This week, may we (and our children) be aware of our humanity—and what it is to be fully known and held by God's forgiving heart and faithful hand.

SPRING

SCRIPTURE
Genesis 3:19; Matthew 16:25; John 10:10; Ecclesiastes 3:19-20

BREATH PRAYER

Inhale: O God of dirt and dust,
Exhale: Bring beauty from ashes.

FAMILY DISCUSSION QUESTIONS

Read Genesis 3:19 together.

- What does it mean that humans are made from dust?

- What do you know about Ash Wednesday? What confuses you about it?

- What do you know about the season of Lent? What do you wonder about it?

- Why do you think some people say things like "passed way" or "lost their life" instead of "died"?

- Tell about a death from a TV show, movie, or book that you remember. What has stuck with you about that experience?

- Who can you talk to when you have a question about death or dying but you aren't sure how to think about it?

- How does making space to reflect and repent help us to grow in our relationship with God?

- What is one thing our family could do to make space in our schedule to observe Lent together this year? (Some ideas to get you started: no screens on Wednesdays, eating a simple meal once a week, going on weekly nature walks, reading through the Gospel of John together, volunteering at the food pantry together, spending one evening a week in quiet reading or journaling, listening to or making music together.)

"God of the Dust, we praise you for being a Maker who is capable of dreaming up glory from dirt. As we journey through this Lenten season, help us to remember our origin story and find ourselves deeply grounded in bodies made from the lowest part of creation, yet alive with gloried breath from the divine."

COLE ARTHUR RILEY

167

FAMILY PRAYER

younger

Dear God, Your great love is a mystery. We know we don't have to have all the answers about death and life because You are with us in all things, and You are making all things new.

Help us to have the imagination to think about what it must have been like when You breathed human beings into life from dust—even us!

Help us to remember that we don't have to be afraid to talk about death with You. Make our home a safe place to share our wonderings with one another too. We know that no matter what happens, You won't leave us. You are good, and we can trust You.

Be with us when we're sad, scared, or confused. We know that You love us so much that You came to earth to be human, too. We love you, God, and we know You love us infinitely more. Amen.

older

God of dirt and dust, we come to You and sit in the midst of Your mystery.

There is much we do not understand about the world and You, the One who made it. We cannot pretend to comprehend life and death. Instead, we marvel at Your great love—a Love that breathed into dirt and dust, and formed us, body and soul. You even became human Yourself, taking on the weight of our humanity.

We come to You aware of the times we have pushed away, neglected, or ignored our need for You. We find comfort in Your loving presence, even when we have shut You out and refused to acknowledge our lack and our need. We are fully human— we know this full well.

Help us to be present to the humanity in ourselves and in one another. In this season of Lent, may we be brave enough to get quiet so You might bring us from darkness to light. Even as we reflect on the depths of our humanity, remind us that we are not alone. Help us to remember that You are the Author, Sustainer, and Redeemer of life. Amen.

There
is no life
apart from death.
There is no
resurrection
without the
tomb.

To Go Without

OVER MAC AND CHEESE and dinosaur-shaped chicken nuggets, I reminded my children that the season of Lent was coming up.

We talked about how some people choose to fast from something that has become a distraction in their lives, and others try to add something in, such as a walk or journaling or making art. Across traditions and denominations, observing Lent is a time to set other things aside and make space for Jesus. To go without or to add in, not because we'll earn favor with God but because we know our lives are noisy. Those forty days culminate in Holy Week, when we observe the final days of Jesus' life; His torture and trial; His death; and, finally, His resurrection.

I wasn't sure my kids were paying much attention when I shared about fasting during Lent. The old cliché is to refrain from sweets, but at its essence, this practice is intended to center one's heart and mind on the reality of Jesus. Fasting can serve as an entry point as we ask God to continue to refine us and shape us.

The Christian year is one of feasting and fasting. While Advent is a time of hope and anticipation, Lent forces us to reckon with the shadow side of Jesus' time on earth. God-made-flesh was misunderstood, mocked, and maligned. More than once, I've wrestled with how to walk through this wilderness time on the Christian calendar with my kids.

Lent is elusive. Personal. Tender. As Christians, we are people of the Resurrection, yet this sober season leading up to Easter invites us to look inward, to reflect on our wounds and to repent of how we've inflicted wounds on each other.

A few days after our conversation about Lent, I found my kindergartener's favorite stuffed animal hidden in a box in our family room. I thought our dog had collected it and added it to his toys. As I tidied, I grabbed the stuffed turtle and placed it on the landing of the stairs.

"Buddy, what's your stuffie doing down here?" I asked. "Will you put him in your room?"

He then informed me that he had decided he wanted to give up the stuffed animal for Lent. I was taken aback. We didn't come from a tradition where Lenten fasting is talked about much or legalistically enforced, especially for children.

On Easter morning, amid chocolate bunnies and pastel eggs, I found my son happily heading to the box to retrieve his little stuffed creature. Then I noticed our eldest son crashed on the couch, video game in hand. I realized I hadn't seen him playing his favorite games in the past couple of months—he had privately committed to abstaining over Lent.

I wondered if I had accidentally coerced my kids into fasting over Lent. But the truth is each of them has a deep well of spirituality, apart from my influence. Yes, I had introduced them to the idea of fasting, but their internal conviction led them to step away from their favorite toys and games.

Our kids don't need us to act as go-betweens—they have access to the Holy Spirit themselves.

I had hoped to go for a walk every day of Lent—through the rain and the sun, the cool climate and the fair temperatures. I started strong, but the weather was uncooperative, and the days got full. Eventually, my commitment fell away.

While forty days of Lent may not sound like much, it often feels much longer. We're in the now and not yet.

Here in the Midwest, Lent aligns with the seasonal ailments and elements of early spring. Trees are barren; skies are gray. Skies have turned to mist, and fields have turned to mush. Yet we are not without the hope that the season can still be redeemed.

Creation's groans are deafening, but we know that someday green shoots of life will burst forth. We'll feel the warmth of the sun on our faces. We'll once again breathe in the smells of tulips and lilacs unfurling after the rain. Babies will be born, and green hope will rise through the dirt.

As we journey through the austere time of Lent, it can be easy to lose the thread of hope we hear about in Romans 15:13: "Oh! May the God of green hope fill you up with joy, fill you up with peace, so that your believing lives, filled with the life-giving energy of the Holy Spirit, will brim over with hope!" (MSG).

My sons could have broken their fast for a trove of reasons, but they held to it. They were committed. When I think about how they made space for a new experience of God on their own, I'm heartened to know that while I can act as a guide to their formation, they can experience God on their own, too. I don't think I would have chosen for them to fast from their favorite things, but it resonated with them and pointed them to divine love.

It's easy to heap insurmountable expectations on ourselves for our children's faith. But faith isn't made up of formulas; we can't simply follow a three-step process and get instant results. It's also easy to assume that our kids won't develop a robust relationship with Jesus

This is the kind of fast day I'm after:
    to break the chains of injustice,
    get rid of exploitation in the workplace,
    free the oppressed,
    cancel debts.
What I'm interested in seeing you do is:
    sharing your food with the hungry,
    inviting the homeless poor into your homes,
    putting clothes on the shivering ill-clad,
    being available to your own families.
Do this and the lights will turn on,
    and your lives will turn around at once.
Your righteousness will pave your way.
    The GOD of glory will secure your passage.
Then when you pray, GOD will answer.
    You'll call out for help and I'll say, "Here I am."

ISAIAH 58:6-12, MSG

if we don't perfectly model spiritual practices. But when we think this way, we're mis-understanding the character of God. God is a God of grace and mercy, not condemnation.

My fasting failed, but God did not. I had planted a seed of goodness in my children's hearts, and their tender hearts were fertile soil. The Holy Spirit is the One who watered that seed. As 1 Corinthians 3:7 says, "It's not important who does the planting, or who does the watering. What's important is that God makes the seed grow."

While we can help color the contours of our children's lives by passing on Scripture and practicing rituals, rhythms, and routines to orient their experiences to their lives in Christ, we also must remember that the way we spend our days and the values we pass on to our children go beyond rote religious experiences.

If the purpose of Lent is to rid ourselves of outside distractions so God may form us inwardly into the likeness of Jesus, we must trust that God will guide us and our families, changing us on the inside so we might reflect the character of Christ in the way we live.

As the prophet Isaiah wrote, may we not become too focused (or performa-tive) with our fasting that we forget the real work of the people of God: to break the chains of injustice and set the captive free (see Isaiah 58:6-7).

As parents, we can heap a lot of pressure on our shoulders to pass on a robust, healthy spirituality to our children. While it's a privilege to be able to share faith with them, we can trust that God will pur-sue our children well beyond our parenting intentions. We don't need to be (nor can we ever be) perfect parents for our kids to cultivate a relationship with God. After all, the One who knit them together in the womb in the first place will continue to draw near to them all the days of their lives (see Psalm 139).

SCRIPTURE
Matthew 6:16-18; Romans 15:13; Psalm 139; 1 Corinthians 3:7

BREATH PRAYER

Inhale: O God of all,
Exhale: We trust You.

A PRAYER FOR LENT

During this season of Lent, O Lord, We turn away from the ways of this world And the lies of the evil one. We put ourselves and our children into Your hands And follow You, The One who leads from death into life.

TO LIGHT THEIR WAY

FAMILY DISCUSSION QUESTIONS

Read Matthew 6:16-18 together.

- ▸ Why do some followers of Jesus observe Lent?
- ▸ What does it mean to fast from something?
- ▸ What is the purpose of fasting?
- ▸ Why might someone fast from something that's not inherently bad?
- ▸ What has become a distraction in your life?
- ▸ When have you felt the Holy Spirit nudge you to take a break from something? What was it?
- ▸ Why can it be helpful for Christians to observe a church calendar year as well as a typical calendar year?
- ▸ Why might some people think God will only show up if they do something "religious"? How does grace tell a different story?
- ▸ What might God be inviting our family into during this season of Lent?

FAMILY PRAYER

younger

Jesus, You are here with us. Help us to remember that we can trust You. Help us to believe that You have good things planned for us.

We want to see You at home, at school, and at work. When we get distracted from what matters most, help us to focus on Your love.

As we observe Lent and wait for Easter, prepare our hearts to receive Your never-giving-up grace. Amen.

older

O God of green hope, be with us as we observe this Lenten season.

Help us to hear You above the noise in our lives and our hearts. Help us to experience Your presence in new ways so we may be more fully formed into Your likeness, receiving Your merciful love.

May we go out and live into Your redemptive truth and resurrection power everywhere we go. We trust You and thank You for your never-ending mercies.

Help us to have the powerful faith of a child. Amen.

Dandelion Bouquets

I TRY TO GET TO THE school pickup line early when I can swing it. I sit in the driver's seat and luxuriate in those twenty minutes. I have nowhere else to be, nothing else to do. Sometimes I follow up on emails; other times I send a voice message to my friend across the country, waiting in her own pickup line. Other times I forget my phone altogether. I'm a busy parent who tends to use any spare time to get things done, but I secretly love forgetting my phone and being a tiny bit disconnected.

When I'm not looking down at my phone, I look up instead. I pay attention in a new way to the drops that form and connect on the windshield, to the dad in the orange construction vest and worn boots standing outside the school doors, ready to greet his kindergartener with open arms. I'm more sensitive to the rhythm of the rain dancing on the roof of my minivan.

Without my phone, I'm less distracted and more in tune with everything around me. I roll down my windows to take in the scent of spring rain mixed with exhaust from the truck in front of me. I have eyes to see, to pay attention, to bear witness to the sacred everyday reality I'm living in. Instead of getting lost in the endless scroll and social media algorithms at my fingertips, I loosen my shoulders. I allow myself to feel bored.

With new anticipation, I watch the door my son's blond curls will tumble out of. I see a group of four children huddled under a single umbrella, their little hands clutching the handle, holding up the protection. They walk in step, leaving no one behind.

Children are innately tuned in to noticing. They are particularly gifted at spotting a need and sharing what they have.

How often are we so distracted by our constant social media feeds that we don't see the raindrops around us? How can we share our umbrellas when we don't even know it's raining?

I get out of the van and pull my sweatshirt around my ears, trying to block a bit of the rain. I wave to my son and his teacher, and he tells his umbrella buddies goodbye. I see he has something in one of his hands.

He runs toward me with all the speed his tiny sneakers can muster, his backpack taking over his whole body. I welcome him into my outstretched arms, no longer caring about getting wet.

"I missed you! I have something for you!" He unfurls his fist to reveal a handful of crumpled dandelions. "I picked these flowers for you at recess! Aren't they beautiful?"

His recess was hours ago. The offering in his sweaty palm reveals not only his delight in creation but also his desire to share that beauty with someone he loves. The offering of paying attention.

At that moment, I'm glad for the rain to disguise my tears, and I vow to pay more attention to the glory springing up all around me. To disconnect from my phone more often. To be more like my son, who delights in the dandelions at recess, who has not yet learned to call the yellow flower a weed, to squeeze work into downtime, and to focus on self before sharing a gift with another.

When we see children delighting in the seemingly ordinary parts of our lives, we'd do well to remember that God does not despise small beginnings (see Zechariah 4:10). Poet Mary Oliver writes that the "wildest and wisest" thing she knows is that "the soul exists and is built entirely out of attentiveness."[12]

Throughout His ministry, Jesus paid attention to the seemingly simple parts of life, coloring His teachings with lilies of the field and ordinary sparrows of the sky, reminding us that God's infinite love stretches across all of creation. God not only notices but cares deeply for the mundane parts of nature we often take for granted (see Matthew 6:26-29). Perhaps Jesus told people to become like children because the youngest among us seem to inherently pay attention to God's presence in all things (see Matthew 18:3).

If God cares deeply for what we so often fail to even notice, how much more does God love us? God might just show up right in front of us if only we will slow down enough to notice.

SCRIPTURE
Matthew 6:26-29

PRAYING THE EXAMEN

Praying at the end of the day can help you reflect on where God was present. In appendix 2 you'll find a guide for helping you and your family prayerfully examine God's presence.

BREATH PRAYER

Inhale: Help me
Exhale: Pay attention.

FAMILY DISCUSSION QUESTIONS

Read Matthew 6:26-29 together.

- ▶ How was God present in your day?
- ▶ Where did you see God?
- ▶ Where did you hear God?
- ▶ Where did you smell God?
- ▶ Where did you taste God?
- ▶ When have you been in a rush and gotten distracted from seeing God's goodness around you?
- ▶ Why do you think Jesus used examples like wildflowers and birds to help us understand God's love?
- ▶ What is a young child like when they are on a walk? What types of things attract their attention?
- ▶ How can technology distract us from paying attention to God's presence?
- ▶ How can our family make time to delight in the small things?
- ▶ What parts of the day feel rushed to you? How could our family rework our daily routine so we have space to slow down?

FAMILY PRAYER

younger

God, if You take care of the wildflowers in the fields and the birds in the sky, how much more do You care for us?

Help us to slow down so we can see, hear, smell, taste, and touch You in our lives.

O Jesus, You said that grown-ups should become like little children. Help our family to remember that. Amen.

older

O God of lilies and sparrows, thank You for the gift of seeing the world through the eyes of a child.

Help us to be childlike—awake and paying attention to Your grace, which fills every fiber of our lives. In our fast-paced world, help us to slow down so we may sense Your sacred presence in the present moment.

Help us to discern what is distracting us and what is an invitation to embrace Your love and tenderness. Amen.

By Any Other Name

ONE OF OUR FIRST ADVENTURES as parents is often naming our children. Websites and books abound with lists of names that are unique but classic, charming yet traditional. We pass on family names, we choose names that have meaning—or, if you're like my mom, you land on a name you heard on *Days of Our Lives*. (Don't worry, my parents chose a meaningful namesake for my middle name.)

My memories of labor and delivery with my babies are hazy. Perhaps they're blurry because I had to remove my contacts and quite literally couldn't see; perhaps it was just the sheer glory and exhaustion of childbirth. But a couple of moments afterward are forever clear in my mind: holding my babies for the first time and speaking their names aloud into the bustling delivery room.

My son Asher was born with big eyes that soaked up everything. He was so quiet that I asked the nurses if something was wrong. Everything was fine—he was just curious. The first time we met, the first time I felt his heartbeat and touched his downy cheek, I whispered, "Hi, Asher. Nice to meet you."

I felt his name on my lips and marveled at all the times yet to come when I would say his name. *Who will he become? What will he look like when he isn't a tiny baby, fresh from the womb in our big, terrible, wonderful world?*

I didn't know. But I did know his name.

My husband and I didn't name our oldest son. We met him when he was six months old and finalized his adoption near his first birthday. His name story is full of meaning—all the way from Nigeria.

Our dear friend Eric turned his childhood home in Nigeria into a safe place for orphaned and vulnerable children. When the government officials brought in a new little one, Eric's brother Osarabo, a volunteer, filled out the intake paperwork. His preschool-age son Jeremiah kicked a ball around, playing and trying to overhear the grown-ups' conversation (as little ones are wont to do).

As Osarabo filled out the paperwork, his pen hovered over the *Name* line on the intake form. What would he write for this little one who didn't have identification paperwork? Osarabo's son came over and tugged on his shirt. "Daddy, I know his name! His name is Joseph." (Jeremiah, it seems, was following in the prophetic ways of the Jeremiah in the Old Testament.)

And so it was that the little boy who would become our beloved son was named Joseph—a name that means "God will add." Joseph was also the name of my husband's grandfather, who had just died, adding another layer of meaning for us.

The names we give—and the names given to us—matter.

In the Creation narrative, we see that the first job God gave Adam was to name the animals (see Genesis 2:20). Artist Makoto Fujimura says that Adam's naming of the animals is the first poetic act. Not only that, but naming is a crucial aspect of humanity's call—even now—to steward the earth and care for creation.

It's amid this naming that God reveals Adam's lack.

The birds of the sky and the fish of the sea are lovely, so incredible that they are worthy of being named, but they're not enough. The array of animals couldn't fill the first human's ache and need for connection with another human. Fujimura puts it this way: "The purposeful and playful educational plan that God had in mind was that by naming, we would find, and by finding, we would know our lack."[13] As parents, we're called to care for God's sacred creation in the form of the children placed in our family.

Parenting is revealing: we see our lack in new ways as we raise children. We become deeply aware of our need not only for our Creator but for help from others, too.

When I was young, I loved playing with dolls. I created elaborate backstories for them in my mind and, following the oldest sister trope, took care of them with diligence and love. I didn't understand why my parents thought the names I gave my babies, which were a mash-up of cartoon characters and added consonants, were funny. I also didn't realize that people could have the same name, so I created my own. I cared for them by naming them. As Lisa Sharon Harper says, "There is power in the act of naming."[14] To grown-ups, my dolls' names sounded like nonsense. But to me, they were perfectly created and selected for them. Imagine my shock when it was time to go to kindergarten roundup and I met a classmate with my brother's name. *How can this be? Another Nathan exists in my very own town?* I was shaken for days.

Parenting is revealing: we see our lack in new ways as we raise children. We become deeply aware of our need not only for our Creator but for help from others, too.

Throughout Scripture, we see the importance of names in milestone moments, even for the oldest among us. In Genesis 17, ninety-nine-year-old Abram becomes Abraham; Sarai becomes Sarah, with a blessed assurance that she would have a baby. In the New Testament, murderous Saul becomes Paul the apostle; Simon turns to Peter. The list goes on.

God names us. As Ephesians 3:15 says, "Every family in heaven and on earth derives its name" from our Maker (NIV).

A Chinese missionary once visited our church and shared that his daughters were named following the tradition of choosing characteristics he and his wife wanted them to embody. He shared that where he was from in China, names had power, reverberating far into the future.

When we live in light of the powerful truth that our names and our identities are found in Christ, it changes our perspective on the day, the week, and the season to come.

SCRIPTURE
Genesis 2:19-20; Genesis 17:1-8; Isaiah 43:1

BREATH PRAYER

Inhale: You call me
Exhale: By name.

FAMILY DISCUSSION QUESTIONS

Read Genesis 2:19-20 together.

- ▸ Why do you think Adam's first act was to name animals?
- ▸ What does your name mean?
- ▸ Is there a special story behind your first or middle name?
- ▸ How do you feel about your name?
- ▸ Why do you think God sometimes gave people new names in the Bible?
- ▸ Have you met someone with the same name as you? What did it feel like?
- ▸ What does it mean to find your identity in Christ?

FAMILY PRAYER

younger

Dear God, we are so grateful that You love us. You never forget who we are, where we go, or what we need.

We thank You for everyone in our family, and we celebrate that You know us inside and out.

Help us to be honest with one another and in our prayers to You. We love You. Amen.

older

O God, You call each of us beloved, and You call each of us by name. In Christ, there is nothing we can do and nowhere we can go that will separate us from Your great love and from our identity as Your children.

Help our family to live in light of the unchanging truth that our identity lies in You.

O Lord, You know us inside and out, and You delight in the swirl of our finger-prints and the unique melody of each of our hearts. We know there is power in naming, so we ask that You would give us the grace to name our feelings and emotions.

May we honor one another in our hearts and in our home, creating daily rhythms that hold each person's belovedness with care. O God, we remember that every family on earth derives its name from You, our Maker, Creator, and Redeemer. Amen.

Lost and Found

I MARK THE PASSING of time with memories of chasing our dog Olive over the years. She's a small fluffball with a need for speed. Part Jack Russell terrier, she has a deep intuition to run. At the crack of a door or the opening of a fence gate, she's there, ready to break free.

One time, when my son left the back door ajar, my husband, wearing only slippers, bolted through the snow and slipped on the ice while chasing after her. Once, a neighbor I'd never met brought emergency beef jerky to lure Olive back as I frantically called for her on a foggy morning. There's the time our furry friend escaped her harness and frolicked on a golf course, the occasion she escaped a fenced-in backyard in the dark of night at the sight of a rabbit, and the sheer terror we felt the Fourth of July she escaped and ran away, in fear of the fireworks.

If cats have nine lives, our dog has nine hundred.

Every time Olive escapes, we run until our sides hurt, and we also pray. We pray that she won't get hit by a car, that if someone finds her, they'll call the number on her tag, and most of all that she'll hear our voices and return home safely to us.

Jesus once told a story (He was a fantastic, if sometimes confusing, storyteller) to describe the extraordinary love of God. He invited them to imagine a shepherd who spent his mornings, afternoons, and nights caring for one hundred sheep (see Matthew 18:12). Then one wandered away from the fold, lost and alone. Jesus asked the people, who I picture to be ordinary moms and dads, village elders, and laborers, "What would a good shepherd do in that moment?" A good shepherd would leave the ninety-nine sheep safe on the hills and go down to the valley to search for the one that went astray.

Over and over again, Jesus told parables to help people fathom how God, in perfect love, pursues them.

In His story about a lost son (see Luke 15:11-32), we meet a man who falls into the entrapments and entanglements of the world's empty love. He abandons the family that has raised him and cared for him, squanders his inheritance, and eventually finds that what he was chasing after has left him empty and alone. At his lowest, he's filthy, full of shame, and living in squalor.

He returns home prepared to beg his father to let him stay as a servant, only to see his Father running toward him, arms open. The father is calling his name, rejoicing that his child has returned home. "While he was still a long way off, his father saw him and was filled with compassion for him; he ran to his son, threw his arms around him and kissed him" (Luke 15:20, NIV).

God's love pursues us.

As we reflect on the season of Lent and Easter, we see the most outstanding picture of God's love in the life, death, and resurrection of Jesus Christ. Colossians 2:9 says, "In Christ lives all the fullness of God in a human body."

In Christ, we find a love that holds a flashlight, finding us in the darkest night.

In Christ, we find a love that transcends time and space to bring us safely home.

In Christ, we find a love that chases us even when there's an ache in His side from running toward us (see John 19:34).

In Christ, we find the fullness of God's love.

In his powerful book *The Return of the Prodigal Son*, Henri Nouwen writes that in his struggle to find, know, and love God, he had forgotten to *be found*, *be known*, and *be loved* by God. "God is looking into the distance for me," he says, "trying to find me, and longing to bring me home."[15] It takes some pressure off to know that God is actively pursuing us in the big and small moments of our lives. Our relationship with God is not dependent on our ability to check all the boxes; it's about the grace of a Parent who won't stop pursuing us.

When our dog is lost, we chase after her because we love her. Time and time again, we keep doing it. Maybe it's a tiny reflection of Christ's pursuant love. Our love exists only because God first loved us (see 1 John 4:19).

If Jesus physically walked in my neighborhood today, maybe He'd gather a group of folks and stand on the sidewalk, spinning a story about a little dog and its owners who kept chasing after her, caring for her, and letting her sleep in their king-size bed even after she led them on high-speed chases.

Maybe the little parable would remind a tired parent—who feels like they're constantly failing themselves, their children, and God—that God is compassionate and merciful, not keeping a record of wrongs but delighting in finding us over and over and over again (see 1 Corinthians 13:5).

Instead of striving, may we begin to see ourselves as little ones God is chasing after. Imagine how our ordinary days would change if we stopped asking ourselves, *How should I love God?* and instead asked, *How will I let God love me?*

SCRIPTURE

Matthew 18:12-14; Luke 15:11-32; 1 John 4:19; Colossians 2:9

The LORD is my shepherd;
I have all that I need.
He lets me rest in green meadows;
he leads me beside peaceful streams.
He renews my strength.
He guides me along right paths,
bringing honor to his name.
Even when I walk
through the darkest valley,
I will not be afraid,
for you are close beside me.
Your rod and your staff
protect and comfort me.
You prepare a feast for me
in the presence of my enemies.
You honor me by anointing my head with oil.
My cup overflows with blessings.
Surely your goodness and unfailing love will pursue me
all the days of my life,
and I will live in the house of the LORD
forever.

PSALM 23

BREATH PRAYER

Inhale: God, Your love
Exhale: Will always find me.

FAMILY DISCUSSION QUESTIONS

Read Matthew 18:12-14 together.

▶ Imagine you are the sheep in this story. How would you feel when the shepherd came to get you?

▶ Imagine you are the shepherd in this story. Why would you leave all the others to get the sheep that was lost?

▶ How do you think a sheep would survive on its own, without a shepherd nearby?

▶ Why do you think Jesus told this story?

▶ Tell about a time you've been lost. What did that feel like?

▶ When have you lost something that meant a lot to you? What happened?

▶ How does it feel to know that God pursues you or chases after you if you're far away?

FAMILY PRAYER

younger

God, You look after us like a shepherd who cares for sheep.

When we wander from Your love, You bring us back. When we're lost, You rescue us. You know us, and You love us with the most enormous love.

Thank You for forgiving us when we make mistakes. Thank You for being kind and gentle with us. Amen.

older

O God, You have chosen to dwell in us and among us. Remind us of Your all-consuming love, which doesn't leave us even when we wander.

Help us to remember that in You, every moment is an invitation to a holy home-coming. Help us to accept Your tiny invitations of grace in our ordinary lives. Help us to be found, known, and loved by You. Help us not to lose ourselves but to journey home to You. Amen.

Truest Time

AS A PARENT, I desperately want to shield my children from deep pain and suffering. And while this comes out of a desire to protect their fragile hearts, I know that in my humanness, I cannot stretch my body to absorb every sorrow and suffering of their world.

The reality is it is not my role to do this. Part of life is death, and I cannot protect my children from this truth. God does not ask me to control the narrative and cover my children in emotional Bubble Wrap. Instead, God is asking me to guide them and to trust God.

When I was around nine years old, my grandpa's health was failing. He was only in his fifties, but already his body was shutting down and his lungs were tiring. One year, I made him a card—I don't know if it was for Father's Day or for his birthday or for Christmas. But I know it said, "Best Papa Ever," and in it, I wrote a little note telling him it was true.

My grandpa, ever the jokester, said, "Well, what would your other grandpa think of this?" He laughed and threatened to mail it to my other grandfather.

At that moment, I couldn't say aloud what I felt in my chest: *I want to tell you this because I know you won't be around much longer. This might be our last holiday together. I don't want you to die without knowing you matter to me. I know this is not the end but only the beginning of a new life. I love you, Papa—very much.*

I didn't say anything. I just smiled, nodded, and gave him a hug.

Children are intuitive. They have an innate sense of what is and what is to come. We often write off the spiritual experiences of the youngest among us, forgetting that they have the same access to God as we grown-ups do. We forget that the Holy Spirit dwells within them and that they experience God in tender ways of their own.

In many ways, children have not yet learned the ways of the world set in data, statistics, and logic. Madeleine L'Engle writes, "Small children do not yet have a sense of chronology and therefore live in eternity; they are far more willing to accept death than we are."[16] While I was not included in adult conversations about my grandfather's prognosis, I didn't have to be. I just knew. I hadn't yet learned the adult urge to fight death. It was something that made me sad, yet I accepted it. I just wanted him to feel my love reflected in the form of a folded-up homemade card.

As a parent to a child the same age I was when my grandfather was dying, my heart aches as I think of my son processing the death of a loved one. But maybe that's not the takeaway. Maybe what I need to learn from this is that as a child, I had a deep trust in eternity. I was able to accept the precariousness of breath, to treasure the memory of being together. I had a relationship with God that didn't stem from the theology books I now have access to; rather, it flowed out of a profound, childlike trust. And God met me there, giving me the spiritual eyes to know what was to come, to say goodbye.

My grandfather died a few months later. I'm so grateful I had the chance to give him that card and all those extra hugs. Glory be to God, who does not give children small doses of His presence.

To be spiritually formed as parents is to unlearn how we have set our watches to the world's time. Spiritual growth means becoming more like the children in our midst—softening our edges and strengthening our tenderness and intuitiveness. Our children have so much to teach us about going deeper in our faith.

When we look at Scripture, we see that Mary had this kind of intuitive, childlike faith. Shortly before Jesus' death, she broke open a perfume bottle and doused Jesus' feet (see John 12:3). This was a burial act, and it made His disciples uncomfortable.

"What are you doing?" they asked her.

But Jesus told them to leave her alone—that she was worshiping.

Artist and theologian Makoto Fujimura says that Mary's intuition perceived Jesus' impending sacrifice before others could see it. Artists, he says, often have the ability to intuit the unseen, to sense the story behind the story, and to exist in and outside of time.

I think that children, regardless of their natural talent, are artists in the sense that they are innately curious and full of wonder. Children, like artists, "have the ability to peek into the true nature of reality and pose questions that may seem irrelevant at the time." Fujimura goes on to say that artists (and, I would add, children) are "dealing with a different set of time: time-fullness that is seen in the moment, even if facing a death."[17] Mary's response to Jesus was intuitive and intentional. She broke her bottle of perfume—worth a year of wages. Judas, meanwhile, formed in his adultness and his ways of the world, betrayed Jesus for merely thirty pieces of silver (see Matthew 26:15).

"Leave her alone. . . . She has done a beautiful thing to me," Jesus says. "She did what she could" (Mark 14:6-8, NIV).

Having a childlike faith reorients us back to the truest time. Not Smartwatch or Google calendar time but a more profound, genuine sense of God's time.

When I remember how I held all these tensions as a child, I think about my own children. What if they stand in a similar intersection of faith and grief one day? Will they try to hold it all alone? Surely, I would want them to tell me about it! While it's good and right for me to be there to guide my children, I wonder if there's something more behind that desire.

I want to create a relationship where my children can trust me and talk about real, heavy, even incomprehensible things, but I don't want to place myself where only God can be. I don't want to overstep and get in the way of their communion with God. My deepest desire is that they would have a relationship with God where they can intuit things firsthand.

As parents, we have to trust God to be God. Our job is simply to make space for our children to experience Christ working in their lives.

What a gift.

SCRIPTURE

John 12:1-8; Ephesians 2:17-18; Matthew 18:10; 2 Peter 3:8-9

BREATH PRAYER

Inhale: O Ruler of all,
Exhale: You are in and out of time.

FAMILY DISCUSSION QUESTIONS

Read John 12:1-8 together.

- ▸ Who cared for Jesus before He died? Who betrayed Him?

- ▸ If you've experienced the death of someone you cared about, what helped you process those emotions?

- ▸ What gives you comfort when you feel sad?

- ▸ What ways do we use to measure time? How do you keep track of what time it is?

A PRAYER FOR
MAUNDY
THURSDAY

O Jesus, You
    promised Your
    disciples this—
That though Your
    physical body
Would soon be gone
And even betrayed
For pieces of silver,
You would leave Your
    presence with
    them
And indeed with us,
    Your church,
In the breaking of
    bread,
In the sharing of wine,
Present each time.
We serve one another
    in love.

TO LIGHT THEIR WAY

▸ What kind of relationship to time do kids have? What kind of relationship to time do grown-ups have?

▸ How is God the creator of time and also bigger than time?

▸ What does spring teach us about time?

FAMILY PRAYER

younger

Dear God, we try to mark the passing of time with clocks and calendars, with days and months and years. But Your love is too big to be trapped in time. As Jesus showed us, Your love is too big to be trapped in a tomb, too.

Help us to remember that, in all the times of our lives, You are with us.

No matter how old or young we are, no matter where we are or what time it is, we can pray to You. Through Jesus Christ, we have full access to You, the Maker of time and the Redeemer of all. Amen.

older

O God, we can't pretend to understand the what and how and why behind time. We cling to the hope that You are the Maker, Ruler, and Redeemer of all.

As we reflect on Holy Week and the death of Jesus, help us to have a renewed sense of the profound love You weave in and out of time.

Help us to be childlike and trusting in our worship. We praise you that, through Christ, even the youngest among us have access to You, O Lord. May we praise Your name forevermore. Amen.

Trouble Sleeping

Content warning: gun violence

WE SINK INTO THE COUCH and flip off the lights. The kids are asleep, and it's finally time to catch up on the latest show we've been binge-watching. We're five minutes in when we hear feet coming down the stairs. Our son stands in the doorway.

"Mom? Dad?" he says. "I can't sleep."

My husband gestures to a spot on the couch. Our long-limbed son sits down and rests his head on his dad's shoulder. He used to be a soft, squishy body, all round belly and round cheeks. The years have stretched him; he's almost as tall as I am now. As he enters adolescence, we enter a new stage of parenting.

We pause the show and ask him what's on his mind.

"I can't stop thinking about what happened," he says, voice low and shaking.

Words tumble out. He had walked by the newspapers at the library and read the front page. It outlined the horrific details of a mass shooting that had killed children and teachers at an elementary school.

"A student survived because they . . . pretended to be dead," he whispers.

My heart drops. We had told him about the shooting when it happened but spared him the most gruesome details. But now he's read about it himself. He can never go back. His looking glass into the world has cracked again. I ache for him—for all our children. For all of us.

"The world isn't safe," he says, curling into his father's arms.

I choke back my own tears as we let him process, being as honest as we can. I resist the urge to make the violence of this world seem less than it is. I promise him that I will do everything I can to make the world better for him, for his siblings, for everyone.

He nods, still visibly upset. "Dad, did you see that guy's shirt at the grocery store?"

My husband shuts his eyes and lets out a breath. I know that whatever the shirt said, it wasn't good. I steel myself. My son looks at me with big brown eyes that have seen too much.

"It said, *Give Violence a Chance*," he tells me, voice wavering. "Why would he wear that?"

I look at my gentle eleven-year-old child, his head in his hands. I have no words. I am heartbroken. And furious. I silently plead with God for direction in this unexpected parenting moment.

He shares his emotions, and we do our best to affirm them. We share our feelings too. We think of ways to process hard things—talking with parents, taking belly breaths, journaling, drawing, praying, turning to a comforting psalm in the Bible, sharing with a therapist.

We talk about evil in the world—and the goodness that exists too.

I work hard to avoid partaking in spiritual bypassing (using faith language to dismiss or avoid hard things) or delving into toxic positivity (minimizing pain by insisting on a positive outlook). But I also share what I believe to be true: that Jesus left us the Holy Spirit, the Comforter, who will never leave us (see John 14:25-31). My husband and I list things that we and other grown-ups have done to make our community and country safer.

Our dogs curl up next to our son, sensing his need for comfort. He asks questions; we answer. We continue to talk until no more words hang in the air. Then we just sit. Together.

It hits me that he trusts us enough to share his fears. I feel tears rush to my eyes all over again.

"I'm so proud of you for coming down and telling us what you were holding," I whisper. "You can always talk to us about what you see or hear or how you feel. We're always here."

After I give him the tightest embrace I can muster, my husband walks him back up to his bed.

When I was a child, I clutched my fears as I stared at the ceiling at night. So did my husband. Neither of us felt like we could say scary things aloud. Our parents were doing the best they could with what they had. If they weren't raised in families that were equipped to create honest space for naming hard things or sitting with complicated emotions, how could they pass on that ability to us? I'm grateful for the many tools our generation has at our disposal for charting a different path.

Dr. Traci Baxley says that children often ask questions and bring up topics we're not comfortable with or prepared to answer. But the way we show up for our kids in those moments matters. "What you tell your children is important, but how you act during those discussions is crucial. Addressing hard topics actually can make your children feel safer," she writes. "I know that sounds counterintuitive, but it gives them some control over the messaging they are receiving, and it gives them a safe place to answer questions and unpack scary or unfamiliar topics."[18]

Though I sometimes dream of wrapping my children in Bubble Wrap, protecting them from the world's hard edges, I know that's not what God asks of me. Though we ache to protect our children's innocence, our role as parents is to guide them and journey alongside them as they traverse this world—a world that is full of great beauty but also marked with injustice, suffering, and death.

Our role as parents who follow Christ is to introduce them to a living Hope that shows us a better way.

In this season of Lent, we're invited to reflect on the last days of Jesus' life on earth. We reflect on how He blessed peacemakers (see Matthew 5:9) and healed victims of violence (see Luke 22:49-51). With reverence, we grieve His last days and, finally, His gruesome death at the hands of those in power.

This season is not all bunnies and chicks and new dresses and warm fuzzies. Like parents wanting to wrap up a complicated conversation with our children in a bow, we ache to go past the uncomfortable realities of Lent and move on to Easter. We sit in the pain as we reflect on the sins of our world and the sins we personally have been part of inflicting. But we must sit in the tension of *not yet*.

Our job is not to shield our children from every heart-wrenching headline; it's to help them make sense of the world around them. As parents, we may feel terrified to wade into complex topics, especially when we haven't seen it modeled well by our peers or our families of origin. Spend just a few minutes on social media, and you'll see that the norm for dealing with the latest trending news is to hurl insults, to harm instead of heal.

If we don't model empathy, nuance, and understanding when we talk to our children about the real pain in our world, they will turn elsewhere to get their questions answered.

Through her research, Dr. Baxley has observed, "As our children grow up, their peers and social media will have more influence over their understanding of these issues than you may, especially if they're not used to having weighty conversations with you."[19]

It's normal to be apprehensive about talking to our kids about hard or uncomfortable topics. But we have to do it anyway. Our children are constantly being formed, and as parents, we have the profound honor of discipling them with tenderness and grace. Their growing hearts and minds are fragile, and we must handle them with care, embracing a posture of listening, as modeled by Jesus throughout the Gospels.

Dr. Baxley describes our responsibility to our children this way: "You are the first person that they will come to with their big questions, the first person they will reach out to, asking for support and encouragement. Don't let your fears drown out their need to question a world that is sometimes frightening and unfair, and in some cases bigoted and racist." She goes on to say that we are to "invest in our children through continuous open dialogue and active listening. It is our job to walk them through the sacredness."[20] Guiding our children through the most sin-riddled parts of our world is not easy. We don't have all the answers. But as Christians, we do not parent without hope. We are living into a narrative of abundant life that goes beyond the news headlines we read.

Theologian Miroslav Volf writes that Jesus "broke the vicious cycle of violence by absorbing it, taking it upon himself."[21]

Jesus died on the cross, but He did not stay dead.

We sit in the darkness of Lent, but we do not stay waiting.

This world, erupting in violence and death, does not have the final word. Because of Christ's limitless compassion, He has won victory not only for Himself but for us, too (see 1 Corinthians 15:55-57.) In light of this truth, we can, along with our children, contemplate pain and then be moved into action, breaking the cycle of sin and death.

No matter what awful nightmares are splashed across the headlines, we can tell our children that God holds our tears in a bottle (see Psalm 56:8). Today we cry out to Jesus, but a time is coming when every tear will be wiped away (see Revelation 21:4). And when we have trouble sleeping, we can return to our beds with the promise that, one day, everything will be made new (see Revelation 21:5).

In other words: Easter is coming.

SCRIPTURE

Matthew 5:9; John 14:25-31; Luke 22:49-51; 1 Corinthians 15:55-57; Revelation 21:4-5

BREATH PRAYER

Inhale: You hold
Exhale: All my tears.

FAMILY DISCUSSION QUESTIONS

Read Matthew 5:9 together.

- ▶ What did Jesus teach about violence?
- ▶ What news have you heard about lately in our world? Our nation? Our community?

- ▸ What have you heard or seen that has made you confused or afraid?
- ▸ What gives you comfort when you're scared?
- ▸ What makes you feel safe? Who do you feel safe around?
- ▸ What do you think it means to have hope?
- ▸ Why do we, as followers of Jesus Christ, have hope?

FAMILY PRAYER

younger

Dear Jesus, be with us when we're scared. Help us to remember that You are with us and that Your Spirit will never leave us. When we're afraid or when bad things happen, remind us that You're near. Thank You for giving us the hope that someday there will be no more tears.

Help us to be brave enough to share when we're sad or scared. Help us to be strong enough to stand up for what's right.

We love You, and we know that You love us with a love that fills every galaxy— and then some! Amen.

older

O gracious God, we come to You with weary hearts and wary minds. This world is not as it should be. All around us, we feel the aftershocks of sin and death.

We lament the ways we have become numb to suffering. We lament how we have contributed to a culture of violence, and we ask for Your forgiveness. Form us into people who make peace.

Help us to bring every part of our lives to You, giving You our questions. May we go out into the world, empowered by Your Spirit, as a healing presence instead of a harmful one.

O Jesus, though the world erupts in violence, we know that death does not have the final word. Thank You for keeping a record of our every tear, and thank You for giving us new hope—and a new way to live. Amen.

A PRAYER FOR GOOD FRIDAY

May our children know a way that chooses mercy
When faced with an enemy,
A way that chooses
Sacrifice instead of comfort,
A way that chooses
Healing instead of violence,
A way that chooses
Loud love instead of hidden hate,
A way that opens their hearts
Instead of closes them shut.

TO LIGHT THEIR WAY

Small Resurrections

"WHO'S YOUR FAVORITE ILLUSTRATOR?" I ask Abram over spaghetti and meatballs. My husband raises an eyebrow, doubtful that our five-year-old son will have an answer.

"Hmmm," he replies with a mouthful of garlic bread. "Probably Eric Carle."

My husband's eyes grow large, impressed at the literary knowledge held inside the little boy with spaghetti sauce smeared across his face. I'm not surprised though.

My kids grew up on a steady diet of books like *Brown Bear, Brown Bear, What Do You See?*, *The Tiny Seed*, and most of all, *The Very Hungry Caterpillar*.

"I just love that caterpillar book, where he eats all the food," Abram confirms. Then he shoots up from the dinner table, inspired. He runs to the kitchen and returns clutching a paper plate with lines separating it into four quadrants, his most beloved art project of the school year.

"Remember the life cycle?" he says, pointing with greasy fingers to the dried pasta glued onto each section. There's a tiny dried pea on a green leaf to represent the egg, a piece of rotini to symbolize a caterpillar, a macaroni shell as the chrysalis, and farfalle pasta for the butterfly.

Caterpillars are curious creatures, capturing our imaginations, making us wonder, *How can a fuzzy little crawler transform into a beautiful butterfly?*

We see themes of transformation and metamorphosis throughout Scripture, culminating with the life, death, burial, and resurrection of Jesus.

When Jesus was crucified, all who loved Him wept in anguish. It's hard for us now, knowing the glorious Resurrection that was to come, to truly wrap our minds around how devastated His friends and family must have felt at His death.

"'Resurrection' is another word for change, but particularly positive change—which we tend to see only in the long run. In the short run, it often just looks like death," says Richard Rohr.[22] As humans created by a Maker God, we are created to be transformed too. But before we can experience the tiny resurrections of our lives, we often have to sit in the darkness. It's the moments of being in the dark—in the chrysalis—that shape, change, and form us most.

"Whenever new life grows and emerges, darkness is crucial to the process," Sue Monk Kidd says. "Whether it's the caterpillar in the chrysalis, the seed in the ground, the child in the womb, or the True Self in the soul, there's always a time of waiting in the dark."[23] Our truest selves reflect Christ, who dwells within. In 2 Corinthians 5:17, Paul says, "If anyone is in Christ, the new creation has come: The old has gone, the new is here!" (NIV).

Makoto Fujimura points out that the Greek word for "new creation" is *kainos*, which he interprets to be a "New Newness"—"akin to a caterpillar becoming a butterfly, but more. Yes, it is transformation, but it is more than that—it is transfiguration."[24] In Romans 12:2, we are reminded not to conform to the world's ways but to be transformed by the renewing of our minds. The Greek word for "transformed" here is *metamorphoo* (the root word for *metamorphosis*).

When we look around at the tiny transformations and resurrections that happen within us and around us, we're reminded afresh that we can trust Jesus' resurrection.[25] We see that all beautiful transformation into new life, from what we see in nature to what we experience within our souls, comes from Christ. "This New Newness breaks into our lives through Christ," Fujimura says. "Christ's death on the cross is a new beginning; Christ's resurrection is a new beginning."[26] As we observe the Lenten season and approach Holy Week (which is its own invitation to be enveloped in darkness), may we reflect on the "New Newness" that is to come.

SCRIPTURE

2 Corinthians 5:17; Romans 12:2

BREATH PRAYER

Inhale: The old has gone;
Exhale: The new is here.

FAMILY DISCUSSION QUESTIONS

Read 2 Corinthians 5:17 together.

▸ What is the life cycle of a butterfly?

▸ Imagine yourself as a caterpillar. How would you feel being wrapped into a chrysalis?

A PRAYER FOR
HOLY SATURDAY

O Lord, may our
children Begin
to fathom a
love Not bound
by earth's
constraints Of
time and space.
May they feel
Your presence
In the waiting.

*TO LIGHT
THEIR WAY*

- ▶ What do you think it means to go through a metamorphosis?
- ▶ What big changes have you been through in your life?
- ▶ Why do you think hard times in our lives can lead to good new things?
- ▶ How has Jesus helped you transform your habits or ways of thinking?
- ▶ What ways of the world are put to death when we become new creations in Christ?

FAMILY PRAYER

younger

Dear God, we thank You for Your creativity in turning a caterpillar into a butterfly. It's just like You to make creation beautiful.

In You, Jesus, we are made new. Help us to not be afraid of the dark but to be transformed by Your big love. Amen.

older

O God of transformation and renewal, we thank You for turning death into life. We thank You for the tiny resurrections all around us.

We thank You for the hope of becoming a new creation in Christ. We confess that we easily get wrapped up in the world's ways. We ask for Your presence in our moments of darkness and waiting, for the times we don't see a way out.

Continue to transform us and shape us into Your beautiful image. Give us wings. Amen.

HABITS OF PLAY

Justin Whitmel Earley says that habits of play are important practices for the Christian household because they echo the Kingdom to come. In his book *Habits of the Household*, he suggests three ways to embrace play with your children:

1. Read imaginative stories to them.
2. Accept their invitations to play.
3. Send them out to play on their own.

Work of the Child

"I'M JUST NOT GOOD at playing with them," my husband confessed as he tossed toy trains and action figures into bins. "It doesn't come naturally to me."

From where I sat, his statement couldn't have been further from the truth. Just that day, I'd heard him make up silly songs in strange voices while making PB&Js, causing our kids to laugh until they snorted milk out their noses.

It's easy to overthink play. As we become more aware of the aches and pains of the grown-up world and get burned by the demands of adulthood, we can lose our ability to embrace play.

The learned desire to quantify and qualify, to explain life away with facts and figures, gets in the way of God's instruction to become like children (see Mark 10:15). Our society never tells us straight up that play is frivolous, but the messaging is in the air we breathe. We work to earn vacation days (and even then, it's hard to disconnect completely). We see play—and its parent, rest—as a reward, not the necessity it really is.

When my youngest kids entered preschool, I worked in the communications department of a nonprofit that provided play therapy to displaced children in refugee resettlement camps in Syria. These children had lost everything and had experienced unfathomable trauma. And yet there in the dust of desert tents, the children created stories with dolls and stuffed animals, held singing contests, and drew pictures.

Play was a form of healing. Play helped them express emotions and imagine a better day. Play was necessary.

Ephesians 5:1 tells us to be imitators of God as beloved children. If God sees us as children, and if play is an inherent part of being a child, then perhaps play is more critical for our souls than we tend to think. Entering into play is accepting a divine invitation to be childlike.

To play is to shed our armor and remove our false expectations of what it means to be an adult. To play is to replace performative seriousness with sacred shenanigans. As followers of Christ, we don't have to earn our value. Our worth doesn't flow from our work or our accomplishments. That frees us to stop the 24/7 striving and integrate rhythms of rest and play into our lives.

Children can turn anything into a toy. My son Abram sees our recycling bin as an endless treasure trove of possibilities. Maria Montessori, known for her work in early childhood development, had a philosophy that play is the work of the child. As parents, we must honor that. Our children begin to understand the world around them—and the One who created it—when they play.

As our kids grow, their play times might change, but the rhythms of play are still vital. When my son was struggling with math homework (and I didn't know if I could break down fractions for one more minute), we took a break and played basketball. Play offers a reset, a respite, a renewal from the output-centered ways of the world.

We grown-ups tend to conflate play with leisure, and then we find ourselves lost in a sea of disappointment or envy when we see other people's versions of the "good life." After all, not everyone can play tennis during long lunch breaks or take the family on a Facebook-worthy vacation "to be a kid again."

But embracing a posture of play is available to all of us. Integrating playful habits into our homes is completely free. We can make silly voices just because. We can play a game of tag or doodle in a notebook. When my kids summon the tickle bugs, I laugh just as hard as they do. I usually think, *Wow. I really needed that laughter.*

Sometimes I wonder if people won't take me seriously if I make jokes or post about silly adventures with my kids on social media. I worry they'll assume I don't care about the real suffering and pain of the world. But being playful doesn't mean we're flippant or trivial. Amid the world's fires, play is a splash of cold water that keeps us going. When we play, we can hear a faint whisper: *Joy is still possible.*

Glimmers of joy and rhythms of rest are markers of life in Christ. If we're called to be awake to the world and move toward suffering, we must also take time to retreat to care for our souls through rest and play. The adults I know who are most tuned in to play are also the most empathetic people I know.

Play is not ignorant. It's necessary.

A PRAYER FOR EASTER

As we celebrate Your resurrection power, We pray our children Would sing and dance In the promise that we are Easter people And we have a living hope in You. May our children Bask in the truth That You have conquered sin and death, And may that living hope Spill into all they do, all they meet, all they are.

TO LIGHT THEIR WAY

We play and laugh to keep us soft, even when we bang our elbows on the world's hard edges. We play so we can keep going.

As parents, we get to learn from the best. Spending time with kids is a master class in relearning play. It looks different through their ages and stages, but children are naturally gifted at play. They have much to teach us about rest, imagination, and creativity. They delight for the sheer reason of delighting. They are much less likely to worry about tomorrow, which is something Jesus said a thing or two about.

Play isn't logical—that's the point. Justin Whitmel Earley writes, "A world without play is a world without magic. And a world without magic is a world without resurrection. And in a world without resurrection, nothing good can come true."[27] When I tell my children the story of Christ's resurrection, they trust it. They have questions (so many questions!), but to them, a world where death does not win and a man rises from the dead is believable. They're tuned in to the miraculous. Their imaginative adventures on the playground are rooted in things that can't be explained away. Their play has prepared them for an appreciation of mystery. Earley says, "To really play—is an exercise of imagining the kingdom, a practice of bearing witness to it right in our own living rooms and back yards."[28]

Our kids—those dragon slayers in living room forts and those brave explorers of backyard jungles—can teach us grown-ups a lot about embracing mystery. As we see clearly in the Easter story, the Christian life is full of mystery. Earley writes, "Let's pause the tasks, then, and play ourselves into Easter people."[29]

May play open our hearts to possibilities, strengthening the bonds between parent and child as we live into our God-given imaginations.

SCRIPTURE
Ephesians 5:1; Mark 10:15

BREATH PRAYER

Inhale: Tune my heart
Exhale: To imagine the impossible.

O creative God, spark in us imagination so we might see the world not just as it is but how it could be.

FAMILY DISCUSSION QUESTIONS

Read Mark 10:15 together.

▶ Why do you think Jesus told people to be childlike?

▶ Why did God give us imaginations?

- ▶ Why is imagination important to grown-ups as well as kids?

- ▶ How can we read the Bible with our imagination? How can our imagination help us connect with the stories of Scripture?

- ▶ What do you think it would have felt like to experience Jesus' resurrection?

- ▶ What was your favorite thing to play when you were younger? What is your favorite thing to play now?

- ▶ What types of things does our family like to play together?

- ▶ How can you spend time playing, imagining, and creating on your own?

- ▶ How can we incorporate more time to play and imagine as a family?

FAMILY PRAYER

younger

God, You've given us the gift of imagination. Help us to use our imagination to create, explore, and connect with You, our Creator.

Thank You for the ways kids can help grown-ups use their imaginations well.

Help us to imagine ways to make our world more loving, joyful, and peaceful. Be with us as we play, together and apart.

Protect us from the world's lie that playing is a waste of time. We know that playing and entering the land of make-believe can be a good gift from You. Help us all to imagine a better world. Amen.

older

We know there is power in make-believe, and we ask for Your help in becoming more childlike so we might glimpse Your majesty in new ways. May all we dream up, all we create, and all we do reflect Your upside-down Kingdom.

Breathe in us new life so we may ask not only "Why?" but also "Why not?" Protect us from the lie that play is wasted time. Cultivate an imagination deep within us and deliver us from the trappings of the grown-up world.

Spark in us holy wonder and prophetic imagination. Move in us so we may be moved to make and create, to embark on adventures, and to start new stories. Amen.

With God's help,
we can tend to our
children's fragile hearts
while also sweeping
away the cobwebs
of our own.

Spring Cleaning

WITH A MUG OF COFFEE in one hand and a novel in the other, I ease into an armchair in the sunroom.

Windows cover the three exterior walls of the room, inviting a deep exhale from all who enter. The kids are occupied outside, and the glow of the springtime sun streams through the tall, century-old windows, casting beams that illuminate the dust particles usually left unseen. Tiny buds form on our magnolia trees while green shoots of grass burst forth on the lawn.

Ah, I think, *a moment of peace.*

I crack open my book. And that's when I see them: sticky, smudged handprints covering a window. I clear my throat and shake my head. Quiet doesn't come easily in our house of six humans and two dogs. Cleaning one window can wait. I return to my spot on the page.

From her perch on the couch, our pup is on high alert. She stares out the window, taking her self-appointed role as protector seriously. A minute later, she spies a neighbor taking a walk and goes on the offensive, letting out a series of high-pitched barks. Annoyed at the interruption, I look up from my book to shush her. That's when I realize that thick smudges cover not just one window but each pane of glass. It's a sunroom—there are *a lot* of panes of glass.

What were my kids doing in here? I stand up to survey the damage and sigh. I spy a thick coat of grime, and I can tell our fluffy guard dogs have also been pressing their wet noses onto the windows. I toss my book and head to the kitchen, grabbing some window cleaner and a rag. Once I start, I realize that I can't remember the last time I dusted this room. I sneeze.

Why are we so disgusting?

As I wipe away the grime, I shudder at the thick coat of dust on the windowsill. I don't want to know what exactly was on my kids' hands when they decided to touch every square inch of glass. I slide open the windows and breathe in the Windex-meets-fresh-air smell. Vestiges of stale winter air fade in the springtime breeze.

An hour later, I've sufficiently scrubbed our windows.

I'm half horrified that the room was so grimy, half proud that I got a jump start on spring cleaning. I sit down, eager to return to my book, when my sons barge through the door.

"What's for lunch?" they ask, kicking off their muddy shoes, their sticky hands covered in another mysterious substance. The dogs greet them with sloppy kisses.

I look at my dirty cleaning rags and have to laugh.

It's a well-worn cliché: "Home is where the heart is." Here in the sunroom, the children's shouts and dogs' barks sound like heartbeats. In the swirl of their fresh fingerprint smudges, I stand in the beautiful rhythm of *us*.

I don't consider myself an award-winning housekeeper. In 1938, prolific writer Brenda Ueland penned a chapter called "Why Women Who Do Too Much Housework Should Neglect It for Their Writing,"[30] and I have to say that, for better or for worse, I've really embraced this idea. But while my baseboards may be neglected and dust bunnies sometimes make their home under my furniture, maybe I can be the keeper of the family's heartbeat.

What does it take to shake the dust from the corners of our hearts? Where have cobwebs settled in while we weren't paying attention? Who or what are we allowing to leave fingerprints on our hearts?

Irish teacher and poet John O'Donohue writes, "Without our ever noticing, the heart absorbs the joy of things and also their pain and care."[31] In Psalm 51, David describes his heart carrying the weight of the pain he has inflicted on Bathsheba and himself. He asks God to sweep the corners of his heart: "Create in me a clean heart, O God, and put a new and right spirit within me" (Psalm 51:10, NRSV).

What does it look like for God to create a new heart in us?

God cares intimately about what our hearts hold. God doesn't want extraordinary sacrifices or lists of good deeds; God wants our hearts.

With God's help, we can tend to our children's fragile hearts while also sweeping away the cobwebs of our own. Jesus taught, "Where your treasure is, there your heart will be also" (see Luke 12:34, NIV). The light of Christ can filter into our hearts, illuminating the shadows and making bright what was once clouded with darkness.

What beautiful and true things have left their fingerprints on our hearts? What has left our hearts bruised and aching?

"The state of one's heart inevitably shapes one's life," O'Donohue says. "It is ultimately the place where everything is decided."[32]

In his letter to the Christ followers in Ephesus, Paul prayed that Christ would dwell in their hearts through faith (see Ephesians 3:17). Though our hearts are heavy sometimes and light other times, we can rest assured that our hearts are beautiful, "precisely because it is where God dwells: the heart is the divine sanctuary."[33] What a comfort that the human heart can be called beautiful by the One who made it, especially when so much of this life can feel covered in grime.

SCRIPTURE
Psalm 51:10; Luke 12:34; Ephesians 3:16-18

BREATH PRAYER

Inhale: Create in me
Exhale: A clean heart, O God.

FAMILY DISCUSSION QUESTIONS

Read Luke 12:34 together.

▸ Jesus said that our hearts will follow our treasure. What do you think that means?

▸ How is your heart? Courageous? Fearful? Heavy? Compassionate? Forgiving? Loving?

▸ Do you believe that God dwells in your heart? How does that change the way you think about yourself?

▸ Why is it important to include cleaning habits in our home, even if it's not always fun?

▸ Why do you think some people choose to deep-clean their homes in the spring?

A PRAYER FOR DIRTY HANDS

We pray for the small, sticky hands
And the fingerprints they leave behind
With each intricate swirl.
May they know the care of their Creator,
And may we remember it too.

207

TO LIGHT THEIR WAY

- What is it about spring that feels fresh or new?
- Have you ever scrubbed or washed something that was dirty and then seen a transformation (big change)? How did that make you feel?
- What happened this week that left beautiful fingerprints on your heart?
- What happened this week that left your heart a little smudged?
- How could we take better care of one another this spring?

FAMILY PRAYER

younger

Dear God, You make all things new. You know our every heartbeat, and we thank You for loving us so much that You, the God of the universe, chose to make Your home in our hearts. Thank You for the gift of Your Holy Spirit.

Help us to remember that no matter what we've done or what we worry about, we can bring our whole hearts to You.

When cobwebs start to cover our hearts and we aren't sure what to do, bring us back to Jesus. Thank You for gently and tenderly sweeping the corners of our hearts and making everything clean like a fresh spring rain. Amen.

older

O God of spring rain, as this season ushers in refreshment and renewal, help us to examine the state of our family's heart.

In Your gentleness, we ask You to hold our hearts, whispering into the cobwebbed corners so we may brush away the old and let You renew a right spirit within us.

What a grace it is that the light of Christ can filter into our family, illuminating the shadows and bringing light to what was once filled with darkness. Forgive us for the ways we have let greed and power, selfishness and pride dirty our hearts.

Create in our family a clean heart, O God, and put a right spirit within us so we may enter into rhythms of righteousness and justice, goodness and peace. Amen.

THE HISTORY OF
SPRING CLEANING

Across the globe, a tapestry of cultures and
religions incorporate cleaning traditions into the
springtime season. Some say the ancient roots of
spring-cleaning stem from the Jewish Passover,
which is observed between late March and mid-April.

The holiday marks when the Israelites were driven out of
Egypt in such a hurry that they didn't have time for their
bread to rise, prompting them to bring unleavened bread
on their journey (see Exodus 12:39). To commemorate
how God freed the people of Israel, tradition dictates
a ritual search to make sure no traces of leaven (called
chametz) are left in the home. This often leads to
deep cleaning in all the home's nooks and crannies.

Good Fruit

"WALK WITH PURPOSE!" our professor shouts, leaving a trail of journalism students in her wake as we make our way through Manhattan crowds.

I do my best to keep up, craning my neck to take in the skyscrapers I've only seen in movies. I breathe in the gorgeous sights (and not-so-pleasant smells) of New York City and try to match my professor's brisk pace. Hordes of people push in all directions. I feel like Dorothy in *The Wizard of Oz*.

I'm not in Iowa anymore, I think to myself as I pick up my pace.

Our speed of life ebbs and flows over the course of our lives, but it isn't sustainable to move at high speed nonstop. Whether you live in Midtown or the Midwest, eventually you have to embrace a slower pace.

When we become parents—bathing babies and helping with homework—we're often forced to slow our steps, to reorient ourselves to a new way of understanding time. Modern life demands that we move fast, and it has a way of warping our understanding of God's time—and God's love. How can we fathom a love that is patient if we never slow down?

Kids have much to teach us about growing in patience. My children, who usually have nonstop energy, tend to move in slow motion when it's time to leave the house. While they sometimes test our patience, kids also help us imagine a life that isn't on-demand. They move through the world to their own rhythms, distracted by a butterfly landing on the car, mesmerized by a bunny hopping through the yard.

Kids tend to have a healthier relationship with time than most adults do. We grown-ups consume productivity apps, time hacks, and best practices. We track our efficiency and our accomplishments. As much as we say kids are impatient, we tend to be the ones who are always shouting, "Hurry up!" We want things *now*, whether it's coffee at the press of a button, breaking news with the refresh of an app, or immediate obedience when we ask our kids to stop wrestling and put on their shoes so we won't be late.

Our high-speed culture offers an insidious question: *Who needs faith when our fast-moving world can meet every want and need (even the wants and needs we didn't know we had)?*

Scripture is chock-full of gardening and farming metaphors, and I wonder if that's because gardeners and farmers deeply understand time. They know the discipline of patience; the work of their hands requires it. No matter how productive and efficient they may be, they can't make plants grow simply by demanding them to.

Growth takes time.

Just as the natural seasons change, the Holy Spirit guides us through the dead of winter into the new life of spring—over and over again.

In the New Testament, James tells followers of Christ to be patient in their faith, to learn from the way farmers wait in the rhythms of spring planting and autumn harvesting. "See how the farmer waits for the land to yield its valuable crop, patiently waiting for the autumn and spring rains," he writes (James 5:7, NIV).

I once saw a photo that tracked a blackberry's growth stages. Each stage was photographed and placed in a circle. I learned it can take up to two years for a blackberry bush to produce fruit. (And here I get frustrated when I have to wait a week for a new episode of my favorite podcast!)

First, a tiny green bud appears, then a larger one and an even larger one until it begins to burst open. At that point the bud shows hints of white until it bursts forth, breaking free and blooming into white blossoms. The petals stretch out and gradually fall, leaving only the green core, which slowly matures into a tiny globe of fruit. The globe grows, cascading into a color palette of greens into reds into purples before culminating in a juicy, plump blackberry, ripe for the picking.

The slow-moving artistry of God's creation took my breath away. I've walked by wild blackberries my whole life and never stopped to marvel at how many times the plant changes—even looking dead at times—before it bears fruit.

The picture reminds me of the pregnancy app that alerted me to the fruit my growing baby's size compared to each week. (When we got to forty weeks, it *did* feel like I was carrying a watermelon everywhere I went.) No matter how much I wanted to speed up those last few weeks, no matter how desperately I ached to fast-forward to having a baby in my arms, I had to be patient. I had to put my faith in the Creator God, who dwells in us and invites us to grow in His perfect fullness of time.

In a letter to fellow believers, Paul wrote, "It's not the one who plants or the one who waters who is at the center of this process but God, who makes things grow" (1 Corinthians 3:7, MSG). The *First Nations Version* renders Paul's words this way: "We are working side by side with the help of the Great Spirit. You are Creator's garden where he grows good fruit, and you are the sacred lodge where he has chosen to live" (1 Corinthians 3:9).

Living into patient rhythms of growth is an act of faith. We see this in the slow work of gardening—and in parenting, too. We nourish our kids with all that we have to give, and then we must trust that, with God's help, their lives will grow the good fruit of love, joy, peace, patience, kindness, goodness, faithfulness, gentleness, and self-control (see Galatians 5:22-23).

"Patience opens us to many different people, all of whom can be invited to taste the fullness of God's presence," Henri Nouwen says. "Patience opens our hearts to small children and makes us aware that their early years are as important in God's compassionate eyes as the later years of adults."[34] If given the choice to craft a dream lunch menu, my son Abram will always choose fruit salad. While peanut butter and jelly sandwiches are more convenient (especially when I'm on a writing deadline), I occasionally bring a chair to the kitchen island, where he can stand beside me. Side by side, we make space to wash the berries, chop the apples, and mix up a fruit salad together. We often sneak bites of fruit as we make our salad. He once popped a raspberry into his mouth and sighed in contentment. "Oh, Mom, it's so good—you have to try!"

When we move beyond our busyness and into a trusting, childlike posture, we can "taste and see that the LORD is good" (Psalm 34:8). This is grace: "something you can never get but can only be given," says Frederick Buechner. "There's no way to earn it or deserve it or bring it about any more than you can deserve the taste of raspberries and cream."[35] When we shut down our productivity apps and push our hands into spring dirt, believing in God's presence through the seasons in our lives, we can embrace the blessing of taking refuge in the One who is holding it all together.

SCRIPTURE
James 5:7; 1 Corinthians 3:5-9; Galatians 5:22-23; Psalm 34:8

BREATH PRAYER

Inhale: It's You, O God,
Exhale: Who makes good things grow.

FAMILY DISCUSSION QUESTIONS

Read Galatians 5:22-23 together.

- Patience is a fruit of the Spirit. What do you think it means to be patient?
- Think of someone you know who is patient. How does that trait show up in their life?
- What happens to a race car that drives fast without refueling?
- Why do you think God cares if we're patient?
- Do you know someone who has a farm or a garden? What do you think would be some of the challenges of that kind of work?
- Have you ever planted something from a seed? What happened?
- What is something that you've had to wait a long time for? What was it like to wait?
- Do you feel like you move too slowly? Too fast? Why do you think that is?
- In what ways could we slow down our daily or weekly schedules?
- How do we know that the Holy Spirit is working in our lives?

"The best time to plant a seed is now. Change is a long, slow march heavenward, with as many twists and turns as there are branches in a growing tree."

MICHAEL CURRY,
LOVE IS THE WAY

FAMILY PRAYER

younger

Dear God, You make good things grow.

Without You, we'd have no trees with green leaves, no flowers with bright petals. When we think about how mighty oaks, fresh lilacs, fruits, and vegetables come from seeds, we are amazed! Even when we can't see growth happening, we know that good work is happening beneath the soil. As we grow, help us to grow in love.

Help us to be patient and kind, loving and joyful. May all we do, all we say, and all we are reflect You, the Giver of life. Amen.

older

O God, as we watch new life sprout and bloom, as we breathe in the fresh air and feel the sun's warmth on our faces, we thank You for the new life of spring.

We thank You for the hope inherent in a spring rain or sun-soaked day that brings buds that turn into blossoms. And when it seems like we're waiting for new hope to grow within us, help us to wait in You, for we know You are working in the unseen soil of our hearts. May our home and our relationships with one another cultivate a spirit of love, joy, peace, patience, kindness, goodness, faithfulness, gentleness, and self-control.

Lessen the pressure around us to perform or be perfect, for in You, all strivings cease. Bring us fresh purpose so our nourished hearts can grow in You and so we might live in a manner that cultivates flourishing for all people. Amen.

Flourishing

OUR NEIGHBORS GATHER for a spring cleanup day, as we do every year, to get our public park and communal green space ready for warmer weather.

We choose a Saturday morning and hope for no rain (and, if we're honest, no late snowfalls either). We emerge from our hibernation, greeting each other in our worn coats and work gloves. Kids carry rakes taller than they are, grandparents push wheelbarrows, and someone inevitably volunteers a truck to collect yard waste.

We get to work.

Retirees and elementary schoolers and everyone in between meet to pick up litter, plant flowers, and prepare our shared public space for the first bits of spring.

The sun melts the final mounds of snow into the earth, leaving us with mud puddles fresh for splashing and revealing last autumn's leaves that didn't make it to the raked pile. There's brush that needs clearing away and fallen branches that broke under winter's weight.

There's never a convenient time for yard work. My son Asher usually has his first soccer game of the year around the same time as cleanup day (yes, I hide under a blanket). But we try to align our schedules so our family can be involved.

As we pack away the remaining Christmas lights from the neighborhood entrance, our cleanup crew has the imagination to see what will be someday. Everything is brown and branches are bare, but soon the tiniest pops of color will arrive, announcing spring's arrival.

We work knowing that a few weeks later, we'll hide candy-filled Easter eggs along the park's crevices, tucking bits of pastel among the pines. My kids will run through the fresh green grass with their kites, delighting in the April wind. But for now, we pick up pieces of shattered glass bottles and discarded bits of trash.

The land is messy as it thaws, and our old sneakers and work boots get caked in mud. Our noses are red, and our cheeks are cold to the touch as we dig, clean, and chat, but we keep going, gathering dirt under our fingernails. Neighbors catch up, laughing, gossiping, and complaining, as folks who have been cooped up are wont to do.

This communal clearing away shakes off the cobwebs from my heart, too.

Winter can feel so isolating—so, well, *cold*. In the blizzards and ice storms, I've felt myself wondering if anyone else lives near us at all. The freezing temperatures hurt our faces, and we run from our vehicles to our homes, sharing quick waves here and there but not much more.

In the coldest months, the frigid temperatures tend to freeze much of my efforts for connection and self-care. I can easily pause relationships and put plans to care for myself on hold until it gets warm again.

When the earth thaws, so do we.

My children, who have been cooped up, too, falling victim to cabin fever, are free. At the first glimpse of spring, they run with glee, stretching their muscles and catching up with neighborhood friends they last saw in snowsuits.

The worst of winter has passed, but we still work as we wait for the warmth of spring.

Our neighborhood's master gardener is a retired teacher and keeps us organized, graciously guiding my easily distracted kids to a patch of space that needs raking. I'm grateful for the community gathered and for another grown-up who takes the time to pour patience and care into my children.

Only a few short months separate the seasons. I reflect as I collect fallen branches, in awe that spring will soon turn to summer and our yard work day at the park will feel like a lifetime ago. The care we put into this little patch of park space will make way for it to become a little urban oasis where kids in flip-flops chase each other, where big brothers push younger siblings on swings, where one-hundred-year-old trees watch over another generation of children, and leafy branches blanket the park under a canopy of shade. We tend to the trees that birds will turn into an aviary, their songs melodies that will meet the thrum of lawn mowers and the giggles of children as they run through sprinklers.

When God told Adam to have dominion over the earth, the Creator of all things was commissioning humans, including us, to care for creation (see Genesis 2:15). We are made in God's image, and we know that God tends to creation with lovingkindness (see Psalm 117:2). So we must do the same.

At creation, God blessed human beings and told them to "have dominion over the fish of the sea and over the birds of the air and

> When I consider your heavens, the work of your fingers, the moon and the stars, which you have set in place, what is mankind that you are mindful of them, human beings that you care for them?
>
> PSALM 8:3-4, NIV

over every living thing that moves upon the earth" (Genesis 1:26-28, NRSV). In her book *The Very Good Gospel*, Lisa Sharon Harper explores the idea of dominion: "If humanity is created in God's likeness, then the way we exercise dominion should reflect God's kind of dominion."[36] As we gather with our handful of neighbors and pull our children away from video games and endless apps, replacing their devices with garbage bags and garden trowels, we're choosing community and the common good. We're committing to care for the living things around us and all who use them.

Our beautiful natural world is God's, and we are given the gift of stewarding it with care and compassion. Psalm 24:1-2 says, "The earth is the LORD's, and everything in it, the world, and all who live in it; for he founded it on the seas and established it on the waters" (NIV).

"God's actions reveal deep love for humanity. Only love would compel a self-existent God who can't be coerced by any higher power to pull out the stops and craft a world that is not only functional but beautiful and abundant. Love does that," says Harper.[37] Unfortunately, humans haven't been the best at receiving this abundant love and caring for God's creation. Because of our lack of care, in a very real way, creation groans (see Romans 8:22). We want our children—and all future generations—to inherit a flourishing world, not a planet marked by famine, dwindling resources, and extinct species.

We are parents who care, who do our broken best to tend to the world (and the children) God has breathed into existence. We want our children to breathe clean air and drink clean water. We want them to inherit a healthy earth, delighting in the majesty of snowcapped mountains and frolicking in fields of wildflowers.

We want them to enjoy the wonder of God's handiwork. We must steward our resources and teach our children how to do so as well, so generations upon generations will continue to live in the shade of mighty oaks and swim among brilliant life-forms in the sparkling blue seas.

We care for creation because, as Deuteronomy 10:14 tells us, all of heaven and earth belong to God. When we care for not just people but our planet, our labor is an act of love to the Lord of all creation.

This is why we plant pollinator gardens: so toddlers can delight at the sight of a fuzzy, fat bumblebee as it weaves in and out of purple flowers that dance in the breeze. This is why we buy used when possible and watch our carbon footprint. This is why we reduce, reuse, and recycle, long after Earth Day passes: so children can catch muddy worms after a spring rain, so we can breathe fresh air and delight in the delicate balance and the connected cycle of four distinct seasons.

This is why we join our neighbors on cleanup day. We show up and roll up our sleeves, working together, because man wasn't meant to be alone. Because community care and creation care go hand in hand.

The Collection band sings a repeat line in their song "The Gown of Green" that comes to mind every time I reflect on caring for creation (and raising my kids to do the same): "We will sow the Earth with diligence and love." First Corinthians 16:14 says simply, "Let all that you do be done *in* love" (NRSV).

Perhaps previous generations thought that caring about our precious and delicate Earth was only for flower children or political activists. But as Christians, our call is to love our neighbor. And as we care for the land our neighbor stands on, the air our neighbor breathes, and the water that nourishes our neighbor's very life, we are following Jesus' command to love our neighbor as ourselves: caring for their flourishing, for their children, and for generations to come.

SCRIPTURE

Psalm 24:1-2; Romans 8:24; Deuteronomy 10:14; 1 Corinthians 16:14

BREATH PRAYER

Inhale: The earth is Yours,
Exhale: And everything in it.

FAMILY DISCUSSION QUESTIONS

Read Psalm 24:1-2 together.

▸ What does it mean that God is the Creator of all?

▸ How many examples of God's creation can you name?

▸ How would you feel if someone ruined something you made?

▸ Why do you think God has given us the earth to take care of?

CELEBRATE EARTH DAY

Earth Day is celebrated April 22. Consider choosing one of these activities to do together as a family:

1. Plant a seed.
2. Feed the birds.
3. Read a book about God's creation.
4. Play nature bingo.
5. Host an eco-friendly party.

For instructions and additional ideas, see https://www.pbs.org/parents/thrive/15-ways-to-celebrate-earth-day-with-kids.

- How is caring for nature a way to not only love God but love our neighbor, too?

- In what ways can our family be more thoughtful about what we consume?

- What is littering? Why is it harmful to the earth God made?

- Ecosystems are connected and rely on each other. Why might have God created nature to be this way?

- How is caring for God's creation an act of praise or worship?

- What could we do this spring to take care of our neighborhood?

FAMILY PRAYER

younger

God, we see You in all seasons, and we thank You for the gift of new life in spring!

Thank You for the buds on tree branches, for the birds that hop on the grass and sing beautiful songs. We feel You in the fresh air from open windows and the dandelions popping up in the grass.

You are the Maker of heaven and earth! Your love is bigger than all the galaxies, yet You care about the tiniest ladybug crawling on a leaf. Help us to take care of the earth You've given us to walk on, the air You've given us to breathe, and the water You've given us to drink.

Help us to be gentle with all living things. Help our family to honor You and take care of Your creation so all living things will continue to experience the beauty of spring for years and years to come. Amen.

older

O God, in You bare branches come to life, birds serenade us in spring's symphonies, and flowers stretch into bursts of color.

Help us to see You in our comings and goings as winter's chill gives way to open windows and fresh air. Jesus, help us to feel Your humanity in the dirt below our feet. Holy Spirit, help us to feel Your comfort in the canopies of trees slowly stretching above our heads.

No matter how old we are, help us to explore You in the world, delighting in Your creation like children discovering the golden bloom of spring's first dandelion. Help us to steward the land, the skies, and the seas well. Help us to be gentle with creation, for we show our awe and reverence for You when we care for all You've made. All of creation whispers Your glory. Amen.

SUMMER

Introduction

LIKE PULLED TAFFY AT the state fair, summer stretches on. The sun is lazy, covering the earth in a yawn and swallowing us whole. Long days turn into longer weeks. Cotton candy clouds dissolve into dusk.

My kids protest bedtime when the rest of the world is still covered in light, before the fireflies have a chance to sparkle. "It's not fair!" they chorus.

Sometimes we let them stay up, sipping lemonade and catching bugs, the bottoms of their bare feet coated in dirt. Their knees are covered in scrapes, their ankles are peppered with bug bites, and their noses betray a sunscreen not reapplied.

How often I've prayed for these summer days—for the cold isolation of winter to melt away into summer's welcoming warmth. Yet now that I have what I've prayed for, I find myself listless. The air-conditioning unit shakes under the pressure, and I'm caught in a midsummer panic: *Have I done enough? Have I made the most of these fleeting months? Why do I keep losing my temper?*

Summer is slipping away like leftover sand from a beach bag. I see an article floating around about "only having eighteen summers with your kids," and it sends me down a mild midsummer spiral. I wonder if I've wasted everything.

Backyard tomato plants break free from their cages, bursting forth and rejoicing in the humidity and heat. The leafy vines climb higher than our kids, giving us fat, round fruit we'll slice on toast and share with our neighbors. Jonny collects cucumbers in an old box, and I think we should make pickles, and then remember I know nothing about pickling.

It's the hottest stretch of the year. We situate ourselves in front of fans, waiting for the fever to break. The heat wave has made us slow. The unstructured mornings amble into lazy afternoons. I reach for popsicles for the kids and linger in front of the freezer's icy chill.

We haven't given our family a multi-week vacation out of state. We don't have a lake house to while away our weekends.

Maybe you've looked around on social media and felt like you were missing out on something or depriving your family somehow. Or maybe you scrimped and saved for a dream vacation only to have it rain the whole time while your family argued.

As adults, we know that sometimes our dreams don't align with reality. We teach our children that you don't always get what you want. The flip side is that sometimes when you do get what you want, it's not what you expected.

Summer offers us a chance to slow down, forcing us to answer the uncomfortable question, *What will we do with our days when they grow longer and lighter?*

Summer invites us to notice—to be outside in the fresh air and feel the prickle of sweat on our skin, the sweetness of a strawberry melting on our tongue. We can take notice of the stubborn lilies that sprout among the weeds in the back alley. We can be like children, lost in the wonder of a butterfly's wings, charmed by a melted sorbet sunset.

"This delicious season can slip by us in our quest for the extraordinary—the perfect vacation, the crossed-off bucket list, the back-to-school countdown," writes Laura Fanucci, who has taught me so much about finding the holy in the seemingly mundane. "But when we lunge after the exceptional, we can let the ordinary beauty pass us by."[1] What ordinary beauty might be nestled in the contours of our families this season, if we're able to slow down enough to notice? What might our children remember years down the road—not about what you did but about how they felt?

The summer months are swathed in what the church calendar calls Ordinary Time. In spring, we observe Lent and Easter. In winter, we celebrate Advent and Christmas. But summer invites us to slow down and relish the reality that God is with us in the slow moments. The sprawl of summer beckons us to see the sacred in the sticky sunscreen, the dripping popsicles, and the stretches of summer boredom. Perhaps, if we allow it to, the slower rhythm of summer can remind us that we are not the sum of what we do or the magical memories we can conjure up for our children. These moments of Ordinary Time invite us to reflect on the glorious truth that God calls us beloved children, desiring our presence.

As you enter this slower stretch of time, may you be open to how the God of all seasons is reminding you that your family needs rhythms throughout the year to simply *be*. An object in motion stays in motion—so we all need to stop sometimes. As the psalmist writes, we need to be still and know that God is God (see Psalm 46:10). We need to be bored sometimes because maybe that's when we hear the still, small voice of God. There are times we need to sit. To wrestle in the waiting. To quiet our physical lives so the spiritual part of us may rest. (And our children need to see us doing this too.)

As a parent, you may feel that rest—even in the lazy days of summer—is out of reach, even laughable. But incorporating true Sabbath is possible—and necessary. May the pages in this section be a resource for you in living out countercultural rhythms of rest.

As you spend time in inner reflection and then shared conversation with your family this season, maybe you'll find ways to take a break from screens and brainstorm how to spend time in nature together. Maybe you'll eat from paper plates or hunker down on the couch with a family movie as raindrops punctuate your afternoon. Perhaps you'll find new ways to extend hospitality and work toward rhythms of family life that make space for the flourishing and the freedom of all people.

Whatever God might speak into your soul and the soul of your family, may this summer bring with it glimmers of growth and glimpses of glory in the seemingly ordinary moments of your life together.

A Prayer for Summer

O God of all seasons,
We thank You for the warmth
Of summer's embrace,
For the sun that stretches over us,
Bathing us in light
And beckoning us
To bask in the glow of Your glory.

We ask You to surround our
    family
In this season of good growth.
Nourish us with Your
Summer rain and help us
To be rooted and established
    in love
As we bear the fruit You have
    for us.

Be near in the birds' morning song
And the dappled sunsets at dusk.

Help us to see You in the sparkle
Of fireflies, whose wonder
Delights kids of all ages.

Help us to see You in the still
    waters
And the crashing waves.
Help us to hear You in the rustle
    of leaves
And breathe Your aroma in the
    lingering scent
Of a bloom bursting forth.

God, be near in the backyard
    games of tag
And the send-offs to summer
    camp.

Be in the worn pages of a library
    book
And in every nook and cranny of
The old wooden treehouse.

Sit with us on the baseball
    bleachers
And in the salty concession-stand
    popcorn.

Be near in the crammed suitcases
And forgotten directions
Of a family road trip.

Help us to be awake to the glory
    surrounding us
This summer.
Draw us to the people and places
You have for us to love,
And may our hearts be tender
To receive love in unexpected ways.

May we establish gentle rhythms
    of rest
In the midst of summer's
    excitement.
Grant us the gift of noticing
The feel of sand
Or blades of grass

Or hot cement
Under our feet.
Help us to slow down so we may
Pay attention to the way
Cotton-candy clouds
Shift their shape.
Give us imagination
To enter daydreams with our
   children.

We thank You for training wheels
On the hand-me-down bike
And for tossing the keys to the
   teenager
Who just passed their driving
   test.

May our hands and feet
Be a blessing
To all who cross our paths
This summer.

Grant us patience when family
   time
Becomes too much.
Grant us creativity
When the days stretch on.
Grant us peace
In all our comings
And goings.

We thank You for the invitation
To slow down

And reset,
For the smell of fresh-cut grass
And the lush green leaves on
   the trees,
For bright blooms
And juicy berries ripe for the
   picking.

We thank You for ice cream
   dripping down
Our children's chins
And for swimming suits
Hanging to dry.

Bless the fans that keep us cool,
And protect those who wipe
   sweat
From their brows.

Thank You for the splendor of
   getting lost in a book
And for the way our children
   grin
When a page transports them
To grand adventures in faraway
   places.

We thank You for bees that
   bumble along,
For sun-ripened tomatoes fresh
   from the garden,
For cannonballs at the pool,
For neighborhood friends,

For bike rides and stroller walks,
For summer jobs that clock in
    and out
As time slowly marches on.

Be with us in our cookouts
And parades,
Our family road trips
And midsummer dreams.

May we not take for granted
Sandy feet,
Bug bites and lemonade,
Fireworks and sunscreen,
And fireflies that light the night
With flashes of delight.

Release us from the pressure
To give our kids a perfect summer,
For we know "flawless" is
Forever out of reach.
Instead, help us to be present
When we are together,
Knowing that memories can be made
On a walk
Or in the kitchen
Or in the garage,
Not just on a family vacation.

Be near in the chalk drawings
And backyard bubble blowing,
In the skipped rocks

And melted popsicles.
Be near in the bike rides
And farmers markets.
And may we never be too caught up
To give thanks for all who labor
So we may rest.

Speak to the oldest and youngest
    among us
In daydreams and fits of summer
    boredom,
Thunderstorms and holy interruptions.
Amid frustrations that boil over,
Sibling rivalries,
And heat waves,
Cool our tempers.

Help us to see that these
    seemingly ordinary moments
Hold Your very essence.
Help us to inhale Your love
So that our every breath
Is a gentle offering of grace
To our children, to our
    neighbors, and to ourselves.

May we live wholehearted
And be wholly present
In the months to come,
Knowing Your extraordinary love
Covers each moment
Of ordinary times.

Sticky Fingers

IN OUR EARLY DAYS AS PARENTS, my husband and I decided to be brave and take a summer weekend road trip with our four (quite young) kids. We had it all planned: a day exploring downtown would culminate at a giant old-fashioned candy store.

At this point, our oldest was in first grade. We also had a three-year-old and two tiny babies under one. Yes, we got those "You have your hands full!" comments all the time. But my husband and I were just bonkers enough to feel like with a double stroller, enough fruit snacks for the kids who could walk, and coffee for the parents chasing them, we could make some family memories and probably not lose our children.

We didn't lose any children. But I wouldn't exactly say that we escaped unscathed either.

We went to an art museum and a sculpture garden—and it was about ninety-three degrees. We were hot, sweaty, and tired. But the day wasn't over yet; it was time to stop at the candy store.

We're not talking about a little shop; it's a gigantic *experience*. Located in a sprawling corner lot in the heart of the city, the store is filled with every kind of candy you (and your grandmother) can possibly remember. It has a nostalgic, vintage vibe and also features a soda fountain, a diner, a vintage pinball arcade, a movie theater, and giant displays of movie memorabilia.

For my six-year-old and three-year-old, it was sensory overload. *The smells! The sights!* It took the phrase "like a kid in a candy shop" to a new level.

As soon as we squeezed our stroller and diaper bags into the store, we noticed security cameras and "NO STEALING" signs everywhere—on every bin of rainbow-hued bubblegum and every stack of candy bars. The signs warned in bold font that theft wouldn't be tolerated: the police would be called, and there would be hefty fines for anyone who had sticky fingers that came from somewhere besides the candy shop's homemade fudge.

Our boys were enthralled with every shiny item and each alluring piece of candy. We gave them a spending limit and let them make their treat choices with the promise that they'd brush their teeth when we got back to the hotel.

Their decision-making time in the candy store was excruciating. They wanted everything and anything that was right in front of them. The shiniest, loudest little toys (that were somehow also filled with candy?) grabbed their attention most. My son Joseph had already settled on his selection of candy, but as we were getting ready to pay for everything, he spotted a spinning Captain America toy that twirled and buzzed and lit up in a rainbow of colors with the press of a button.

It was overpriced, and I could see it would somehow be used as a weapon on his brother. Plus, it barely contained any candy. We told him to put it back because he'd already made his choice. Now it was time to pay, get our little zoo of humans to the ice cream shop, and head back to the hotel.

There were tears, of course, but we finally bought a giant bag of candy and were ready to head out. As we walked across the street to the ice cream shop, my husband and I laughed at all the "NO STEALING" signs plastered at every conceivable nook and cranny of the store.

Wow, they're really taking theft seriously, I thought. *No one would steal after all those signs!*

We made it to the ice cream shop and then back to our hotel, where it was time for showers and pajamas. The two older boys jumped on hotel beds while we fed the babies. And, of course, we had to dump out our bag of candy and divvy out the treasures.

That's when we saw it. Or maybe when we heard it: the whir of a light-up, rainbow-colored spinny toy. A Captain America one, in fact. A Captain America toy we did *not* pay for.

Our six-year-old had sticky fingers!

I was mortified. And a little panicked. Shoplifters would be prosecuted! Were they tracking our minivan? Was our son on a fast track to a youth of petty theft, leading to a life of crime?

I think my husband and I gasped simultaneously before I choked out, "WHAT . . . IS . . . THAT?"

Our son's eyes had turned into giant saucers. He immediately started crying.

Since I'm slightly paranoid, I grabbed our bag of candy and used the hotel phone to dial the candy shop and confess our sins.

My son watched me on the phone. Based on the look on his face, he was sure he was going to jail.

The candy shop manager was gracious to this frazzled, embarrassed mom. He said there was no need to come in or take our debit card number. We were forgiven. I thanked him profusely and hung up.

I took a breath, got the three other kids settled with a TV show, and led my little culprit to the hotel chair on the other side of the room. I sat with him and reminded him that God teaches us not to steal because when we take what isn't ours, we don't just harm others; we harm ourselves, too. I told him that the store owners lost money.

He confessed he'd tucked the toy away at the bottom of a stroller.

I wiped his tears and gave him—and myself—some space to process. I left him with a stack of children's books we'd brought along and went back to talk with Jonny.

When we returned to check on our son, he was still sniffling, quietly reading a story-book Bible. We talked about what had happened and asked him what he'd learned about forgiveness, and then we prayed. He had a debt that was forgiven, and I'm pretty confident he learned about actions having consequences and the radical grace of forgiveness.

I have four kids who are learning, growing, and figuring things out. As a parent, a wife, a neighbor, and a writer, I'm figuring things out myself—and I'm in need of forgiveness too. There are moments when my words or actions harm others and myself. But in those moments, Christ is already there, ready to forgive me and receive me with the outstretched arms of a father.

In the story of the Prodigal Son, we read this line about the son who went astray: "While he was still a long way off, his father saw him and was filled with compassion for him; he ran to his son, threw his arms around him and kissed him" (Luke 15:20, NIV).

This is the kind of forgiveness God has for us. We are not just welcomed into forgiveness; we are pulled in with compassion. We are covered with kisses and embraced in the arms of a loving Father. The Father doesn't just put up with us; He runs toward us.

As a parent, I am able to connect with this idea when I think of my love for my son and his theft of the spinny toy. It's much harder to think of myself as the child in this scenario. But the grace of Jesus is lavished on us the way a compassionate parent forgives their children. Because that's what we are: children of God.

Our family was recently talking about God's forgiveness at the dinner table. To illustrate his point, my husband lifted up his can of sparkling water (a drink our kindergartener always pines after), held it out, and said, "Here."

My son immediately grabbed it and took a drink. That is forgiveness. It is *given*. And by the grace of God, we can receive that forgiveness—for the seemingly minor transgressions and for the deep sins in our lives too. It is not earned by good deeds or some cosmic point system. It is grace. It is given.

I am forgiven. You are forgiven. We just have to receive it, like a child.

SCRIPTURE
Ephesians 4:32; Colossians 3:13; Psalm 86:5; Daniel 9:9

BREATH PRAYER

Inhale: Help me to forgive
Exhale: As You have forgiven me.

FAMILY DISCUSSION QUESTIONS

Read Ephesians 4:32 together.

- ▸ What does God tell us about forgiveness?
- ▸ Can you tell about a time you needed forgiveness? What happened? What does it feel like to be forgiven?
- ▸ Can you tell about a time you forgave someone? What happened? Why is it difficult to forgive?
- ▸ Why is it important for us as followers of Jesus to forgive?
- ▸ Think about the thief on the cross (see Luke 23:32-43). How do you think he felt when Jesus forgave him? Why do you think Jesus forgave him? What does this story teach us about Christ's love?
- ▸ What's at stake if we don't forgive our family members?
- ▸ What's the difference between forgiving and forgetting? Does forgiveness mean there are no consequences?
- ▸ Is forgiveness a one-time thing, or is it something we keep choosing to do? Why do you think this is?

We are not just welcomed into forgiveness; we are pulled in with compassion . . . The Father doesn't just put up with us; He runs toward us.

FAMILY PRAYER

God, You are gentle and kind. You are quick to forgive and slow to anger.

We are sorry for the times we have harmed one another (and ourselves) through our words or actions. [Pause for reflection.]

Thank You for Your big, beautiful forgiveness. In light of the forgiving love of Christ, will You help us to forgive others as You have forgiven us?

Please help us to release what we're holding on to and live into the ways of Jesus at home, at school, in our neighborhood, and at work. Amen.

O forgiving God, we come to You aware of our propensity to get it wrong. We grieve for the ways we have not honored You, harming others and ourselves in the process.

And while we know it is important to confess our sins to You, our stories do not stop there. You do not leave us a long way off; You move toward us.

O God, You are the author of forgiveness—true forgiveness, which feels like a new beginning and looks like having our slate wiped clean.

Thank You for your compassion, which moves toward us, not away from us, in our darkest moments and our most profound transgressions.

Help us to receive Your forgiveness so we, too, may forgive those who have sinned against us. Amen.

231

In the Garden

SOME PEOPLE ARE BORN with a green thumb. They're at home with their favorite pair of gloves and little packets of heirloom seeds. They seem to have an encyclopedic knowledge of sunlight needs and watering schedules.

And then there's me.

I love plump tomatoes plucked fresh from the vine and have never refused a farmers market bouquet. But I stick to the cultivation of words and stories, not vegetables and plants.

One year, my husband and kids planted a garden for me as a late Mother's Day gift. They built the beds and chose a selection of vegetables. They watered and tended it, but the patch of land was too shady and the soil was too sandy to produce much fruit. On top of that, it was too tempting to the neighborhood rabbits and a few deer, which nibbled and munched on the fledgling plants while stubborn weeds strangled the growth.

My family did their labor in love, but it just wasn't working.

A few years (and a few homes) later, we decided to attempt a low-key backyard garden. We didn't put too much time or effort into it; we chose a sunny patch of our backyard, planted a few varieties of tomatoes and cucumbers, and hoped for the best.

By midsummer, we had more tomatoes than we knew what to do with. We ate an overwhelming number of BLTs and delivered brimming bags of sun-ripened tomatoes to everyone we knew.

How could this happen? We worked so diligently and had such high expectations for our first garden, which failed, and the one that took little effort yielded a beautiful harvest.

As parents, we often think that if we just do the right things the right way, our children will make good choices. *Struggle, adversity, and teenage rebellion won't touch our family!* But as much as we want our families to flourish, we don't always get to make those calls.

Maybe you grew up in a church where memorizing Scripture or following a strict set of rules was the equivalent of having a relationship with Jesus. Maybe you were taught that the more you knew (or the more you did), the more worthy or holy you were in God's eyes. Henri Nouwen said that instead of asking ourselves how we can love God better, perhaps the better question is: "How am I to let myself be loved by God?"[2] I wonder how this flipped perspective might change the way we approach parenting. What if we loosened our grip on our measuring sticks and instead asked ourselves how we might create a space where children could love out of an overflow of God's love? How might the ways we talk about Christ and measure our spiritual growth change if we cultivate homes where children are reminded that they can receive and grow in God's grace, love, and compassion?

It's not about making a fence for the rabbits; it's about finding a better space for the garden—a more holistic view of what makes life grow.

As I reflect on our gardening adventures, I know we had good intentions on that first try. But instead of pivoting or recalibrating when growth didn't happen—instead of getting to the root of the problem—we blamed hungry creatures, shady trees, and imperfect soil. We believed we'd followed the rules, so when the garden went awry, it felt a lot like failure.

This can be a dangerous mindset to take into parenting. Ask any parent far along on their parenting journey, and you'll hear the same refrain: you can't control every (any?) circumstance in your children's lives.

As parents, we cultivate instead of control. We don't have to toil; instead, we can tend. And tending our kids' hearts and minds, bodies and souls, even as the world throws the unexpected at them, even as they make mistakes and find their way, is a lot like gardening. It's a lot like cultivating the soil, pivoting when needed, and trusting God with all we have and all we are.

"There is something profoundly stable and rooted about faithfulness in family. We must be available to provide a dwelling place, a home, for those persons we are given to love intimately," says Wendy Wright in *Seasons of a Family's Life*. "Children need roots before they can sprout wings."[3] The sitcoms I grew up watching told me parenting came down to serious conversations, those "Hey, kiddo" moments with a grown-up sitting on the foot of the bed, talking through an important life lesson with their child. Yes, we have essential conversations at times, but the everyday moments we cultivate are what make up a life together.

What are your everyday moments looking like in this season? We can tell our kids so many things about our faith and our values with our words, but are we living it out? Are we living out of our belovedness and embodying our love for God and neighbor in our daily lives?

As Justin Whitmel Earley writes, "No one habit or blessing or prayer or conversation is going to magically change their life or relationship with God. That is (thank God!) up to the divine regeneration of the Holy Spirit (which allows us peace), but what these habits of the household are doing is giving our children windows into what we mean when we talk about faith."[4] Beyond teaching facts and figures, faithful parenting is living out the heart behind the rules. It's how we spend our time, energy, and resources. It's integrating curiosity and compassion into the fibers of our family, into the makeup of the moments we share with our children. Parenting in the rhythms of God's abundant love is a giant lesson in letting go, in realizing control was never really ours in the first place. We do what we can do, but we also have to trust that the Holy Spirit is with us, even when things go awry and we can't see whether any fruit is growing.

In Galatians 5, Paul encourages the church, reminding them that they were called to be free (verse 1). This freedom, he says, means that rules and regulations are no longer the most important things in our lives. Instead, the only thing that matters is "faith expressing itself through love" (verse 6, NIV). As the passage progresses, it becomes clear that when we tend the soil of our hearts, the Holy Spirit grows fruit there. The same is true of our families. As we live out our faith together by loving our neighbors and being loved by God, we will find our gardens being filled with the fruit of the Spirit.

Instead of relying on religious rules to give scaffolding to the soul of our families, what if we began to trust the Holy Spirit to help us cultivate goodness in our rhythms together— for the flourishing of not just our family but all people?

"I want to raise these amazing, beautiful, frustrating children to become wise and strong, kind and generous, loving and whole individuals who love God and love their neighbors well," writes Sarah Bessey. "And just as I mother my children with that endgame in mind, I do believe the Holy Spirit mothers us with an endgame. It's not only our own wholeness, it is also for the wholeness of the world."[5] In this season of parenting, may the Holy Spirit nurture and guide us as we nurture and guide our families in the season ahead.

SCRIPTURE
Galatians 5

BREATH PRAYER

Inhale: Tend the soil of my heart, O God.
Exhale: Grow good fruit within me.

FAMILY DISCUSSION QUESTIONS

Read Galatians 5:1 together.

- ▸ What do you think Paul meant when he said we've been set free? What have we been set free from?

- ▸ Can you think of a time you followed a recipe, instructions, or rules for something but the outcome wasn't what you had hoped for?

- ▸ What can we do or where can we turn when we need guidance or help?

- ▸ Why do you think God doesn't give parents instructions for raising kids?

- ▸ Why might God prefer us to make room for a relationship instead of following a rigid set of rules?

- ▸ What does a garden need to grow? What does the human heart need to grow?

- ▸ What challenges do gardeners face when they're taking care of their gardens?

- ▸ How long do you think it takes your favorite fruit or vegetable to grow?

- ▸ What happens if we get so set in following the right rules for God that we stop loving God?

- ▸ What is the fruit of the Spirit (see Galatians 5:22-23)? Why does God give us the Holy Spirit?

- ▸ What habits does our family have that make space for honoring God?

A PRAYER FOR A MEAL TOGETHER

For access to abundance
And the hands that farmed each field
And picked each fruit and each vegetable,
We give thanks.
For clean water to scrub the dirt away,
For soil that helps good things grow,
And for sun that shines its face upon the earth,
Revealing Your glory,
We give thanks.

TO LIGHT THEIR WAY

FAMILY PRAYER

younger

God, You have given us Your Spirit to help us and guide us.

Just as a gardener takes care of seeds that become sprouts that become plants that become flowers or fruit, Your gentle love cares for us. You are the Living Water and the Light of the World, helping us grow. When we feel the growing pains, help us to remember that You will never abandon the gardens of our hearts.

Help us to receive Your love so we can live freely and lightly, and extend that love to others. Amen.

older

O God, we thank You for making Your home in our hearts.

Nourish us with Your goodness. Nurture us in Your lovingkindness. We know we cannot work our way to Your love—it is already there, in us and among us in Christ.

O God of abundant love, help us to abide in You. Holy Spirit, we ask for Your guidance so that all we do, all we say, and all we are would be an overflow of Your great and gentle love.

In You, may we bear the fruit of love and joy, peace and patience, kindness and goodness, faithfulness and gentleness, and self-control. Amen.

Constellations

WE NEEDED A CHANGE OF SCENERY, to breathe new air in our lungs. Our trip wasn't fancy—most of it was spent in a camper in a friend's driveway—but it offered us space to reorient our hearts. On the final night of our visit, we lugged well-worn camp chairs to our friend's backyard, surrounded by families of trees and a breeze off the waters of Lake Superior. A fire roared as we passed around sticks and marshmallows in the ever-widening circle of chairs.

Big kids told spooky stories, and little ones crawled into our laps. Twinkle lights danced over our heads. The pictures I have from that night are mostly blurry: the flash too bright, the kids too high on sugar to sit still, and the grown-ups too content to care about a perfectly staged photo. But the most magical part of that night, the memory no photo could capture, was what happened next.

As the daylight faded, stars emerged.

Bright white pinpricks glistened and glowed, popping up all around us, puncturing the sky and reminding us how big the world is and how small we are.

I love those reminders of the vastness of our cosmos because they remind me that I am a child of the Creator God. That the Maker holds me the way a mother holds her sticky, sweaty five-year-old on the last day of a camping trip.

In those moments when it feels like I can touch the vastness of creation, I can almost smell the essence of heaven here on earth. I exhale, remembering I'm a beloved daughter of the Maker of the heavens and the earth. I'm held in all my exhaustion and frustration, my wonderings and doubts, wrapped in the arms of the One who breathed it all into existence—the mighty oaks, the lapping blue waters, and even the pesky Northwoods mosquitoes.

The stories started to grow quiet (undoubtedly, one of us parents realized we'd stayed up well beyond bedtime), the cicadas hummed to their own beat, and a blanket of darkness hemmed us in as dusk turned to a deep, inky blue, dotted with pinpricks of glittering stars.

One by one, we began to look up, noticing the beauty we couldn't see in the light of day.

"There's the Little Dipper!"

"I see the North Star!"

The kids connected the dots, squinting an eye and tracing their fingers in the air, piecing together stories and stars.

Soon we were all on our backs, the crackle of the dwindling fire the soundtrack to our awe. We remembered an app that uses technology I don't understand to scan the skies in real time with a phone's camera, overlaying the constellations on the screen. The more we looked, the more we saw—pictures coming alive before our very eyes. We all hold stories that aren't always seen.

We often forget how much others are a part of our own constellations. But here we are, living and breathing under the same sky, looking up. As we see in Colossians 1:17, God is in all things and holds all things together. In Christ, we are more connected than we know.

It's easy to forget the wonder in our daily comings and goings, to miss the sparkle of God's connected love in the dark seasons of our lives. For one magical night in the Northwoods, there are thousands of evenings of takeout and doomscrolling and collapsing on the couch after a long day.

We notice the glory around us because we need every ounce of strength we can muster not to get pulled into the black holes surrounding us—those consuming feelings of cynicism, overwhelm, and dread. As Job 12:22 says, our God "reveals the deep things of darkness and brings utter darkness into the light" (NIV).

We seek glimmers of God's glory that peek through the darkness of our lives because we know what's at stake if we don't: we're prone to wander, get distracted, and forget our interconnectedness and the glory of God in it all.

"People who notice the stars in the sky or take an extra moment for the sunrise haven't known only joy in their lives," writes poet and artist Morgan Harper Nichols. "They usually have experienced the cold, black-blue waters of struggle and the long quiet hours of sorrow. . . . They learned not to take things for granted. They learned to treasure where they saw the light."[6] When the bills are due, your kids are whining, and you can't stop your head from spinning, you won't always be able to escape into a Northwoods nature retreat. But you can step outside.

As day dissolves into night, I hope you'll stand on your front steps or your fire escape, letting the fresh summer air fill your lungs as you look at the stars and connect the dots. I hope you'll remember that you are not alone, that the Spirit of God goes before you and your family.

May the words the psalmist wrote so many years ago speak to your soul as you dwell in the mystery that the One who made it all is not finished making Your story. May you remember that God's love is the string that connects the dots in the story of your life, creating a brilliant picture you may not always see but is always, always there.

> When I look at the night sky and see the work of your fingers—
>   the moon and the stars you set in place—
> what are mere mortals that you should think about them,
>   human beings that you should care for them?
> Yet you made them only a little lower than God
>   and crowned them with glory and honor.

PSALM 8:3-5

SCRIPTURE
Colossians 1:17; Job 12:22; Psalm 8:3-5

BREATH PRAYER

Inhale: When I look at the stars,
Exhale: I see Your handiwork.

FAMILY DISCUSSION QUESTIONS

Read Psalm 8:3-5 together.

- ▶ Why do you think that, for thousands of years, people have been inspired by the stars and named constellations in the sky?

- ▶ Where have you seen the most stars in the sky? How did it make you feel?

- ▶ Why is it easy to forget the beautiful things in our lives when we're experiencing things that are difficult or overwhelming?

- ▶ How can paying attention to glimmers of beauty in our lives be an act of worship?

- ▶ When have you looked back on your life and realized that God was connecting things in ways you didn't realize?

- ▶ What is at stake if we forget how we're connected to each other as a family?

In all our
exhaustion
and frustration,
our wonderings and
doubts, we are
wrapped in the arms
of the One who
breathed it all into
existence.

- What is at stake if we forget how we're connected to each other as a community?

- When you think of the ways your life is connected to others', how does that make you feel? Why?

- Where are you seeing the light in your life right now? (Think about places, people, activities, or situations.)

- How might remembering that we all sit under the same stars lead us to act more compassionately in our community and our world?

FAMILY PRAYER

God, the world is so big. When we look at the stars, we're amazed at how wonderful Your creation is and how big Your love is. As we look up at night and trace our fingers over the stars, imagining shapes and stories, we are reminded how connected our world is—how connected we are to You, to our family, and to our neighbors.

We may not see the stars during the day, but that doesn't mean they don't exist. We can remember that even when we can't see You, You are with us.

Help us to be on the lookout for good, beautiful things so we can tuck them in our pockets and remember them when we feel sad, afraid, or overwhelmed. Help us to remember that Your light shines, even when we can't see it. Help us to remember just how connected we are. Amen.

younger

O God who sets stars into motion, who forms families in beautiful ways, we can't pretend to understand the why and how and when behind all that has happened in our lives. From the darkest nights to the most brilliant sunrises, we know there is much that is not ours to know.

Even in our most doubtful moments, we hold on to a stubborn trust that Your presence has been with our family all along, connecting our stories the way children trace their finger against a backdrop of stars.

Help us to remember to look up so we may experience the gift of Your wonder in the daily comings and goings of our lives. Help us to remind one another to notice, to pay attention. Help us to remember that we all sit under the same canopy of stars. Help us to fathom how we are connected to our local and global neighbors. Amen.

older

Parades and Pentecost

I SLING TWO CAMP CHAIRS over one shoulder, balancing a cooler in the crook of my arm, pushing the stroller as I do a quick head count.

Yep. All kids accounted for.

My oldest carries a quilt; my youngest hasn't run off yet. I squint in the sun, surveying the blocked-off downtown street.

"There's room over there!" I lead my crew in and out of crowds, securing a spot on the curb.

We get settled, and I take a deep breath, inhaling the smell of summer: a swirl of sunscreen, cotton candy, barbecued ribs, and bug spray.

Our hometown throws off the heavy mantle of winter with a big hurrah, welcoming summer with a weekend festival. Neighbors reconnect with one another, trading snow boots for flip-flops. Friday night brings members of our racially and socioeconomically diverse community together with a parade. I have sweet memories of marching down these same streets when I was in elementary school, and now I get to pass on a bit of nostalgia to my children.

The kids get in position, ready and willing (and hopeful) to catch a few Tootsie Rolls.

The parade is about to begin. And then it doesn't. I glance at my watch.

"Mommmmm, I'm booooored."

"It'll start soon."

We wait. We keep waiting.

My eldest rolls his eyes. My youngest spots a child holding a snow cone and flies into a fit of jealousy.

Finally, when I'm almost ready to pack it all up and head home for the sake of my sanity, the police escort rolls down the asphalt. The crowd full of young families, clusters of too-cool teens, and groupings of grannies all cheer.

The parade begins.

A beautiful hodgepodge of community groups, small businesses, schools, and churches make their way down the street wearing matching shirts and offering enthusiastic waves. We watch as the local meatpacking plant employees, many of whom are immigrants and refugees, wave to my children as they ride on a float decked out in flags representing their home countries. A semitruck lumbers down the road, driven by a woman with blond hair and tattoos.

A group of families walks past us, holding printed photos of smiling faces, and my heart falls when I realize they're with a local hospice group, walking in remembrance of those they loved. Gymnasts make the street their tumbling mats, wowing the crowd (and stressing me out) with their series of flips.

An elementary-school-age boy zooms past in his wheelchair. Dancers and drumlines woo the crowd. Politicians I agree with—and ones I don't—sit on the back of old-school convertibles and perfect their smile-and-wave. A float sponsored by an African American church rolls by while children lead us in a chant against gun violence. I see the Catholic school walk by, followed by the city's most charismatic megachurch. A group of white-haired women in cardigans and khakis sit atop the retirement home's float and flash thousand-watt smiles, waving at the wrist like royalty.

At some point, I realize I'm crying.

This is what the church is like, I think. God's family is a living, breathing ragtag mix of all this. Our perspectives, backgrounds, gifts, and talents may vary, but we're all journeying the same path. We're speaking different languages but hitting the same pavement, the Holy Spirit uniting us amid our differences.

Summer brings the day of Pentecost, an observance in the Christian year that comes fifty days after Easter. On this day, we celebrate "the outpouring of the Holy Spirit and the ongoing life of the Holy Spirit in the church today."[7] Christians across the globe celebrate what we read about in Acts 2—the breaking in of a new reality (God's Spirit poured out on everyday people). This was a moment that changed everything—and is still changing everything.

In Acts 2, we see a wild scene play out. I wonder if the early church, like my family waiting for the parade to begin, was worshiping but perhaps growing tired in the wait. Jesus had promised that while He was leaving them, He'd leave behind something better: His Spirit (see John 14:15-31). And His followers believed it. Even if they couldn't fathom it, they clung to hope. They gathered. They worshiped. They waited.

And then, *boom.* Or should I say, *whoosh.*

"When the day of Pentecost came, they were all together in one place. Suddenly a sound like the blowing of a violent wind came from heaven and filled the whole house where they were sitting" (Acts 2:1-2, NIV). All the women and men were filled with the

Holy Spirit, who breathed in them the gift of divine presence. They even began speaking new languages (see Acts 2:4).

It was like they were on fire—full of different words, united in something bigger.

Lisa Sharon Harper writes, "At Pentecost, God brought the languages together, but not in the way we would imagine. God did not unite the world under one imperial language. Rather, the power of God made it possible to have unity in the midst of diversity. God made it possible for people to speak languages that were not their own and to understand one another."[8] Maybe that's why our hometown parade, full of ordinary folks marching down a pretty unspectacular main street, felt a bit extraordinary to me. It was a cobbled-together picture of something sacred—a bunch of beautiful, sweaty people across age, ethnicity, race, theology, politics, and ability, gathering together to celebrate.

We worship a God who still breathes life in us today. A God who does not erase our differences but uses them to make something beautiful.

I don't think I'll look at our hometown summer festival and community parade the same way in the coming years. I'll keep bringing my kids and telling them about Pentecost and the church's birthday. No doubt one of them will trip and another will complain, but in the midst of the ordinary, we will praise God for a gospel spoken in thousands of different languages, lived out in billions of different ways.

SCRIPTURE
Acts 2; John 14:15-31

BREATH PRAYER

Inhale: Holy Spirit,
Exhale: Breathe new life into me.

FAMILY DISCUSSION QUESTIONS

Read Acts 2 together.

▶ Why is the day of Pentecost considered the birthday of the church?

▶ Acts 2 says there was a loud rushing like thunder and God's Spirit was like fire. How do you think people who were worshiping felt when they experienced this?

- Scripture says the people were utterly amazed. What is so amazing about Pentecost?

- On the day of Pentecost, the Holy Spirit gave people different languages they could speak and understand. Why do you think that happened? Why didn't God just give followers of Jesus one common language?

- Have you ever watched a parade? What kinds of floats or groups of people were there?

- Why do you think parades are a tradition in so many cultures?

- Has anyone ever made you feel bad because you were different in some way? Have you ever been excluded because you were different? Have you ever excluded someone else? What might the Holy Spirit have to teach us about unity?

- Can you speak more than one language? What challenges come with learning a new language?

- How could our church or our family celebrate Pentecost?

FAMILY PRAYER

younger

Dear God, Your Holy Spirit is a gift for all who believe. Thank You for that gift!

We can't see You or smell You or touch You, but we still believe that You are here, surrounding us and guiding us.

We celebrate that the family of Christ is like a giant parade full of people who are different but also united in You. Help us to celebrate the ways we are both alike and different. Amen.

older

O God, we thank You for the Holy Spirit. Breathe new life into Your church, our family, and our hearts.

Help us to live into who You've called us to be. Thank You for the sacred differences You've given the family of believers. May we declare Your wonders, as the first church did long ago. Help us to celebrate in one accord. Unite us in Your peace. Guide us in Your power. And send us out in our native tongue: love. Amen.

CELEBRATING PENTECOST AS A FAMILY

Go to a parade with your family this summer.

Light a candle at dinner. As you talk about Pentecost, reflect on the tongues of fire that descended on members of the early church.

Look up how to say *Holy Spirit* in multiple languages.

Attend a fireworks display, reflecting on the sights and sounds of that first Pentecost.

Honor the birthday party of Christ's church by baking a birthday cake. At the party, wear red, the liturgical color of Pentecost.

Attend (respectfully) a church service held in a language that's not your first language.

Create an origami bird out of white paper to symbolize the Holy Spirit, who descended like a dove at Jesus' baptism.

Draw a comic strip to tell the story of Pentecost (don't forget the *boom!* and the *whoosh!*).

Paper Plate Hospitality

JONNY AND I LAUGH ABOUT how we thought we were so busy before we had kids. In a way, we were—we were busy figuring out how to do life on our own as adults, learning how to face the world together as a couple, trying to navigate friendships and new jobs and taxes.

Also.

It's almost laughable how much downtime I once had. I used to be able to go to the bathroom in peace, without little fingers creeping through or a teen pounding on the door.

Parenting is an all-consuming occupation. I don't know a parent (to a newborn or a teen or anything in between) who isn't exhausted in one way or another. Raising humans takes truckloads of mental, emotional, spiritual, and physical energy. (Raise your hand if you've ever done a load of laundry with a toddler hanging on your leg or if you've ever lugged a Costco-size pallet of Gatorade across a mile-long field to your child's soccer game.) Parenting takes grit, not to mention time and presence.

Jonny and I are both fairly extroverted (*people! places! conversations!*), and we were incredibly social in our pre-children days. We could clean the house in about an hour (the square footage was minimal, and there were no wayward LEGOs or gym socks to clean up), and we loved having people over for just about any reason.

Our relationships were rich and robust. We hosted game nights, theme parties, backyard barbecues, and small groups from church. I tried my hand at new recipes and decorated tablescapes with breakable items. We laughed until our sides hurt and cried ourselves into boogery messes. It was wonderful.

Then we got older. Some friends moved away. Others had babies. Jonny and I became parents and moved away too. Friendships got complicated. Suddenly our days were filled in other ways: with the needs of one child, then two, then three, then four. We celebrated the beauty of this messy parenting season but grieved the loss of what had been too.

Making (and maintaining) friendships as a parent can feel impossible.

Years down the road, we found ourselves back in the same town as our friends Nick and Ashley, a couple we'd become close friends with back in our newlywed days. Now we had eight kids between us. Life looked a bit different from the days when we'd linger over a leisurely brunch after church or stay up late after having dinner together on a work night. This time, they invited us over for a summer barbecue with both our families. We found an evening to circle on the calendar between Little League games and work meetings.

I was thrilled to put something on the calendar that featured interaction with other grown-ups. I planned to bring homemade cookies, chips, burgers, and paper plates. Our idea of hospitality had changed and deepened into a more holistic (and, dare I say, holy) idea of creating a space for honest, no-frills community to happen.

I planned to make cookies on the cookout day, but I was coming up against a writing deadline and got busy with work. I screamed when I looked at the clock. We were supposed to be at our friends' house in fifteen minutes! Store-bought would have to do. I came into the kitchen to pack up what we were bringing, only to find that half of the cookies had already been sneaked from the package and eaten. I had no time to make new ones or go to the store. And as always, we were running late.

My daughter needed a diaper change, and my son had decided now was a great time to get out (and spill) paint. I grabbed some generic ice cream from the freezer as my husband and I rallied our crew.

"Time to go!" I shouted as I cleaned a spill with one hand and grabbed my sandal with another.

When we finally arrived at Nick and Ashley's house, we tumbled out of the minivan—sweaty, frazzled, and late. Our kids had been loud and grumpy on the ride over. I was still focused on my deadline and secretly (and unfairly) fuming that Jonny hadn't kept our family on schedule. While I'd been looking forward to this time together with friends, I now just felt like our chaos was on display. The frozen block of ice cream melted in my hands.

I took a deep breath as the kids ran to play on the trampoline, and we went to greet our friends.

"We brought ice cream," I said with a shrug, handing it off to someone to place in the freezer.

Nick had just gotten home from work and grabbed his keys. "Sorry, guys, I guess I'm running back to the store for hamburger buns."

Ashley popped her head out of the kitchen. "We ran out! I tried to make my own, but they turned out . . . like rocks."

Our friends looked as frazzled as we felt.

Jonny rummaged through our bag of frozen burger patties and chips, remembering that he'd thrown an extra package of buns into our bag at the last minute. *Score!* We all exhaled.

As we started to eat and drink, vestiges of real life began spilling out around the table.

"Can you believe he said that to me at work?"

"What does it look like to get an ADHD diagnosis?"

"KIDS! BE GENTLE!"

Ashley looked down and noticed her shirt was smeared with mustard from the sticky hands of a toddler. Our eyes met, and I laughed, telling her it was nothing compared to our anniversary dinner the week before, when I realized much too late that my tank top had streaks of not only yogurt but Vaseline, too.

The more we let ourselves be honest with each other, the more relaxed we feel.

Making time to invest in friendships is complicated enough as it is—we don't need the pressure of perfection hanging over us too. Nobody has it all together, and it's refreshing not to have to hold ourselves up to some unattainable standard.

When we invite our friends and neighbors into our everyday messy reality, with bills stacked on the desk and simple food served on paper plates, we give them permission to be real too. The God of all things could have broken through in any time, place, or context. God didn't choose a highly sanitized human life. Instead, His ministry was marked by ordinary moments with ordinary people.

Much of Jesus' most profound and beautiful moments with His disciples took place at the table. Even in the thick of His demanding ministry, Jesus embodied hospitality (and He didn't even have his own house!). He cared about relationships with flawed, real-life humans who probably walked around with stains on them too.

Jesus made space for others and invited them to the table. I wonder what He has to teach us about building relationships even now.

Though my social media algorithms beg to differ, hospitality and community around the table don't equate to candlelit tablescapes or weed-free backyards. It's in the midst of our mess that we can exhale and laugh. As Dietrich Bonhoeffer says, it's "through our daily meals He is calling us to rejoice, to keep holiday in the midst of our working day."[9] The workday of a parent is never-ending. We're always on the clock—many of us have jobs, callings, and vocations that intersect with domestic duties but also take us outside the constant push and pull of parenting at home.

The demands we carry are heavy. But we can lighten the load for others—and accept a lightened load as well. We need to break bread (or hamburger buns) and relax in the company of others.

These moments of imperfect community are invitations from God to laugh at ourselves, to stop taking ourselves too seriously, and to remember that if God really is in all things (see Ephesians 4:6), then we can see the divine in our messy emotions, our messy families, and our messy homes. We can gather around a folding table in the backyard, and it can be beautiful. We can show up when it's easier to silo ourselves, and it can be sacred.

We can give friendship, and we can receive it. We can throw caution to the cobwebs and rejoice in real-life hospitality and community, even if it doesn't look the way it once did.

Finding authentic friendships can often feel out of reach, especially during certain seasons of parenting. We just found out that Ashley and Nick are moving. Jonny sighed. "Now we'll have to make new friends again," he said with a laugh.

Whether you skew introverted or extroverted, we are all made for community. Keep looking for ways that work for you to gather around the table, even in the thick of parenting. If you wait until you have it all together, you'll be waiting until eternity. The good news is that Jesus is setting a table for us even now (see Revelation 19:8-10).

Romans 12:13 tells us to give to those who have need and to be "inventive in hospitality" (MSG). That means we can show up as our truest selves. We can clothe ourselves in humility (mustard stains optional). We can share what we have. We can bring more people in. We don't have to take ourselves too seriously. We can laugh heartily. We can accept the invitation.

And don't forget the buns.

SCRIPTURE
Ephesians 4:5-6; Romans 12:13

A PRAYER FOR A CHILD'S FRIENDSHIP

We pray for
    friendship
To be extended and
    received
All the days of our
    child's life.
May their
    relationships
    build bridges,
And may they dance
    across divides
To the tune of a new
    friend.

TO LIGHT THEIR WAY

BREATH PRAYER

Inhale: O God, there is one body
Exhale: And one hope in You.

FAMILY DISCUSSION QUESTIONS

Read Romans 12:13 together.

▸ What could our family do to be "inventive" in our hospitality, as *The Message* puts it?

▸ When have you felt welcomed at a meal?

▸ What makes someone a good friend?

▸ When has a friend seen something you did that made you embarrassed? How did they react?

▸ How does friendship change in different ages and stages?

▸ Why do you think Jesus frequently had important conversations with His friends while sharing a meal?

▸ Imagine a giant feast fit for royalty and a simple meal at a picnic table. Where do you think Jesus would have eaten when He was on earth? Why?

▸ Jesus was full of hospitality even though He didn't have a home. How can we honor this kind of hospitality in our own lives this summer?

FAMILY PRAYER

younger

God, thank You for the friends You've given us. Help us to be kind and loving to the people You've put in our lives.

Help us to love our neighbors, our classmates, and our family members. Help us to remember that we love because You first loved us. Amen.

older

O God, thank You for the gift of community. Thank You that we do not have to go through this world alone. When we are lonely, remind us that we are wanted.

Help us to be the kind of friends who make others feel welcome and at peace. Help us to make space the way Jesus did, extending warmth and reminding others that their presence is wanted. Help us to live in vulnerability so that others feel permission to do the same. Thank You for giving us Jesus, who broke bread and invited everyone, even those who were most often forgotten, to join in the feast. Amen.

Language of a Dream

TO OBSERVE CHILDREN on the beach is to watch dreams unfurl. Children haven't yet unlearned their God-given imaginations the way we grown-ups have. They inherently and intuitively accept the slow rhythm of a sun-soaked summer afternoon.

Kids create whole kingdoms out of grains of sand and accept the divine invitation to get swept up in a dream. They lie flat on long stretches of sand, burying limbs and burrowing bodies. With closed eyes and slowing heartbeats, they feel the sun warm their faces. And in that moment, they're transported somewhere magical, to a dream both in and out of time.

As children, we're told to dream big. This is a sentiment we pass along to our children. But as we grow older ourselves and our worlds grow colder, we forget the wisdom nestled in a dream.

How easy it is to refuse those God-given invitations to imagine something better! As time marches on, and we with it, cynicism seeps into our souls. We forget to dream of the world as it could be and become consumed by the sorrowful ways the world *is*.

As we grow older, perhaps we realize that to dream is to be vulnerable, to be like a child. It's a fragile thing to hold on to hope for beauty to break in, for healing to come. So to protect our hearts, we harden them against dreaming.

But what if God is ready to do something new through a dream—if we dare to hold it? The prophet Isaiah invited the people of Israel into a divine dream:

See, I am doing a new thing!
    Now it springs up; do you not perceive it?
I am making a way in the wilderness
    and streams in the wasteland.
ISAIAH 43:19, NIV

We live in a time of spiritual wilderness and wastelands. All around us, we see suffering and sorrow, discouragement and darkness. Why bother dreaming when everything is so . . . wrong? Bishop Michael Curry says that's exactly why we must dream—that dreaming is what saves us from falling into despair and destruction when the world is at its darkest, when evil seems to have had the final say.

"Dreams are love's visions," he says, "the boundless faith that the world can be remade to look more like what God hoped for his creation."[10] With God, our dreams can remake the world. When we soak in the pastel colors of a sherbet sunset or close our eyes in the sun, we are not wasting time. We are making space to hear God in a new way.

Throughout Scripture, God gives ordinary people extraordinary dreams. Dreams have meaning—then and now.

When my son turned one, I took him to a medical clinic in Nigeria, where he was born. The nurse asked me his name.

"Joseph," I told her.

"Ah," she replied with a gleam in her eye, tossing her braids over her shoulder, "like the dreamer in the Bible."

Maybe you haven't dreamed of bundles of wheat like Joseph did, but God is still speaking through dreams. And perhaps the dream God is whispering into the hidden parts of your soul is the antidote to the despair we see and feel all around us.

How many children have been told by a grown-up to get their head out of the clouds? How often do we hear "You're a dreamer" hurled as an insult?

How wrong we've gotten it.

As children of God, we are called to dream, no matter our age. The youngest among us seem to understand that dreams aren't futile or superfluous but rather a natural, necessary part of our lives.

Every morning, I ask my children what they dreamed about, and their tales of adventure and woe tumble out. Some are beautiful; some are scary. Their dreams tell me what they're afraid of, what soothes them, and what sets their hearts ablaze.

Having the audacity to hold a God-breathed dream in our hearts often grows out of being awake to the injustice and inequity around us. Dr. Martin Luther King Jr.'s oft-quoted "I Have a Dream" speech showed that he did not ignore the world's suffering but entered into

Perhaps the dream God is whispering into the hidden parts of your soul is the antidote to the despair we see and feel all around us.

people's very real pain—and then dared to cast a sacred vision for something better. The insidious evil baked into the racist systems and structures he and other civil rights leaders worked against could have brought them to despair, but instead it lit a holy fire for something better.

Before King shared his dream, he spoke into the suffering. "Now is the time to rise from the dark and desolate valley of segregation to the sunlit path of racial justice," he said as he addressed the crowd at the Lincoln Memorial in the sweltering heat on August 28, 1963. "Now is the time to lift our nation from the quicksands of racial injustice to the solid rock of brotherhood. Now is the time to make justice a reality for all of God's children."[11]

Sometimes our dreams come when we're sitting on a serene spot on the beach. But other times they come when we witness the most heartbreaking parts of humanity. I look around at the very real racism and so many other *isms* that still fester today, and I know that, for the sake of all God's children, we must keep working for the dream. And that takes faith. Maybe even bold, powerful, tender faith, like a child who climbs backyard trees and slays imaginary dragons.

Jesus told His followers to become more like children. He said that in becoming childlike, they would welcome Him (see Matthew 18:1-6). God wants all of us to have a pulsing, powerful faith that allows us to see things not just as they are but as they could be. When we dream like a child, we're welcoming Jesus.

The prophet Joel told the people that in the narrative of God's redemption, even "old men will dream dreams" (Joel 2:28).

When we imagine, we dream. And when we dream, we taste the Kingdom of heaven—speaking (and living into) sweet, true, just, and beautiful words, even as creation groans. As Bishop Curry aptly says, "The language of a dream is the language of hope."[12] Imagine what we might dare to dream if we loosened our adult understanding and replaced our cynicism with childlike faith. Hope might be born, even today.

SCRIPTURE
Isaiah 43:19; Genesis 37:1-17; Matthew 18:1-6; Joel 2:28

BREATH PRAYER

Inhale: Breathe a new dream
Exhale: Into me, O Lord.

FAMILY DISCUSSION QUESTIONS

Read Genesis 37:1-17 together.

- ▶ Why do you think God used dreams to speak to Joseph?

- ▶ Share about a dream you had that remains vivid in your memory. What happened? Who was in it? How did it make you feel?

- ▶ What is a daydream? Have you ever gotten in trouble for daydreaming?

- ▶ Many artists and creators say their ideas started as a dream. Why is it vital for us to pay attention to our dreams—both the ones we have at night and the ones that hold our hearts captive during the day?

- ▶ Why is it important to dream in the face of evil and injustice? What's at stake if we forget to dream?

- ▶ Who tends to be more in tune with their imaginations: kids or grown-ups? Why do you think that is?

- ▶ Why do you think Jesus told His followers to be more like children? Dr. Martin Luther King Jr. shared his dream for an anti-racist America for all God's children, even though racism was baked into his society. Why do you think his dream still resonates with people today?

- ▶ Fill in the blank: I have a dream that _____.

- ▶ How can our family use our imagination to help our community?

FAMILY PRAYER

younger

Dear God, You have given us the gift of dreaming big dreams. Be in our dreams at night and in our dreams during the day. Thank You for the gift of imagination.

Help us to use our imagination to explore and create. Jesus, You told people to be more like children because the faith of a child is beautiful. Thank You, God, for giving us dreams. Amen.

older

O God who dwells in dreams, be near in the darkness of our world. Help us not to fall into cynicism or despair, but illuminate in us the beauty and vulnerability of dreaming new dreams. Give us the powerful, profound faith of a child, and make us brave enough to speak the language of hope.

O God, help us to imagine a new way, rooted in Your justice and anchored in Your truth. We believe You are doing a new thing! Help us to listen so we may be prompted by Your Spirit to dream new dreams for the flourishing of all creation. Amen.

Waves like Thunder

I KICK OFF MY SANDALS and feel hot grains of sand under my feet. I walk toward the waves, marveling that the southern stretch of the Baja California peninsula, full of intense sunshine and sea breeze, exists at the same time my children are back at home, entering the first mild days of an early Midwest summer.

The breeze topples off the white-capped waves, shaking the earth. I walk closer, eager to touch the water, to dip a toe into the ocean. A lifeguard blows his whistle, gesturing toward the ropes and barricades I was too distracted, too in awe, to notice.

I stop. Shaken out of my thoughts, I turn my gaze from the golden sand to the blue waters whose waves touch the sky. I stand at the edge of the rope and watch the tide rise and fall with booms that echo a Midwestern thunderstorm.

Rise. Fall.

Fall. Rise.

Like a laboring mother, the wild waters hold the groans of creation. I remember how my body bent and folded as I labored through contractions, timing my breaths, co-creating with God.

Pain. Joy.

Joy. Pain.

Inhale. Exhale.

Scripture tells us that creation groans: "We know that the whole creation has been groaning as in the pains of childbirth right up to the present time" (Romans 8:22, NIV). We don't have to look far to see that people are in pain all around us. Our hearts are heavy. Our breaths are shallow as we bear down and hold the aches, believing with hope that joy will follow.

The lifeguard nods, gesturing from his tower to the fifteen-foot swells. "Those waves will pull you under," he shouts between booms. "They'll take you with them."

I stand at the edge where land meets the sea, in awe of our Creator God.

I do not understand how beauty and evil commingle on the same planet, how winter and summer somehow exist all at once in the same plane, depending on where you are in the world. I feel the mist on my face and wonder how we can breathe through the pain and ride the waves without being pulled under.

When I was in labor with my son Asher, I experienced debilitating back pain. I thought I was dying. I could not sign the consent for pain medicine—I choked out an answer, giving my husband verbal consent to sign the medical release on my behalf.

The waves that were bringing in a new life were pulling me under, giving me only brief moments of reprieve as the contractions rolled in, wave after wave, their crashes like thunder.

The moments between contractions gave me a space to catch my breath. In those slivers of time, I felt safe instead of scared.

All creation groans.

Headlines full of suffering crash into my heart like waves thundering onto the shore. War, political infighting, abuses of power—wave after wave.

Somehow we have to figure out a way to hold the line. To stay present and tender to the groans while also resting in the moments of stillness, catching our breath. We have to exist in a world where bare feet get buried under sun-soaked sand and other feet squish into last year's snow boots.

When Jesus said that the poor will always be among us (see Mark 14:7), He was not giving us a free pass to discard the care and keeping of our neighbor; instead, He was reminding us to stay present. The way of Christ is to stay awake to suffering—to the rise and fall of creation's labor pains.

Jesus went toward: toward the woman at the well, toward the children in the crowd, toward the poor at the party. He went toward those being pulled under by the waves.

People accused Jesus of spending time with the wrong kind of people. But He continued to journey toward the waves. And in the literal waves, He also knew how to rest (see Mathew 8:24).

"Wake up, Jesus!" the disciples yelled.

But He breathed in the pause between the rise and fall of life's pain. *He rested.*

Jesus gives us a perfect picture of how to hold the many tensions of life. At this very moment, a baby is taking their first breath, and someone else is taking their last. The sun rises, casting warmth and light, and in another part of the world, the sky darkens. A couple holds hands and says, "I do," while another marriage dissolves with a final signature. A child makes the team, and another goes to their room and cries. A pregnancy test result brings rejoicing for one and sorrow for another.

We live in an ocean of beautiful and terrible; we live on a planet that cries out like a laboring mother.

If we want our children to follow the way of Jesus, we must look inward and ask our beating hearts if we're willing to do the same. Will we bear witness to the pain while staying soft to the sacred?

Although I remember the deep pains of labor and delivery, my memories are hazy—swaddled like the gauzy blanket I held close to my chest. Physical suffering brought forth great beauty.

"I have been wholly in joy when I have been in pain—childbirth is the obvious example. Joy is what has made the pain bearable and, in the end, creative rather than destructive."[13] This is life on Earth: great suffering punctuated by profound joy. *Toil and rest. Iniquity and justice.* Our lives are complicated.

On the beach, as the ocean roars, I feel the rhythm of crashing waves.

Push. Pull.

Crescendo. Decrescendo.

Speak. Listen.

Work. Rest.

There's a popular phrase that stems from the Old Testament admonition in Micah 6:8: "Do not be daunted by the enormity of the world's grief. Walk humbly now. Do justly now. Love mercy now. You are not expected to complete the work, but neither are you free to abandon it."[14] As parents, we help our children navigate the choppy seas of this life. We point them toward Jesus, who knew when to move toward and when to retreat.

These are the rhythms of our lives. We repeat this litany in moments of anguish and in times of peace.

God is good,
All the time.

All the time,
God is good.

As followers of Christ, we mourn with those who mourn; we rejoice with those who rejoice (see Romans 12:15). In the following line, Paul encourages people to "live in harmony with one another. Do not be proud, but be willing to associate with people of low position" (verse 16).

This is what it is to be fully human: present to the tear-soaked faces and the deep belly laughs. Aware of the waves that crash and the waters that are still. Knowing that the sun casts its rays on one side of the world while darkness cloaks the other side.

Creation groans. But Jesus is with us, timing contractions, bearing witness to the pain of our stories and the beauty birthed by that pain. At His voice, strivings cease, and the waves return to their slumber.

May Jesus be in the pain. May Jesus be in the joy. May Jesus be in every season, every story of our lives.

SCRIPTURE

Romans 8:22-24; Micah 6:8; Matthew 8:24; Romans 12:15-16

BREATH PRAYER

Inhale: You are with me
Exhale: In the waves.

FAMILY DISCUSSION QUESTIONS

Read Romans 12:15-16 together.

- ▶ When has someone sat with you when you were sad or having a hard time? What did they do or say that was helpful?

- ▶ When have you felt celebrated? What did someone do or say to make you feel special?

- ▶ What does it mean that God is present in our pain and also in our joy?

- ▶ Have you ever felt both sad and happy at the same time? Why do we sometimes cry happy tears?

- ▶ Have you ever been near the waves of an ocean or a large lake? What did you hear, feel, taste, see, or smell? How does that memory make you feel?

This is life on Earth: great suffering punctuated by profound joy.

▸ What can we learn about God's character when we are around water?

▸ Do the waters of your life feel full of waves or still and calm right now?

▸ Jesus moved toward people. What people or work might God be calling you to move toward?

▸ How can we bear witness to pain while staying soft to the sacred this week?

FAMILY PRAYER

younger

Dear God, You are with us when we feel happy and when we feel sad. There is no place we can go that will separate us from You and Your big love.

Help us to notice the beautiful parts of our days, and help us to remember that when things happen that leave us feeling frustrated, scared, or confused, You are still with us. Jesus, You are near when the oceans of our lives are full of giant waves, and You are near when everything feels calm and still.

In all things, help us to care for others the way You care for us. Amen.

older

O God who is present to every sorrow and every joy, we come to You.

As sure as the tides that rise and fall, You are with us in the pain and the beauty of our lives. You are near in our tear-soaked faces and our deepest belly laughs. You are in the crashing waves and the still waters.

Help us to remember that in all seasons, You are good, and we can trust You. In the rhythms of our days and the push-pull of our lives, give us the grace to sit in the tension, holding on to the hope that You are our Redeemer, Restorer, and Rescuer. Amen.

REFLECTION 8

Divine Interruptions

I'M MAKING SPAGHETTI when the first interruption hits. I move the phone from the crook of my neck and hit the stop button on the messaging app. The voice message I was leaving my friend Patty will have to wait.

"Mom, I cracked it!" Asher runs into the kitchen and, with all the pride he can muster, shoves his Rubik's Cube—the one he's been practicing all day, all summer—toward my face.

"That's great, bud," I tell him as the pot of water begins to boil.

"Watch!" he says, scrambling the blocks and starting from scratch. I toss the pasta into the boiling pot and watch him make the color squares dance in his palm.

I try to be thankful for the interruption. Someday, I know my son won't run to me, but today he's still small enough to run his knobby knees into the kitchen to show off to his mom.

I joke with Patty that I should leave text messages instead of audio ones because my kids are expert interrupters. They seem to have a sixth sense when I pick up the phone. (My mom tells me it's generational; I was the same way.)

Something else captures my son's attention, and I'm alone again. I grab my phone with one hand and attempt to open a jar of spaghetti sauce with the other. I tap the record button to resume my message.

"So, where did I leave off?" I start, rehashing the weekend, the novel I just finished, my processing of the latest national news, my reflections on the cool breeze that broke up our midsummer heat wave.

"MOMMY!" I look down to see a mop of blond curls at my waist. It's Abram, newly six and full of effervescence that bubbles over like the pot of spaghetti.

"Mom, is it time for supper?

"Mom, can I taste a noodle?

"Mom! Mom! Mom!"

I stop recording my message. I don't even bother telling Patty I have to go. She'll hear the whole scenario. She's a mom of three—she'll understand.

I send my six-year-old on his way, drain the pasta, and set the table. I feel guilty for not making any sides, but it's a Sunday evening in the summer. My husband is impressed I'm cooking at all, because he grew up one of six kids, and his mother, who fastidiously made three meals for six kids every day, took Sunday dinner off, and Jonny and his siblings usually ate popcorn or cereal. So a hot meal (on real plates!) is impressive all on its own.

Abram has been begging for spaghetti for weeks, but with temps in the nineties and our Iowa humidity, the kind that hangs thick in the hair and coats every crevice of your body, neither Jonny nor I wanted to heat the house with garlic bread or load steaming piles of pasta onto our plates. We wanted watermelon, grilled chicken, and potato salad. But today was mild, and Abram got his wish.

I test a noodle and laugh at the thought of the recorded interruptions, one after another.

As parents, it's easy to feel like we're bombarded by requests—because we are. Domestic life is rife with interruptions, and it's easy to feel like we're bearing this burden alone.

So much of the ministry of parenthood is invisible. Our labor is unseen; our care is unseen. The Sunday meal prep ripe with interruptions when you just want to connect with a friend? Unseen.

Something in me decides to replay the messages I left for Patty. As I listen, I hear the voices interrupting me—voices that sound so small, so young. My sighs sound exasperated as I listen to the playback. My heart stings.

Dietrich Bonhoeffer's words on life together hold new meaning now that I'm a parent. "We must be ready to allow ourselves to be interrupted by God," he says. "God will be constantly crossing our paths and canceling our plans."[15]

Today God is interrupting me in the form of two little boys. I don't always receive these divine beckonings with welcome or desire. I'm often exhausted and lacking patience.

Parenthood is a giant interruption filled with tiny interruptions. But we can let ourselves be spiritually formed by our fractured plans, welcoming Jesus in the form of a nine-year-old showing off his skills or a six-year-old hungry for dinner.

That old cliché says if you want to make God laugh, tell Him your plans. The truer sentiment is that if you want to see God, pay attention to the interruptions in front of you.

I try to remember this when I change my disabled daughter's diaper for the tenth time in a day. The adage from the grandmas in the church nursery isn't always true: babies don't always grow out of that stage.

Interruptions aren't always cute. Sometimes they represent dashed dreams, disappointments, and defeats.

Maybe there's charm and whimsy in seeing God interrupt us on a relaxing summer Sunday. But what about when your disabled child needs to visit another specialist? What about when your teen gets in another fender bender and you get the text just as you're sinking into the couch after an already exhausting day? What about when the colicky baby wakes up for the sixth time in the night?

In these moments, we choose to believe that God has something to say to us—not because God *needs* anything from us but because God *wants* to be with us.

God is speaking to us in the cry of an infant, the text of a teen, and the demands of a kindergartener. God doesn't leave us to deal with these interruptions alone; God is already there. This reframing reminds us that the unseen way we show up in our lives is holy. God doesn't only dwell in sanctuaries; God shows up in our actual lives.

And maybe, if we're lucky, we'll wipe the spilled sauce from our phone, play back the interruption, and upon relistening, find it holy too.

Will we resist the urge to fight interruptions? Will we welcome the tiny, sacred interruptions in our lives? It's who we are in those scattershot moments that make up a life.

In Revelation 3:20, we see a picture of Christ's presence in our lives: "Here I am! I stand at the door and knock. If anyone hears my voice and opens the door, I will come in and eat with that person, and they with me" (NIV).

Maybe that knock on the door pulling you away from your inbox is bringing you where you've needed to be all along. Perhaps Christ is tugging at your shirt while you make spaghetti, waiting to be invited to the table.

Bonhoeffer writes, "As long as there are people, Christ will walk the earth as your neighbor, as the one through whom God calls you, speaks to you, makes demands on you. . . . Christ is standing at the door; he lives in the form of a human being among us. Do you want to close the door or open it?"[16]

When we are interrupted this week, will we open the door to these divine invitations?

SCRIPTURE
Revelation 3:20; Proverbs 19:21

RING THE BELLS

For centuries, community bell ringing has played an important role in many monastic traditions. As the daily bells toll, marking the passing of the hours, members of the monastery stop whatever they're doing to enter a time of prayer or faithful practice. "The bells stop us in midflight to prod us to ask ourselves again if what we are doing is what we are really meant to be doing," Benedictine Sister Joan Chittister writes in *The Monastic Heart: 50 Simple Practices for a Contemplative and Fulfilling Life*.

As parents, what if we reframed our interruptions—a baby crying in the night, a kindergartener demanding a snack, a teen texting you during your workday—as a monastic bell to reorient your heart back to where (and who) God might be calling your attention toward? Responding to divine interruptions isn't just for the super religious, for monks or nuns belonging to a particular order. The family is, in its own way, a bit of a monastery.

In *Domestic Monastery: Creating a Spiritual Life at Home*, Father Ronald Rolheiser writes, "A parent hears the monastic bell many times during the day and has to drop things in mid-sentence and respond, not because they want to, but because it's time for that activity and time isn't one's own, but God's."

BREATH PRAYER

Inhale: Awaken me
Exhale: To Your interruptions.

FAMILY DISCUSSION QUESTIONS

Read Proverbs 19:21 together.

- ▸ When were your plans interrupted this week? What were you doing? How did you feel?

- ▸ When have you interrupted someone else recently? What happened?

- ▸ What is your typical reaction when someone distracts you from what you're doing?

- ▸ Why can interruptions be good at times?

- ▸ Why is it important to remember that time is God's, not ours?

- ▸ What do you see when you imagine Jesus standing at a door and knocking (see Revelation 3:20)?

- ▸ What does it say about God's character that God wants to be with you?

- ▸ How can you pay attention to the needs of people around you this week?

- ▸ What things have been getting your attention this week? Which of these things honor God and call you back to who you're meant to be?

FAMILY PRAYER

younger

Dear God, it's easy to focus on what we want to do or what our plans are.

Help us to remember that when we're interrupted or when our plans change, we can trust that You are still with us. Help us to stay curious and open to what You're telling us through the interruptions in our lives.

Give us the ability to pay attention to the people we meet and the places we go. Help us to receive Your love and pour it out on others too. Amen.

older

O God, we're familiar with the many interruptions of life—the sights and sounds that distract us from focusing on what we think is important. When the world is loud, whisper into our souls that the most important work is to stay awake to love.

Help us to find You in all the parts of our lives, especially the ones that seem like distractions—in the dishes that need washing, the floors that need sweeping, the appointments that need keeping. Jesus, You are welcome in our home. Who would You have us love? Where would You have us go? Grant us sacred curiosity to ask where You are in our changed plans and our interrupted routines.

Help us to make space in our hearts and in our schedules to experience Your presence in the people and places that fill our days. In the forest of our lives, slow down our days so we might marvel in the trees.

Help us to pay attention to what You have to teach us. Help us to remember what matters. Amen.

All God's Children

WE WALK HAND IN HAND down the tree-lined street. Historic architecture surrounds us, each tall column and carefully laid brick whispering stories of the past. The vintage-style lampposts flicker on as the sun begins its descent.

I look into his eyes and smile. At this moment, I know I'm smitten.

"I can't believe I didn't know this neighborhood even existed," I whisper-shout at my husband, breaking the spell and peering inside the charming brick two-story with a "For Sale" sign in the front yard. (He opts out of my suggestion to climb onto his shoulders so I can peek in the backyard. It's probably for the best.)

We're back in our hometown visiting my parents. I stumbled upon the house listing online and convinced him to put the address in Google maps so we could check it out ourselves.

Returning to my parents' house, I am a woman obsessed. I have to learn more. Leaning into journalist mode, I dive deep, researching the neighborhood's past and present. I find that the area has been home to neighbors varying in every imaginable way, spanning income, race, and religion.

Long story cut incredibly short: we unpacked our moving truck six months later.

"Why would you move *there?*" Well-meaning friends and family asked every iteration of this question as our family of six packed up our belongings (in a pandemic! in a blizzard!) and moved from the comfortable suburbs of the state's capital to our considerably smaller, considerably less cool hometown two hours away.

(I argue that it's cool in its own way, but it's true: we don't have Trader Joe's.)

No neighbor—no neighborhood—is perfect. That's why it was so radical when Jesus said (my paraphrase), "You want to know the greatest commandment? Okay. Love God and love your neighbor as you love yourself. Yes, *that* neighbor. Love the person right in front of you. And when you love them, you're loving me."

After the snow melted and we all thawed out, we started to get to know our neighbors, who exuded warmth and welcome. After we went through an intense season of loneliness,

God pieced together our view of community and belonging through each kindness and grace extended by these new neighbors, who invited us over for dinner and even invited a newcomer like me to join the neighborhood board.

As the summer sun stretched over us and air-conditioning units began to hum throughout the neighborhood, we started to see that the small park in our neighborhood square was often a haven for unsupervised kids who had nowhere else to go. Unfortunately, some of them were getting into trouble, elevating fear in a few of our older neighbors, both Black and white, who have been part of the community much longer than we had. I respected them, but some of their suggestions to call the police on children who hadn't, to my knowledge, caused harm or broken laws didn't sit right with me either.

I sat in a weird tension. My neighbors weren't monoliths. Everyone had a unique perspective, a specific way they saw the world—and a thousand reasons for their point of view. I wondered what Jesus would do in this spot. The easiest thing would be to shrug and ignore what was happening. Or perhaps I could write a passionate post on Facebook. Thankfully, God saved me from myself.

How could I love *all* my neighbors well?

I began to sense that this looked a lot like listening and showing up. Our family moved to the neighborhood not just because we loved the historic houses but because we wanted to be part of a vibrant community. We wanted to know the people who lived not just in the beautiful Craftsman-style houses but also in the mobile homes a few blocks down and the rental duplexes a bike ride away.

I tried to listen well (not always my strong suit) and to grow in understanding (also something I'm working on). I couldn't make choices for anyone else, but I could show up and be present. Jonny and I agreed that as temperatures rose, we would try to simply be outside whenever we could that summer. If our kids were playing in the backyard, we'd make space for others to join us. We learned each other's names. We had pickup basketball games. We played backyard baseball, shared Sam's Club pizza, and chugged gallons of lemonade.

We didn't do anything profound—we're not citizens of the year. We just hung out, trying to play a small part in our community to ensure that everyone was a little more cared for and known.

This process isn't always pretty, and it certainly isn't perfect. Making space for kids to hang out in your backyard on occasion doesn't fix systemic issues; it doesn't save the world. I'm not a hero—I'm just a mom sitting on the patio swing. My kids push my buttons sometimes, and other kids do too. Sometimes I'm ready to retreat into the air-conditioning in the evening, but a few of my son's friends are lingering. In those moments, I try to think of how I hope others would treat my children and then treat our young guests the same way.

From the very beginning, God has been giving the same message: "Love your neighbor as yourself" (Leviticus 19:18).

Writer Shannan Martin explores what it is to pay attention to ordinary places and be present in the lives of our literal neighbors. She asks some compelling questions: "Do you believe your child deserves nutritious food and plenty of it? A vibrant education? A life free from discrimination and violence? Do they deserve basic kindness and respect? Do they deserve life itself, free from trauma and marginalization?" She goes on to say, "Assuming your answer is yes, let the same be said for all God's children. And you are uniquely positioned to work toward that goal in your ordinary life."[17]

My neighbor Sarah had been following the neighborhood conversations about rabble-rousers at the park. "I've noticed you've added some extra children to your back-yard hangouts," she said, smiling down at her newborn baby the way only a new mom can. "We've wanted to get to know the kids hanging out at the park, but since we don't have kids that age, I'm not sure how."

I invited her to come over any time. As a writer, I have the privilege of working from home. We have a big backyard and plenty of toys and sports equipment stacked in the garage. I'm uniquely positioned to be present—to show up in my weed-infested yard and let others show up too.

As Shannan Martin says, "Beginning to live as though there's no such thing as other people's children might be our most critical, significant contribution to the flourishing of our world."[18] In the past several months, the troublemaking in the park has gone down. Maybe it's the presence of the police cars some of our neighbors requested. Maybe having neighbors be more present has helped. Perhaps it's a mix of both—or something different altogether. I don't know. And I don't know what tomorrow holds either.

I will continue getting to know my neighbors and letting them know me too. (Vulnerability is scary!) I'll keep listening to them, old and young, and I'll keep listening to God's still, small voice that invites me toward humility instead of self-interest. I'll show up, mess up, and keep going. I'll chase my kids, mix lemonade, and try to do my small part in contributing to the flourishing of our world.

SCRIPTURE

Mark 12:31; Leviticus 19:18; Isaiah 1:17; Proverbs 14:21; 1 Corinthians 10:24

BREATH PRAYER

Inhale: O God, help me to love others
Exhale: The way You love me.

FAMILY DISCUSSION QUESTIONS

Read Mark 12:31 together.

- ▶ How many neighbors around us can you name?
- ▶ How would you describe what makes a neighbor?
- ▶ What do you appreciate about our community? What challenges does our community face?
- ▶ What do you know about the history of our neighborhood, community, or town?
- ▶ What is challenging about getting to know our neighbors?
- ▶ Why is it so important for us to love our neighbors?
- ▶ When has a neighbor done something kind, generous, or thoughtful for you? How did that make you feel?
- ▶ How has God uniquely positioned our family to extend compassion and kindness in our neighborhood?
- ▶ What can our family do this summer to extend hospitality to our neighbors?

ALL OF GOD'S CHILDREN

Consider listening to Jon Foreman's song "All of God's Children" as a family. The lyrics talk about believing in a world that's beyond us, a world we haven't seen.

FAMILY PRAYER

younger

God, thank You for our home and the people we share it with. Thank You for those who live near us.

Help us to be kind, generous, and helpful to the people in our neighborhood. Help us to share and to let others know we care about them. We love because You love us. Help us to show that love to others. Amen.

older

God of lovingkindness, we love because You first loved us.

We will never fully fathom the depths of Your great compassion, but we ask You to help us love more like You do. We pray that our neighbors would know our family by our love. May we be known not by our perfection or our achievements but by how we show up in the world, extending patience and cultivating peace in our community.

This summer, spark in us new ways to share what we have, for in doing so, we are warmed by the fires of friendship and community. Help us to love our local and global neighbors the way Jesus did. Give us listening spirits and soft hearts so we may be knit together in kinship with our neighbors. Amen.

Life Abundant

THE SUMMER I LEARNED how to ride a bike without training wheels was the summer I tasted freedom. I pushed my sneakers on the pedals with all my might, my tires carrying me across the sidewalk and into the great unknown. My pigtails and handlebar ribbons danced in the breeze.

I wasn't flying—I was *soaring*.

I was free.

When do you feel most free? Maybe you're uninhibited when you're at the edge of the ocean or in the mountains. Perhaps you feel liberated when you crack open a fresh journal or when you find yourself swept inside a song. (Some people feel free when they run long distances, which is something I've never understood.)

We have a hard time grasping what it is to be free in Christ because our cultural understanding of freedom is so small. In the US, we often hear the word *freedom* wrapped in political jargon.

But a liberated life in Jesus is so much bigger than any flag we could wave, any T-shirt we could wear, or any banner we could sit under.

My childhood memories of July Fourth are chockful of glowing sparklers, whizzing fireworks, buzzing mosquitos, and melting popsicles. I stopped riding my bike just long enough to learn that in the US we celebrated freedom and honored the country's birthday with picnics and parades and cookouts.

Case closed! Pass the bug spray.

Over the years, I've learned to approach the Fourth of July—and my definition of freedom—with deeper nuance and a broader understanding.

History and empathy must be intertwined.

It wasn't until college that I read abolitionist Frederick Douglass's poignant, passionate (and still highly relevant) speech now known as "What to the Slave Is the Fourth of July." Douglass, who lived through the horrors of slavery firsthand, worked nonstop for the emancipation of enslaved African Americans.

"Your high independence only reveals the immeasurable distance between us," he said, addressing a room full of white women on July 5, 1852. "The blessings in which you, this day, rejoice, are not enjoyed in common. The rich inheritance of justice, liberty, prosperity and independence, bequeathed by your fathers, is shared by you, not by me." He went on to say, "This Fourth July is yours, not mine. You may rejoice, I must mourn."

He went on to share that he stood with God and those who were enslaved. He denounced "everything that serves to perpetuate slavery the great sin and shame of America."[19] Douglass, who had a robust relationship with God, shared a specific word for white Christians who celebrated freedom and independence while other humans who likewise bore the image of God were being treated as property. Maybe one of my ancestors sat in that room, and maybe they were as convicted by the Spirit then as I am now. "Shouts of liberty and equality? To God, it's hollow mockery. Prayers and hymns, religious parades? To God, it's fraud. Deception. Impiety. Hypocrisy. There is not a man beneath the canopy of heaven that does not know that slavery is wrong for him."

Douglass's admonition reminds me of the prophet Amos, who wrote that God was sick of the show, sick of the performances and pretense of the people of Israel. They weren't acting like free, beloved children of God; instead, they were hypocrites, making a show of worship while being shackled by their selfish sin, harming not just themselves but others, too.

> I hate all your show and pretense—the hypocrisy of your religious festivals and solemn assemblies. I will not accept your burnt offerings and grain offerings. I won't even notice all your choice peace offerings. Away with your noisy hymns of praise! I will not listen to the music of your harps. Instead, I want to see a mighty flood of justice, an endless river of righteous living.
> AMOS 5:21-24

It wasn't until I became an adult that I learned about Juneteenth, the celebration of the effective end of the scourge of slavery in the US—thirteen years after Douglass's speech.

"Two years after President Lincoln's Emancipation Proclamation, Union soldiers marched into Galveston, Texas. They spread the news that the Civil War was over and the people were free," Lisa Sharon Harper says in her book *The Very Good Gospel*. "The Hebrew word for 'light' (*owr*) in the Genesis text can be translated as 'happiness.' I imagine that on

June 19, 1865, there was uncontrollable happiness."[20] Galatians 5:1 says, "It is for freedom that Christ has set us free" (NIV). This is freedom! This is good news.

The love of Christ swings wide the gates of oppression, releasing us from the bondage of violence and hate. As I write this, politicians are screaming at each other, refusing to let history and empathy meet. As they shout with red faces and turn their backs on justice, they're losing sight of humanity—of God's reflection in others and themselves.

As followers of Jesus, we must stand firm in the truth that this is not the way. Jesus sets us free from legalism and tribalism. Jesus sets us free from a scarcity mindset and a lust for power. In Jesus, God invites us into a better way.

Jesus gives us life—and life abundant (see John 10:10). This is freedom! This is good news.

Lisa Sharon Harper says that God broke into the universe to disrupt humanity's reign. A confrontation had long brewed between what she calls the "dominion of humanity and the dominion of God."[21] In the person of Jesus, God confronted the rulers of this world.

This is the freedom we stand firm in. This is the freedom that compels us to lay down our weapons.

I teach my kids that if you're going to go to jail, go to jail bearing witness to what's true and right, like many civil rights leaders did in the 1960s. If you're thrown to the lions, let it be because you worship the ways of God and refuse to worship the ways of the world. This is freedom! This is good news.

In 1972, Madeleine L'Engle wrote,

> I wouldn't mind if to be a Christian were accepted as being the dangerous thing which it is; I wouldn't mind if, when a group of Christians meet for bread and wine, we might well be interrupted and jailed for subversive activities; I wouldn't mind if, once again, we were being thrown to the lions. I do mind, desperately, that the word "Christian" means for so many people smugness, and piosity, and holier-than-thouness. Who, today, can recognize a Christian because of "how those Christians love one another"?[22]

Freedom in Christ means throwing off all that entangles us. Freedom in Christ means trading pious performances for the peace of the Spirit. Freedom in Christ means replacing hypocrisy with humility, hurt with healing, selfishness with care for another.

This good news can't be packaged and sold at fireworks stands (though I am a fan of dazzling displays of bursts and booms that make us all go "Ooh!" and "Aah!").

Freedom in Christ is spiritual and physical freedom, like I tasted as a child when I sped down the hill on my pink bicycle. This is freedom worthy of every celebration. This is good news.

Pass the bug spray.

SCRIPTURE

Galatians 5:1; John 8:32

BREATH PRAYER

Inhale: It is for freedom
Exhale: That I am set free.

FAMILY DISCUSSION QUESTIONS

Read Galatians 5:1 together.

- ▸ What activity helps you feel free?
- ▸ What places make you feel free (the backyard, a park, near the water, the library, your room)?
- ▸ What does the word *free* mean to you?
- ▸ What different types of freedom can we have in our lives?
- ▸ How might God define freedom differently from the way a political leader defines it?
- ▸ What does it mean to have freedom in Christ?
- ▸ Do you think Christians are known by their love in our community? In our state? In our country?
- ▸ Who in our community is oppressed?
- ▸ How can our family love those who are oppressed and work toward freedom for and with them?

THE STORY OF JUNETEENTH

My family and I appreciate the children's book
The Story of Juneteenth by Dorena Williamson,
coplanter of a multiracial church in Nashville called
Strong Tower Bible Church. This little board book uses
simple, age-appropriate language to introduce children
to the events of June 19, 1865, when Union General Gordon
Granger arrived in Galveston, Texas, to inform the people
of Texas that all enslaved people were declared free and
the Civil War had ended. The book connects these events
and creates an opportunity for further
family conversations.

FAMILY PRAYER

younger

God, in You we are free to dance and sing. We are free to worship and wonder. We are free to work for the good of all people.

Thank You for the good gifts You've given us. We know that, in You, we can make mistakes and learn from them. We can be free from trying to be perfect. In You, we are free from the small boxes the world wants to put us in.

We know deep in our souls that You made us and love us. In You, we are free to reflect Your image to the world. Your freedom allows us to love ourselves, You, and the people we share this world with. Amen.

older

O God, what is freedom if it is not for everyone? O Christ, in Your abundance, help us to be a family that loves the people across from us—and the people around the world from us.

Help us not to lose sight of Your reflection in our local and global neighbors. Help us to hold the tension of who we are and who we could be. Free us from what entangles us so that, in You, we may love others and work for the flourishing of all people.

O God, thank You for reauthoring our small notions of freedom and for offering a better way. Amen.

Holding the Memory

I'M IN MY SWEATPANTS, eyeing down a work deadline and exhausted by yet another of my daughter's diaper blowouts when I pull up last night's photo on my phone. My husband and I are standing next to each other in a botanical garden, a sea of green sprouting up around us, surrounded by the lush expanse of summer. Our cheeks sport a sun-kissed glow from a day at the ballpark, where we cheered ourselves hoarse during our son's final baseball game of the season.

In the snapshot, I've changed from a simple T-shirt and shorts into a flowy red dress. I'm leaning into Jonny, and we share relaxed, easy smiles that come from simply *being*. While the kids reveled in a movie night at their grandparents' house, we enjoyed an alfresco dinner date, the skies transforming from sugar-spun clouds to a dark blanket covering us in the cool summer night.

In a few swipes, I've uploaded the photo, getting an alert that I can pick up a printed copy in an hour. I want the tangible reminder that while so much of parenting is tuned to our children, my husband and I are also full humans who exist outside of the care and keeping of children.

I need to remember that while I've been entrusted with loving and cherishing my kids (and washing their baseball uniforms, refilling their water bottles, and shuttling them to practice), it's also true that my children are not wholly mine. And in some mystery of divine love, I am not wholly theirs.

Each of our children has their own identity—their particular personality, their individual strengths, and their unique struggles. While we can marvel at the sparkling ways our kids exist in the world—and rejoice at our front-row seats to that wonder—we also must remember that our identity is not entirely wrapped up in parenting. And the kids in our lives are more than their identity as our sons or daughters.

Each of us belongs to the One who knows us and loves us more widely than we can fathom—the One who knows every hair on our heads (see Luke 12:7) and who knit us together, stitch by stitch (see Psalm 139).

When we clutch this reminder of God's love like a beloved photograph in our hands, we can get through the most challenging, exhausting, and demanding seasons of parenting. We can rest in the truth that God cares. God will not leave our children—or us. In John 14:18, Jesus tells His disciples that He won't leave His dear ones as parentless children. Instead, Jesus says, "I will come to you."

As we cycle through different seasons of parenting, we may be overwhelmed by the demands on us, but we cling to the promise that Jesus is pursuing us in our parenting—and He is pursuing our children in their growing too. Jesus is here in the wins and losses, in the warmth of summer and the chill of winter.

Our children must meet God in the reality of their own lives and experiences. Yes, it's up to us to be there, caring for them, being a soft place to land for all the days to come. But it's also up to us to let go—to loosen our grip on what was never ours to clutch so tightly in the first place. As followers of Christ, we trust that in the *before*, *during*, and *after* of our children's lives, Christ *was*, *is*, and *will be* there.

As soon as I whip out my phone, my family and friends groan. They know what's happening. I take too many pictures for just about everyone.

I never regret taking the pictures.

I don't want to forget. I want to remember. I want to remember how the ice cream cone dripped off my six-year-old son's chin. I don't want to forget how my daughter's curls danced in the soft breeze of a midsummer day. I want my hands to hold the brief moment when I truly entrusted my life—and my children's lives—to the hands of a loving God.

I want to run my fingers along the memory. I want to fold it up and turn it over in my hands until the edges are soft. I want the captures of summer so I can tuck them in my pocket when storms surround me and I wonder if the sun will ever shine again. I want to turn to them when winter's cold hands cover my eyes from the promise of spring.

In the early seasons of parenting, I doubted that there would ever be a time when I would get to shower in peace, let alone enjoy an impromptu patio dinner with other grown-ups. I wish I could share

FAMILY JOURNAL

Keep your personal and family memories close by capturing your reflections in a journal. The Examen is a set of spiritual questions you can enter into daily, weekly, monthly, seasonally, or yearly. Turn to appendix 2 to learn more about how to integrate this time of introspection into your days.

some snapshots of my life with that exhausted mother who rocked pieces of oatmeal in her hair and doubted her place in the world.

We can't time-travel to the past. But we have the gift of caring for ourselves now, even as we care for our children in the very real demands of life together. In a thousand little ways, we can frame the spiritual photographs, placing them on the mantles of our lives, letting the reminders of Christ's tender, compassionate love surround us for all the days to come.

SCRIPTURE
John 14:18; Luke 12:7; Philippians 4:8

BREATH PRAYER

Inhale: Help me to remember;
Exhale: I don't want to forget.

FAMILY DISCUSSION QUESTIONS

Read Philippians 4:8 together.

- ▸ What summer memory brings up good feelings for you? Who was there? Why is this memory special?

- ▸ How can holding on to special memories help us when we feel sad, lonely, or discouraged?

- ▸ What are ways we can keep track of our memories (photos, videos, drawings, letters, mementos, etc.)

- ▸ What object holds special memories for you?

- ▸ When you look back, is there a time when God's presence helped you through something difficult?

- ▸ Many of our holidays focus on remembering something. Why is it important to honor shared memories?

- ▸ How can we as a family help one another remember what is true and good?

FAMILY PRAYER

younger

God, it's so easy for us to forget. We forget to brush our teeth, make our beds, and say thank you. It's easy to forget that You are with us, that You love us, and that You will never leave us.

Help us to take pictures with our minds and hold close the memories of times we felt safe, known, and loved. Help us to remember that You love us—that You have a purpose for our lives. Remind us that we are Your children and that You are with us in our struggles and our joys. Amen.

older

O God of memory, help us to remember what matters, for we are prone to forget.

We so easily forget Your promise to love us and never leave us. We forget that You are good and that we can trust You. We forget that who we are lies in You, not in what we produce or the image we project.

Help us to hold the memory of Your presence in our lives so we may be present to our current reality. Help us to be awake to the people in our lives and the places we go. Help us to remember the good time shared among our family. Let those memories surround our hearts and sustain us for all that is to come. Amen.

Snapped

"AND THEN I SCREAMED AT THEM," she tells me. "I mean, *really* screamed. My voice is still hoarse."

She pauses. "So much is happening. I'm not at my best." Her voice breaks. "I'm worried I'm a bad mom."

My heart aches to reach inside my phone and wrap my arms around my friend. From where I sit, she's a caring parent who fiercely loves her daughters. But my heart aches for another reason: because I've been there, broken under the weight of frustration, exhaustion, and unmet expectations, letting anger snap me in ugly ways.

Parenting can be a pressure cooker, and our kids know exactly which buttons to push, causing temperatures to rise until we eventually pop. Being human means making mistakes, but there's nothing like the guilt—and the resulting spiral of shame—that comes from getting it wrong and letting our emotions control us.

Sociologist and research professor Brené Brown has spent decades researching vulnerability and shame. She writes that guilt is "an emotion that we experience when we fall short of our own expectations or standards."[23] All of us have done it. We've all gone astray, falling short of the glory of God (see Romans 3:23). This is, of course, never an excuse for inflicting verbal, spiritual, or physical abuse. But it is a comfort that we all get it wrong sometimes.

In other words: you aren't the only one who has snapped at their kids.

When I become irritable and impatient with my kids—or when I lose my patience and raise my voice so loudly that the whole neighborhood can feel the aftershocks of my shouts for them to "GET IN THE VAN NOW"—I feel an immediate flash of guilt. My kids don't deserve that. I know I need to take a breath and apologize.

Brown says that while shame takes us down dark paths, guilt isn't always bad. It doesn't feel good, but it can be helpful. When guilt meets empathy, it can throw us a rope to help us climb out of the pit, shining a light and whispering into our souls, *This is not who you are. What you did doesn't align with your values, and your kids didn't deserve to be treated that way, but you are more than the sum of your parts. You can apologize. You can do better next time.*

"Empathy and guilt work together to create a force that is adaptive and powerful," Brown writes.[24] She says that guilt is often what propels us to apologize, make amends, and change our behavior.

Maybe you grew up in a home where apologies weren't given or where humility wasn't valued. Many in my generation (and generations before me) are figuring out how to parent children with compassion and kindness when their families of origin left them without a model for living the way Paul commissioned the people of God to: "holy and dearly loved, clothed with compassion, kindness, humility, gentleness and patience" (see Colossians 3:12).

You can change the narrative. You can take a breath and forge a new path, following Christ into a better way. It's not too late. (It's never too late.)

I wonder how many relationships could be repaired if we as parents embraced the humility, vulnerability, and maturity it takes to own our mistakes. How much healing could come in our families—and in our world—if we sincerely and honestly apologized to our children, whether they're still in diapers or have long ago flown the nest?

There's no such thing as a perfect parent, but we can be transformed in Christ. We can choose another way, asking Jesus to reauthor the stories we write about ourselves. We can ask Him to shape us into parents who are compassionate and kind, humble and gentle—and patient, too.

In their work with families from a variety of backgrounds, Molly Baskette and Ellen O'Donnell have concluded that "apologizing is a kind of superpower. It makes us vulnerable, but in its vulnerability there is a curious strength, as we own our humanness rather than go into denial and ego-protective mode."[25] Jesus went first. He embodied vulnerability, blazing a path for us to do the same. We have a God who entered our world as a tiny infant, born to seemingly ordinary people, and died a violent death on a cross. In Christ, we can make ourselves vulnerable and apologize to our kids for the times we get it wrong—the times we aren't true to ourselves and we allow our stories to be written by our sin.

A PRAYER FOR WHEN WE'VE GOTTEN IT WRONG

When we have done harm
With our presence or with our absence,
Give us tender hearts to apologize—
When we have shouted,
When we have snapped,
When we have forgotten,
When we have projected,
When we have failed.

TO LIGHT THEIR WAY

"The thing about sin is: It's something we do (or fail to do). It's not who we are," Baskette and O'Donnell write. "We believe in a God of infinite second chances, a God who is working on us to be people of courage and character and who will keep working on us until the day we die."[26] If we want our kids to be people of courage and character—people who apologize, own their mistakes, and make amends when they've harmed another person—we have the opportunity to live into this ourselves (even when we're triggered and feel our blood boiling).

"It is hard to take another person's perspective when you are flooded with emotion and feel that your own feelings and perspective are being ignored. This is true for you, the parent, as it is for your child," Baskette and O'Donnell write. "But pausing, taking a deep breath, and simply saying, 'I'm sorry I reacted so quickly,' can do wonders for your relationships with your children."[27] No family is conflict-free. No parents or kids get it right all the time. That's just the natural way of things. But when we get it wrong and feel the strain on our souls (just like we do on our vocal cords after losing our cool), we can honor God, ourselves, and our kids by naming it, apologizing, and making it right.

With God's help, we can raise families that live into rhythms of "grace, mercy, and peace" (2 John 1:3).

SCRIPTURE
Romans 3:23; Colossians 3:2; 2 John 1:3; 2:15-16; Ephesians 4:26

BREATH PRAYER

Inhale: I give You my anger;
Exhale: Give me Your peace.

FAMILY DISCUSSION QUESTIONS

Read Ephesians 4:26 together.

▸ Why can anger be a helpful emotion?

▸ Why is it important to pay attention to the things that make us angry? What might those things teach us about ourselves?

▸ What are healthy ways we can express anger?

▶ Why do you think the Bible says so much about forgiveness?

▶ Why is it important to apologize when we have hurt someone with our actions or our words?

▶ Why is it important for grown-ups to apologize to kids?

▶ Why does it sometimes feel embarrassing to apologize?

▶ When has someone apologized to you and meant it? How did you know they were genuine in their apology?

▶ Why is it sometimes difficult to accept forgiveness when we mess up?

▶ Why is it important to remember that our mistakes do not define us?

▶ How can our imperfections help us to be kinder when someone else makes a mistake?

▶ How can we as a family be more proactive about solving conflicts with one another?

FAMILY PRAYER

younger

Dear God, we know You love us. Help us to make choices that honor You, ourselves, and others. When we're angry, give us space to breathe. When we make a mistake, help us to learn from it.

Give us the bravery to say we're sorry when we've hurt someone with our words or our actions. We know that everybody messes up sometimes, and we thank You for being full of forgiveness and kindness. Help us as a family to make peace with one another.

Help us to be gentle and kind, caring and honest. We want to learn Your ways of grace, mercy, and peace. Amen.

older

O God, we come to you aware of the ways we have gotten things wrong this week. We bring our mistakes to You. Forgive us for the ways we have been quick to anger and slow to forgive others.

Help us to apologize when we have hurt another person. May we be a family that reconciles and sets things right. Help us to learn from our weaknesses. We know that we all mess up sometimes. Release us from any false guilt or shame we might be carrying. We know You are a God of fresh starts and new beginnings. Thank You for always welcoming us back into Your loving, merciful arms. Amen.

HOW TO APOLOGIZE
TO YOUR KIDS

Jessica Grose, a parenting writer for the *New York Times*, interviewed leading professors in psychiatry and psychology about how to come back from saying things you regret to your kids, how to empathize with your kids, and how to cut down on snapping at your kids. Here are their tips:

1. Acknowledge your mistake.
2. Give yourself a time-out.
3. Remember that kids struggle with impulse control.
4. If your snapping is frequent, try to get help.

REFLECTION 13

Be Still

"I'M BOOOOORED!"

You've heard the refrain. Chances are, you're triggered by it too.

When my kids hit me with the boredom proclamation, I usually reply with something like "If you're bored, you can clean your room!" or "All these toys and you're still bored? Then I'll get rid of them!"

My husband takes the dad-joke route with his response: "Hi, Bored. Nice to meet you! I'm Jonny."

Our retorts don't go over well. Granted, these aren't the most helpful responses, but by the time we get into the stretch of midsummer, the chorus of our kids' complaints seems to transform into a never-ending cacophony. The kids have already worn out all the warm-weather fun they were so eager to embrace just a month before. The sprinkler has lost its luster; the neighborhood friends have worn out their welcome.

Everyone is hot. Everyone is grumpy. And everyone is very, very bored.

It's almost impossible to resist the allure of screens in those whiny moments. I want to zone out and scroll on my phone. They want to pick from the treasure trove of TVs, tablets, computers, and video games.

In a culture that awards busyness, boredom doesn't just feel uncomfortable; it feels *wrong*—for both kids and grown-ups. When we don't have anything to do or anywhere to go, we get itchy and turn to the nearest numbing cream in the form of distraction.

Over and over again, God's grace tells us we're beloved children—a title we don't have to earn or work for (see Ephesians 2:8-9). But we're constantly absorbing a counter-narrative that says we are what we do. As parents, we're bombarded with endless options to fill kids' schedules, beckoning them to go and do. While structured activities and even screen time have their place, downtime has its benefits too. This goes for the youngest and the oldest among us.

"One of the new challenges for our generation is the impact of technology on our spirituality. This warrants serious consideration," writes Ruth Haley Barton, who has spent decades ministering to the soul-care needs of Christian communities. "If we are not careful, technology has a way of compromising our ability to be present to ourselves, to God and to each other—all of which are fundamental elements of the spiritual life."[28] When I was approaching a writing deadline recently, my parents offered to spend some one-on-one time with my youngest child, Abram, who had recently graduated from kindergarten and was melting under the boredom of summer. As one of four children, he gets a lot of quality time with family, but usually it's alongside a sibling or two. My parents brainstormed how to make their time with Abram extra special, researching movie times beforehand. They beamed with pride as they offered to take him to a new animated movie in the theater.

"That would be fun," he told them, pushing a blond tendril away from his brand-new blue eyeglasses, "but what if we stayed here and played?"

My mom looked at his round eyes and saw what I had been too busy to see. He didn't want entertainment. He wanted presence.

So Grandma, Pop-Pop, and Abram stayed home. My mom hauled out a giant box of old-school Hot Wheels tracks, and they spent a couple of hours building tracks down the stairs and around the living room, experimenting, laughing, and simply *being*.

The gift of presence was better than movie theater popcorn, which is saying something.

Here's what Molly Baskette and Ellen O'Donnell found in their research: "When kids are surveyed and asked what they really want from their parents, the most common answer is not the one you might expect. They want time: quality time. They want time spent together as a family, meaningfully engaged in an activity. Even more, they want you to be less stressed, more present, and focused."[29]

Reading that stings a bit. I want to give my kids the best of me, but sometimes I'm wrung out, and they get only the dregs of what's left of my attention. At the end of the day, as the world continues to erupt into political flames and seemingly endless tragedies, I default to distracted and stressed, my phone glued to my hand as I refresh my Twitter feed to get the latest second-by-second updates. In my exhaustion from meeting life's demands, I forget to be present to the people God has placed right in front of me.

Whatever the reason, maybe you've found yourself distracted from your family too. Whatever drains you—mentally, emotionally, or spiritually—and draws you away from the people right in front of you, resist the urge to drown in feelings of guilt. We're all human. Work deadlines are real. Being awake to what's happening locally and globally is integral to being a good neighbor.

Instead of letting guilt or defensiveness take over, I wonder what it would look like for us to consider how we might add more breathing room into the days and weeks ahead, carving out moments to simply delight in being with our families: playing games, cooking together, making a mess in the living room. I wonder how our families might be filled, parent and child alike, by the gift of slowing down and being bored together.

Making time to simply be present with our kids—and with God—takes intentionality. If we assume downtime will just happen organically, chances are it never will. And if we don't make space to be still, we might end up covering our eyes, missing the glory of God all around us.

In Psalm 46, we are given the reminder that though "the nations are in chaos, and their kingdoms crumble" (verse 6), we are to "be still, and know" that God is God (verse 10). May that be a comfort to us when everything seems like it's erupting into chaos and we find ourselves tempted to zone out on the nearest screen.

Just as we need to be awake to God in our lives and present with each other, we need moments of stillness, too. We need to allow ourselves downtime to get a little bored—parents and kids alike.

Pastor Rich Villodas says that getting quiet and spending time with God can often feel a little lackluster—but that's precisely why the spiritual practice of silent prayer is so essential: it purifies us from the idols of distraction and disconnection. "Silent prayer is often uneventful; it's what I refer to as normalized boredom," he writes. "In a society driven by sensory stimulation, distraction, and activity, silent prayer is an alien practice; it's not from this world."[30]

Slowing down and getting quiet—both in our spiritual lives as beloved children and our domestic lives as loving parents—can feel uncomfortable. Those quick hits of dopamine we get when we distract ourselves with screens can become the false god of "good feels."

If we feel a bit antsy and out of sorts when we spend time in silent prayer, Villodas suggests we think of our boredom as "an act of purification."[31] And we need that purification. While social media hits can feel good in the short term, they're not only addicting but also detrimental long term. In fact, Harvard studies show links between scrolling on our phones and increased levels of anxiety, depression, and poor sleep quality.[32] This summer, may we make space for more boredom with our kids and our loving Creator. May we be surprised by the healing, purifying grace of saying, "Hi, Boredom. Nice to meet you."

We need to allow ourselves downtime to get a little bored—parents and kids alike.

SCRIPTURE
Ephesians 2:8-9; Psalm 46

BREATH PRAYER

Inhale: Help me to be still
Exhale: And know that You are God.

FAMILY DISCUSSION QUESTIONS

Read Psalm 46:10 together.

- ▶ When was the last time you felt bored?
- ▶ How can boredom be a good thing? When has boredom led to creativity in your life?
- ▶ Why do you think Scripture tells us to "be still"?
- ▶ How much time do you spend on a screen every day? Every week?
- ▶ How do your brain and body feel after you've spent a lot of time scrolling on your phone, playing video games, or watching TV?
- ▶ How do you know when it's time to turn off a screen? What boundaries do you have in place? How can our family hold each other accountable when it comes to screen time?
- ▶ What are things you can do by yourself when you're feeling bored?
- ▶ What activities can you do with a friend or family member when you're feeling bored?
- ▶ What is the quietest part of your day during the week? How could you add a rhythm of silent or reflective prayer to those moments?
- ▶ Why is unstructured time important for both kids and adults?
- ▶ How can we as a family do a better job at creating healthy rhythms of down time?

FAMILY PRAYER

younger

O God, we come to You with our feelings of boredom. While boredom is often uncomfortable, we recognize that it can sometimes be a good thing for our hearts and bodies, minds and souls. You have created us to rest!

You invite us into moments of quiet and calm. We know that You are with us in the loud moments—in the laughter and the shared stories—but sometimes we forget You are with us in the quiet times too.

Thank You for the simple gift of spending time together as a family. Thank You for the times we can get quiet by ourselves and remember that You are with us. Help us to remember that a little boredom can be a good thing. Amen.

older

God, our lives are loud. Help us to get quiet so that we can hear You more clearly. Help us to add rhythms of rest into our days.

You lead us to quiet waters and invite us to be still, reminding us that all beauty and glory and power are Yours, and Yours alone. We admit that sometimes we make things into little gods, like what we accomplish or the entertainment we consume. But You invite us to be still and know that You alone are God.

In Your mercy, You invite us to rest, to simply breathe. We admit that we sometimes avoid boredom because we don't want to sit with the discomfort that comes from being quiet. But we know that in the silence, You are with us.

Help us to be mindful of the way we spend our days. Help us to enjoy unstructured, unscheduled time with one another. Give us space in our days to be fully present with You, with ourselves, and with each other. Amen.

APPENDIX 1

Rule of Life

DECISION FATIGUE IS REAL. Weekday mornings used to be riddled with anxiety for one of my sons—finding the clothes he wanted for any given school day left us scrambling more than once. We now live in a school district with an established dress code for students: plain polos and pants. The dress code provided the structure he needed. Weekday mornings became a lot less stressful for everyone when we got into the routine of simplifying his outfit choices.

Creating a rule of life for your family is less about developing hard and fast rules and more about taking time to prayerfully, faithfully, and honestly reflect on your family's beliefs and values so you can examine how your life choices—big and small—reflect what you hold dear.

A rule of life can give you a framework for significant decisions (Should I take this job? Should we move? Are we ready to become foster parents?) to small ones (Should we host our neighbors for a barbecue? How much money should we spend on birthday gifts? Should we sign our child up for soccer?)

Returning to what matters most can lead you to freedom when you're stuck.

Bishop Michael Curry points out that the word *rule* is from the Latin *regula*, which "suggests a gentle pattern or framework—not a hard and fast rule. This is a way to create tangible habits that support our heart's intentions."[1] When you sketch out a rule of life, you create scaffolding to give your family stability as you build your life together. When you need discernment in making choices (both the everyday ones and the monumental ones), this gives you a place to turn to remind you of what's most important—and why. It might help to consider your rule of life an always-changing, ever-evolving values statement.

Creating a rule of life is a spiritual practice that goes back thousands of years to Saint Benedict, and it has been a helpful practice for Christians across tradition, denomination, and background ever since. I don't know about you, but my family life is loud, and our rhythms of everyday life couldn't feel further from the lifestyle of Benedictine monks.

Thankfully, we can distill and borrow the essence of Benedict's seventy-three-chapter rule to help us order our life together "around the values, practices and relationships that keep us open and available to God for the work of spiritual transformation that only God can bring about. Simply put, a rule of life provides structure and space for our growing," writes Ruth Haley Barton.[2] Take time to reflect on your own or with your family to determine what you hold most dear so you can order your days, develop household habits, and intentionally integrate thoughtful rhythms to reflect your values—for whatever season of life your family is in.

Simply put, a family rule of life boils down to two questions:

Who do we want our family to be?
How do we want to live so we become more who we want to be?[3]

A rule of life should be a helpful resource to turn to, not a measuring stick of religious perfection to hold your family up to. Bishop Curry points out that developing and committing to a rule of life isn't about "achieving someone else's idea of the right way to live. This is about living more fully in values you already hold by building some habits that fit comfortably into your regular life."[4]

Bishop Curry suggests four steps inspired by the Rule of Saint Benedict. Here I've adapted them into simple terms to make them accessible for your family.

Before you begin writing your family's rule of life, take a moment to pray—on your own or with your children. Ask God to be a light to your path, guiding you as you journey deeper into your family's journey of faith together. Let any stress about getting it right or shame about not living into your values fall away. Be honest, and remember that God is full of mercy and compassion.

The goal isn't to whip up a never-ending report but to thoughtfully create a simple, one-page sheet you can place somewhere (I suggest the refrigerator!) to remind your family of what matters, rooting you back into God's love.

Creating a Family Rule of Life

1. Identify one to three core values you want your family to live more deeply into during this season. What matters most to you? Why?
2. Write simple vows that summarize what the values mean in your family's real-life context. Make sure to include the reason behind your vows. For example, if your value is listening, you might write: "Because we value listening in our family,

we vow to listen to ourselves, one another, God's Word, and our neighbors with greater curiosity and compassion."

3. Brainstorm actionable habits that might help you live out your vows. What can you do to embody these values as a way to love the Lord with all your heart, soul, mind, and strength and to love your neighbor as yourself (see Mark 12:30-31)? To build off the example of listening, perhaps your family might invite a neighbor over for pizza once a month.

4. Look at your family calendar. How can you incorporate these habits into your rhythm and routines? How will you incorporate these habits daily?

Consider setting aside time annually or at the beginning of each season to revisit and examine your answers to the above questions.

May you grow alongside your family in Christ as you create your own rule for this season.

QUESTIONS TO CONSIDER

Where do you spend your time in a given week?

How do you spend your resources?

Where do you live?

How do your life choices reflect
   (or deflect from) your values?

In what ways are your values cultural?
   In what ways are they of Christ?

What do you want your kids to reflect on and remember about the rhythms of your shared life?

APPENDIX 2

The Examen

LIFE IS LOUD. You're bombarded with demands and needs at home, at work, and in your community. A child cries, laundry overflows, and dishes pile up. Your boss is waiting on you for an email, and the world news highlights another global crisis.

How do you stay awake to the presence of God in and around you if you can barely hear yourself think?

At the end of the day, once my kids are in bed and the house is quiet, my brain often feels overloaded. Instead of sitting in the stillness, I usually attempt to relax by scrolling on my phone or streaming a show on TV. But instead of feeling refreshed as a result, I feel more overwhelmed than ever.

How might we experience more peace if we took time to reflect rather than add to the noise at the end of the day, the week, the month, the season, or the year?

The Examen is a way of getting quiet inside. It's a rhythm of prayer that Christians have used throughout centuries (popularized by Saint Ignatius's *Spiritual Exercises*) to help us examine where, how, and when we experience God's presence in our lives. I think of the Examen as a guide to help me stay awake to God's presence and promptings.

I'll be honest: sometimes praying the Examen feels like more work on my to-do list at the end of a long day. But when I take the time to prayerfully be still, I never regret it. This prayer time brings me closer to myself and to the One who made me. As I play back my comings and goings—the beautiful moments and the heartbreaking ones too—I experience glimmers of clarity and comfort. I feel more rooted in the past, more peaceful in the present, and more energized for the future.

"The examen of consciousness involves taking a few moments at the end of each day to go back over the events of the day and invite God to show us where he was present with us and how we responded to his presence," writes spiritual director Ruth Haley Barton. "We might ask ourselves, How was God present with me today? What promptings did I notice? How did I respond or not respond?"[5]

There are several types of Examen prayers:

daily
weekly
monthly
seasonal
annual

When I pray the Examen, I close my eyes, get comfortable and quiet, and take a few deep breaths as I rewind and play back the comings and goings of my day. I also pray through the Examen at each season's end. As I pray, I think of the psalmist's prayer: "Search me, God, and know my heart" (Psalm 139:23, NIV).

Father James Martin says the Examen is one of the most helpful prayers he knows. He writes, "The examen works against our tendency to view our lives as a series of problems to solve, challenges to surmount, or obstacles to overcome. It also invites us to pause to appreciate God's presence in our lives, which works against the urge to put today behind us and plow ahead to tomorrow. Mainly it helps us notice."[6] Everyone has their own way of praying the Examen. You might try borrowing this take on the five-step Examen that Saint Ignatius practiced.[7]

1. Become aware of God's presence. As you begin, remember that God is with you. It may be helpful to pray something like "God, be with me" or to imagine that Jesus is gazing on you in tenderness and love. Think of God being physically with you, sitting on the couch among the folded laundry and your kids' stinky sneakers, delighted to be in your presence.

2. Begin with gratitude. Start your prayer by giving thanks. Use a lens of appreciation as you recall and reflect on your day—this acts as an antidote to despair, cynicism, or the eternal cycle of fixing or problem solving. Savor these moments of thankfulness, and let God begin to repair your weary heart as you give thanks.

3. Review the day (or week, month, season, or year). As you play back your time, get curious about how God has spoken to you through the places you've gone, the people in your midst, and the events that have happened. Notice where God was with you. Who showed you love? Who did you extend love to? How did you

experience God? How did your day begin? Where might God have been inviting you into something? Pay attention to your emotions as you reflect.

4. Get honest. As you pray, remember that God cares for you with compassion. In light of Christ's mercy, you don't have to hide the parts when you may have hurt or dishonored yourself, God, or someone else with your words or thoughts, your action or inaction. Ask God to help you grow in humility. It may feel uncomfortable to name your sin, but as I often remind my kids when they make a mistake, it's important to remember that making a bad choice doesn't make you bad. Remember that the grace of God frees us from the shackles of shame.

5. Look toward tomorrow in grace. Reflect on the coming day, month, season, or year as you close your prayer. Name what you're anticipating, and ask God to extend grace to you. As you prayed, did you realize you're struggling with patience toward your family? Did you realize you've been quick to anger as you approach that work deadline? Invite God to help you with the burden you're holding.

May the Examen offer you another way to encounter God, who is always with you. May you reflect and be changed by God's grace, experiencing a more peaceful heart so you can cultivate peace within your family and bring peace to your community and world.

You don't have to be Catholic to borrow from the Christ-centered wisdom and spiritual practices of Saint Ignatius and the early church. To learn more about the Examen, visit ignatianspirituality.com or read Father James Martin's book *Learning to Pray*.

APPENDIX 3

Lectio Divina

WE CAN MEET GOD in new and beautiful ways through Scripture. But reading and praying alongside the Bible can sometimes feel daunting or overwhelming, especially if you grew up in a context where the Bible was weaponized or used in harmful ways.

Maybe you're wondering, *How can I read and pray through these ancient, holy texts wisely and well? And how can I help my children learn to do the same?*

A spiritual practice called *Lectio Divina*, which simply means "sacred reading" or "holy reading," gives us (and our kids) a gentle guide to borrow as we read Scripture and grow closer to God. Lectio Divina is an ancient Christian practice used across different traditions and backgrounds. It invites us to intentionally engage in the reading of God's Word, using the text as a jumping-off point to enter into an ongoing sacred conversation—the back-and-forth dialogue God has with us in our daily lives.

As a mom to four delightful children who tend to be making noise and needing things constantly, I find that Lectio Divina helps me slow down and intentionally, prayerfully approach Scripture instead of just making Bible reading another thing to check off my to-do list.

As Joan Chittister writes, "Sacred reading is what stops us from dashing through spiritual ideas without stopping to consider exactly what they mean to us today."[8] When I take the time to engage in Lectio Divina, I begin to glimpse how Scripture is, as Hebrews 4:12 says, "alive and active" (NIV) in my life. When we participate in Lectio Divina, we begin to unravel the mystery that somehow a passage penned thousands of years ago can still connect us with God today.

Though there's no one correct way to approach this practice, it tends to follow a loose pattern of reading, meditation, reflection, and contemplative action. (Even if this approach is new to you, you may realize you've intuitively taken these steps while reading and praying through a passage such as a psalm.) As you read, you'll explore what's happening, you'll grapple with what the reading brings up in you, you'll question yourself and God, you'll listen to what the Holy Spirit might be leading you toward, and you'll share your praises and sorrows with the One who exists in and out of time. You may be surprised by where God leads the conversation.

Each week of this book includes passages or verses to turn to for further reading on your spiritual journey through the seasons. You may find it helpful to borrow these prayerful Lectio Divina steps as you turn to these texts.[9] Some people like to journal; others prefer to close their eyes and cut out distractions.

Consider integrating some of these questions when you read Scripture with your children. You could even adapt the questions to go along with a Bible storybook for young kids.

May you feel God's presence as you prayerfully read, and may you be encouraged as you grow in your relationship with Christ.

Lectio Divina Steps

1. Reading. Read through the text. First, ask yourself, *What does it say?* Next, read through the passage again, this time to grow in understanding. What's going on? What is the context of the passage? (If you're unfamiliar with a phrase or are unsure of the historical underpinnings, check a trusted commentary or turn to the introduction of the book of the Bible you're reading.)

2. Meditation. Lean into your curiosity as you wonder what God might be saying to you through the text. What words or phrases stand out? What about the text gives you pause? What draws you closer? What do you notice?

3. Reflection. Enter into prayer with God, sharing your petitions and praise. What is your response to the questions you meditated on after you read the passage? What is your reaction to God? What tension does this bring up for you? What stirs gratitude in your soul?

4. Contemplative Action. Consider the difference this Scripture makes in your life. What might God be inviting you into, and how will you get there? What implications does this passage have for the life of your family or your community? What possibilities or challenges does it bring up?

Lectio Divina is an opportunity for God to bring things up for you to notice and then for you to respond to God about those things.

JAMES MARTIN,
LEARNING TO PRAY

APPENDIX 4

Daily Prayers to Share

CHANGE CAN BE BEAUTIFUL—and it can also feel brutal. As seasons shift, children grow, and headlines turn over faster than we can fathom, staying in a rhythm of family prayer can help you and your children remain rooted in the rich soil of God's love.

Nourishing the souls of our children takes intentionality, and prayer plays an important part in that nurturing.

Daily prayer isn't magic. It's not a supernatural bandage for fixing wounds or ensuring that life will work out the way you hoped (or planned). But praying together can remind your family that all you do and all you are comes from God. And in the moments when we can barely find our footing, those glimmers of grace we sometimes glimpse when we pray can be downright sustaining.

The shortest of prayers (yes, even amid wailing babies, warring siblings, or wayward teenagers) can offer a moment of stability. Praying together can remind your family that as you embark on different paths in our beautiful, heartbreaking world, your roots connect in Christ. As Colossians 2:7 says, "Let your roots grow deep into him, and then your faith will grow strong and your steps will become firm on this path that you've learned to follow" (FNV).

If we want to raise kids who thrive and honor God, their neighbor, and themselves as they show up in the world, then we must care for their roots. "God longs for us to be fully alive, soaring into the sky and bearing witness to God's good life that is available to us," writes Rich Villodas. "But if we hope to be shaped and changed in this way of life, we must have a root system powerful enough to hold us together."[10]

You don't have to turn your home into a convent to add little rhythms of prayer into your comings and goings. Consider how God might be inviting you to add this habit to your rhythms or routines at home. Could you share a quick prayer before school drop-off? Could you enter mealtime prayer over pizza and plastic cups of soda? Could your messiest, most imperfect times of prayer help your children stay rooted in Christ in ways you never imagined?

301

You can bookmark these prayers and borrow them to connect deeper into the love of Christ.

As Paul said, "I pray that as you trust in him, your roots will go deep into the soil of his great love, and that from these roots you will draw the strength and courage needed to walk this sacred path together with all his holy people. This path of love is higher than the stars, deeper than the great waters, wider than the sky. Yes, this love comes from and reaches to all directions" (Ephesians 3:17-18, FNV).

May these prayers help your family remain deeply rooted and established in love.

A Prayer for Morning

O God of hope, we thank You
For the breath in our lungs
And the gift of a new day.

As surely as the sun rises,
Your mercy covers the earth.
We ask You to help us start fresh
As we embark on the adventures
You have for us.

May all the people we meet today
Know us by our love.
May all the things we do today
Be in worship to You.

Thank You for the gift
Of another morning
On Your big, beautiful earth.
Where there is pain,
May we bring healing.
Where there is suffering,
May we bring hope.

Be with each of us
As we go about the day.
And when the day is done,
Bring us home safely
Under the shelter of Your wings.
Amen.

A Prayer for Midday

O God, we know that to You,
No time is wasted.
And in You, even the most
Ordinary afternoons are holy.

In the middle of this day,
We pause to remember
Your unfailing mercy.
We thank You
For this day—
For all that has happened
And all that is to come.

We ask for Your help
To focus on what You have
    for us,
To be awake to today.
Help us be attentive
To the work of our hands,
And help us be present
To the people You've put
    on our path.

Give each of us comfort
In knowing we are so much
    more
Than the work we do
At school, at our jobs, or
    at home.

As we pause this day to pray,
And as we prepare to enter back
Into the world
That holds so much beauty
And so much pain,
We ask that the light of each
Beloved member of our family
Would shine like the noonday
    sun to all we meet
So that all would know
Your gentle
And glorious
Love.
Amen.

A Prayer for a Shared Meal

God, we thank You for all
Who gather here
And for the meal
We're about to share.

We thank You for the hands
That made this food
And for all who labored
So we may eat.

May the space between us
Be filled with quiet listening
And loud laughter.
May the space between us
Be filled with life poured out
Between family and friends.

As we eat and as we drink,
May we remember Your love
Is in us and among us, always.

God, we thank You for all
Who gather here
And for the meal
We're about to share.
Amen.

A Prayer for Evening

O God, as the sun
Begins its descent
And we gather together,
We come to You,
Kind and compassionate God,
And we thank You for this day.

We pause to reflect
On the beautiful glimpses
Of You
That this day held.
And we stop to remember
The difficult moments
That met us
In the comings and goings of
    the day.

We thank You for this time
    together—
This time to be near
To those we care for
And those who care for us.
We ask that You would bless
Our evening together.
Amen.

A Prayer for Bedtime

O God, we come to You
At the end of the day
And give all we're holding
Back to You.

As the moon and the stars
Illuminate the night
And we begin to rest,
We turn today's worries and fears
And today's joys and celebrations
Over to You, for You care for us.
No part of our day
Is too big or too small
To share with You.

Forgive us for the ways
We brought harm into this day
With our words, thoughts, or
    actions.
And we ask for courage
To make things right tomorrow.

As we get quiet and turn off the
    lights,
We're comforted in knowing
That in the day's most beautiful
    moments,

And in the disappointing parts
    too,
You held us in Your love
And You never left us.
We thank You for Your kindness
And Your unfailing mercy.

As we end this day together
And gather under the comfort
Of cozy blankets and warm
    beds,
We pray for those who work
    during the night
And those who are lonely
Or have nowhere safe
To lay their heads.

May this night bring peace
For all who need it.
Guard us from bad dreams
And untrue thoughts.
Guide us as we sleep
So we may rest
And be renewed
For another day.
Amen.

UNSURE WHAT TO PRAY?

*At bedtime, we often end our prayers
with the words of Jesus that Christians have
been praying for centuries, often referred to as
"The Lord's Prayer" (see Matthew 6:9-13). As you pray,
encourage your family to visualize the words or
to think in pictures. After you're done praying,
share the images that come to mind.*

Our Father, who art in heaven,
Hallowed be Thy name.
Thy kingdom come,
Thy will be done,
On earth as it is in heaven.
Give us this day our daily bread.
And forgive us our trespasses,
As we forgive those who trespass against us.
And lead us not into temptation,
But deliver us from evil.
For thine is the kingdom,
The power, and the glory,
For ever and ever.
Amen.

Writing Your Own Family Liturgy

AS CHILDREN OF GOD, we are all created to enter the ongoing conversation our Maker is having with us. Sometimes we call this divine dialogue—this sacred listening and sharing—prayer.

We can pray at any time, anywhere we are. We don't have to have the right words (or any words at all). Sometimes we pray alone, silently. Other times we pray with our tears or laughter, our very breath becoming prayer. In other moments, we express our praise and petitions through written prayers or liturgies, letting our hearts beat in sync as we lift our voices together.

Like a giant, cozy blanket stretched across the whole family on the couch, communal prayer provides comfort and unites us under a shared covering of God's grace.

Kids are talented liturgists. The youngest among us often bless us (and surprise us) with the creativity and compassion they bring to their prayers. When I was in the thick of writing *To Light Their Way*, I invited my son Asher (who was seven at the time) to join me in writing a prayer. We sat at the kitchen island, passing a journal back and forth.

We started with the prompt, "God, You are . . ." and took turns adding our endings to the sentence. He surprised me (and taught me) by drawing an infinity symbol to describe God. His prayer invited me into a deeper imagination as I marveled at the mysterious glory of God. What a gift!

In Matthew 19:14, Jesus said, "Let the little children come to me" (NIV). Creating family prayer is a way to move toward Christ with your children—together.

Here you'll find some prompts for penning prayers alongside your family.

You can fill in the blanks and tweak the prayers to fit your needs. Feel free to grab a notebook, sketch out your prayers on the back of an envelope, or write them in the margins of this book. You can return to them in new seasons or at the start of a new year. You might craft a prayer at dinnertime and pray through it as a family throughout the week, or you might borrow them for bedtime prayers. Consider dating your shared prayers and saving them as a way to mark the passing of time. Do what works for you and your family in whatever season of life you're in. Use them as scaffolding as you build your prayers together.

May moments of communal prayer be sacred in all seasons of your family life. As you bring your prayers to paper, may you be delighted in the creativity—and the sheer presence—of one another. May your family's offerings of praise, confession, and lament in these liturgies bring you closer to the One who delights in each one of you.

As you enter this divine dialogue, may Christ wrap your family in the blanket of His love. And as your children grow and seasons change, may your hearts be transformed and your imaginations renewed through these prayers.

Prayer Prompts for Families

A PRAYER FOR NEEDING GOD

O God, we come to You

Feeling _____ and _____.

Forgive us for the ways we have _____,

And help us to _____ when we feel most _____.

We _____ You, O God.

Amen.

A PRAYER OF PRAISE

O God of _____,

We praise You and thank You

For the _____ in our lives.

When we think of Your _____,

We want to _____.

We thank You for each member of our family.

Bless _____ and be with them.

Bless _____ and be with them.

Help us give _____ to one another

As an act of worship to You.

Amen.

A PRAYER FOR REMEMBERING

O God, help us to remember that

You have _____ ,

You are _____ ,

And You will _____ .

Amen.

A PRAYER FOR THE CHANGING SEASONS

As the _____ [season that's ending]

Turns to _____ [season that's beginning],

We thank You for the _____ and the _____ [nature attributes, weather changes].

In all Your creation,

We know You are _____ [descriptive word].

As we continue to grow,

Bless this season of _____ [beginning season].

Gather us in Your _____ [attribute of God].

Help our family _____ [verb].

Shape us with Your _____ [attribute of God, such as kindness, goodness, or mercy].

Send us out with _____ [positive emotion] in our hearts,

And bring us home with _____ [positive emotion] spirits.

Amen.

A LITANY FOR THE WORRIES YOU HOLD

Parent: In all your _____ ,

Child: God is _____ .

Parent: In every _____ ,

Child: God is _____ .

Parent: When you hold _____ ,

Child: God is _____ .

Parent and Child: Amen.

A CALL AND RESPONSE FOR THE MORNING

Parent: As you go out into the world, remember you are _____.

Child: I will remember I am _____.

Parent: As you go out into the world, remember God is _____.

Child: I will remember God is _____.

Parent: As you go out into the world, remember I _____.

Child: As I go out into the world, I will remember you _____.

Parent: As you go out into the world, remember the _____ of God surrounds you.

Child: I will remember that the _____ of God surrounds me.

A PRAYER FOR THE END OF THE DAY

O _____ [name for God],

You are _____ [attribute of God].

In You, we are _____ [past-tense verb].

When we are _____ [emotion],

Give us _____ [noun]

So we may _____ [action verb].

Amen.

Acknowledgments

Whether we are aware of it or not, we are drawing from every human being we
have ever known, have passed casually in the street, sat next to on the subway,
stood behind in the check-out line at the supermarket.

MADELEINE L'ENGLE

THE STORIES IN THIS BOOK REFLECT THE IMPACT of many people I've known
throughout my life. I'm grateful for those whose paths I've crossed on the wild and winding journey from being a young child to becoming the parent I am today. To friends and
family I've met along the way: you might not have known, but your memory was a comfort
to me as I wrote. I hope you feel it on these pages.

I'm humbled by the parents and readers who take time out of their full days to share
glimpses of their joys and sorrows with me. It's an honor to pray for you and alongside
you. Thank you for allowing my words to be part of your lives.

To my mom and dad: thank you for all the time, energy, and care you've given throughout the years to make me feel safe, known, and loved. I hope it's okay that I shared some
memories. Thanks for loving me. I love you.

I'm infinitely grateful for a publishing team with a heart of gold. Jillian Schlossberg,
thanks for understanding the depths of this work not only as an editor but as a friend.
Sarah Atkinson, thank you for believing in me and trusting me to steward these words.
Stephanie Rische, you've once again brought my heartbeats into the world with care and
intention—I'm forever grateful. Amanda Woods and Cassidy Gage, your help is so appreci-
ated. Eva Winters, thanks for bringing dreams to life and artfully crafting this book's design
(including the front cover, inspired by windows in our home).

To my agent, Rachelle Gardner: thank you for your guidance and wisdom, time after time.

I write a lot about where we live, and I want to extend an enormous Highland thanks to each of my neighbors, both the young and young-at-heart. A special thanks to Joyce, Sarah, Kas, and ReShonda, who peeked at some early pages of this book. You make that whole love-your-neighbor thing pretty easy!

Patty, how do I capture friendship in a few lines? Thanks for being the best of the best—and the first reader of so many of these pages. You made this book better. Cat, thanks for being you—and for helping keep the ship afloat. I'm grateful for the laundry list of friends just a text away. You know who you are (some of you are mentioned in these reflections!).

To Jill and the Christian Parenting team, and to Nate and the team at Bethany: thanks for inviting me to share my words alongside your work. I'm also grateful to my fellow writers at (in)courage. Thank you to the creative women who help me process how to show up well as a writer in Internet spaces.

It's a gift to live in a historic home that has lived many lives. While writing this book, my family had the joy of meeting Sister Victoria Ann Arndorfer, who lived in our house when it served as a convent for the Sisters of Mercy. Sister Vicky, as we take shelter inside these four walls through the freezing winters and sweltering summers, we feel the prayers of all who have come before us. Thank you for sharing your memories and ministry with us.

I wasn't sure I could write this manuscript with four children at home for the summer. Molly, thank you for being an answer to prayer and for spending summer days with Eliza (and making sure the boys stayed alive too). Your presence matters!

Though most of this writing happened at the dining room table among scattered LEGOs and endless kids' craft projects, I had the gift of taking a small retreat to Prairiewoods Franciscan Spirituality Center to tackle some deep writing. Thank you for your hospitality and for cultivating space for me to get quiet in a noisy world.

I'm grateful for the open arms extended by all who call Westminster their church home. Thank you for welcoming Jonny and all of us—what a full-circle moment! The gift isn't lost on me that you were a place where I first began to learn about God's love—and now you're making space for my kids to explore their faith too.

To Abram, Eliza, Asher, and Joseph: every paragraph I write, every prayer I create, is for you. Someday maybe you'll read this and feel the love I've held (and will continue to hold) through all seasons of being your mom. When I'm with you, I feel God's love. I hope you

feel God's love with you too—even when you go on your own adventures! Thank you for being who you are and for letting me cheer you on. I learn so much about myself, God, and our world when I'm with you. Thanks for asking big questions and for sharing your thoughts and feelings with me. I love you! (I wrote the promise in the "Remember Your Vows" reflection thinking of each of you.)

To Jonny, my husband of fifteen wonderful, weird, wild years: I cannot imagine navigating this life without you—and I don't want to try. It's a gift to grow alongside you and parent with you through all the changing seasons. You make it easy to spot the sacred. I love you, and I really like being with you too. Thanks for supporting and loving me in every chapter of this holy, messy life.

And to the God of all seasons, thank You for calling me Your beloved child. I hope the words on these pages are an offering of love.

Notes

INTRODUCTION

1. Vicki K. Black, *Welcome to the Church Year: An Introduction to the Seasons of the Episcopal Church* (Harrisburg, PA: Morehouse, 2004), 2.
2. Jan Richardson, *Circle of Grace: A Book of Blessings for the Seasons* (Orlando: Wanton Gospeller Press, 2015), xviii.
3. Richardson, xix.
4. Ruth Haley Barton, *Sacred Rhythms: Arranging Our Lives for Spiritual Transformation* (Downers Grove, IL: IVP Books, 2006), 49.
5. Dietrich Bonhoeffer, *Life Together: A Discussion of Christian Fellowship*, trans. John W. Doberstein (New York: Harper & Row, 1954), 52.
6. Morgan Harper Nichols, *Peace Is a Practice: An Invitation to Breathe Deep and Find a New Rhythm for Life* (Grand Rapids, MI: Zondervan Books, 2022), 15.
7. Traci Baxley, *Social Justice Parenting: How to Raise Compassionate, Anti-racist, Justice-Minded Kids in an Unjust World* (New York: HarperCollins, 2021), 173.
8. Bonhoeffer, *Life Together*, 62.

FALL

1. Morgan Harper Nichols, *Peace Is a Practice: An Invitation to Breathe Deep and Find a New Rhythm for Life* (Grand Rapids, MI: Zondervan Books, 2022), 129.
2. Nichols, 143.
3. Andy Crouch, *The Tech-Wise Family: Everyday Steps for Putting Technology in Its Proper Place* (Grand Rapids, MI: Baker Books, 2017), 126.
4. Wendy M. Wright, *Seasons of a Family's Life: Cultivating the Contemplative Spirit at Home* (San Francisco: Jossey-Bass, 2003), 18–19.
5. Miroslav Volf, *Exclusion and Embrace: A Theological Exploration of Identity, Otherness, and Reconciliation* (Nashville: Abingdon Press, 1996), 291.

6. "The Challenge of Peace: A Challenge to Parents—A Reflective Resource for Parents," Family Life Renewal, vol. 1, United States Catholic Conference Commission on Marriage and Family Life, Department of Education, 4.

7. Osheta Moore, *Shalom Sistas: Living Wholeheartedly in a Brokenhearted World* (Harrisonburg, VA: Herald Press, 2017), 32.

8. "The Challenge of Peace," 4.

9. Adapted from Kayla Craig, *To Light Their Way*, "A Prayer for Peace" and "A Prayer on the Feast Day of St. Francis of Assisi" (Carol Stream, IL: Tyndale House, 2021), 170–71, 133–34.

10. Dominique Dubois Gilliard, *Subversive Witness: Scripture's Call to Leverage Privilege* (Grand Rapids, MI: Zondervan, 2021), 103.

11. Gary Thomas, *Sacred Parenting: How Raising Children Shapes Our Souls* (Grand Rapids, MI: Zondervan, 2017), 66.

12. Traci Baxley, *Social Justice Parenting: How to Raise Compassionate, Anti-racist, Justice-Minded Kids in an Unjust World* (New York: HarperCollins, 2021), 31.

13. Baxley, 172.

14. James Martin, *Learning to Pray: A Guide for Everyone* (New York: HarperOne, 2021), 46.

15. Anne Lamott, *Help, Thanks, Wow: The Three Essential Prayers* (New York: Riverhead Books, 2012).

16. Lamott, 4.

17. Martin, *Learning to Pray*, 57.

18. Gerard Manley Hopkins, "Pied Beauty," *Poems and Prose* (New York, Penguin Classics, 1985), https://www.poetryfoundation.org/poems/44399/pied-beauty.

19. Wright, *Seasons of a Family's Life*, 97.

20. Richard Rohr, "Utterly Humbled by Mystery," This I Believe series, NPR, December 18, 2006, https://www.npr.org/2006/12/18/6631954/utterly-humbled-by-mystery.

21. Traci Smith, *Faithful Families: Creating Sacred Moments at Home* (Saint Louis: Chalice Press, 2017), 6.

22. Ruth Haley Barton, *Sacred Rhythms: Arranging Our Lives for Spiritual Transformation* (Downers Grove, IL: IVP Books, 2006), 11.

23. Frederick Buechner, *Beyond Words: Daily Readings in the ABC's of Faith* (New York: HarperSanFrancisco, 2004), 267.

24. Baxley, *Social Justice Parenting*, 10–11.

25. Phuc Luu, *Jesus of the East: Reclaiming the Gospel for the Wounded* (Harrisonburg, VA: Herald Press, 2020), 225.

26. Buechner, *Beyond Words*, 228.

27. Bonhoeffer, *Life Together*, 68.

28. Kat Armas, *Abuelita Faith: What Women on the Margins Teach Us about Wisdom, Persistence, and Strength* (Grand Rapids, MI: Brazos Press, 2021), 137.

29. Luu, *Jesus of the East*, 125.

30. Buechner, *Beyond Words*, 228.

31. Mark and Jan Foreman, *Never Say No: Raising Big-Picture Kids* (Colorado Springs: David C. Cook, 2015), 129.

32. Foreman, 128.

33. Madeleine L'Engle, *A Circle of Quiet* (New York: HarperCollins, 1972), 174.

34. William Martin, *The Parent's Tao Te Ching: Ancient Advice for Modern Parents* (Cambridge, MA: Da Capo Press, 1999), 127.
35. "The Children We Mean to Raise: The Real Messages Adults Are Sending about Values," Harvard Graduate School of Education, executive summary (2014), 1, https://static1.squarespace.com/static /5b7c56e255b02c683659fe43/t/5bae774424a694b5feb2b05f/1538160453604/report-children-raise .pdf (https://mcc.gse.harvard.edu/reports/children-mean-raise.
36. Foreman, *Never Say No*, 54.
37. Baxley, *Social Justice Parenting*, 161.
38. Kate Bowler, "Death, the Prosperity Gospel, and Me," *New York Times*, February 13, 2016, https:// www.nytimes.com/2016/02/14/opinion/sunday/death-the-prosperity-gospel-and-me.html.
39. "As He Gets Hollywood Walk of Fame Star, Snoop Dogg Thanks . . . Himself," Reuters, November 19, 2018, https://www.reuters.com/article/us-people-snoop-dogg/as-he-gets-hollywood-walk-of-fame-star -snoop-dogg-thanks-himself-idUSKCN1NP02F.
40. "Giving Thanks Can Make You Happier," Harvard Health Publishing, Harvard Medical School, August 14, 2021, https://www.health.harvard.edu/healthbeat/giving-thanks-can-make-you-happier.
41. "Giving Thanks Can Make You Happier."

WINTER
1. Katherine May, *Wintering: The Power of Rest and Retreat in Difficult Times* (New York: Riverhead Books, 2020).
2. Jan Richardson, *Circle of Grace: A Book of Blessings for the Seasons* (Orlando: Wanton Gospeller Press, 2015), xvii.
3. Morgan Harper Nichols, *Peace Is a Practice: An Invitation to Breathe Deep and Find a New Rhythm for Life* (Grand Rapids, MI: Zondervan Books, 2022), 20.
4. May, *Wintering*, 239.
5. Henri J. M. Nouwen, Donald P. McNeill, and Douglas A. Morrison, *Compassion: A Reflection on the Christian Life* (New York: Image Books, 1982), 13.
6. Aundi Kolber, *Try Softer: A Fresh Approach to Move Us out of Anxiety, Stress, and Survival Mode—And into a Life of Connection and Joy* (Carol Stream, IL: Tyndale House, 2020), 34.
7. Aundi Kolber, *The Try Softer Guided Journey: A Soulful Companion to Healing* (Carol Stream, IL: Tyndale House, 2021), 58.
8. Amy Kenny, *My Body Is Not a Prayer Request: Disability Justice in the Church* (Grand Rapids, MI: Brazos Press, 2022), 116.
9. Wendy M. Wright, *Seasons of a Family's Life: Cultivating the Contemplative Spirit at Home* (San Francisco: Jossey-Bass, 2003), 43.
10. Madeleine L'Engle, *A Circle of Quiet* (New York: HarperCollins, 1972), 245.
11. Wright, *Seasons of a Family's Life*, 79.
12. Wright, 40.
13. Wright, 41.
14. Rob Garner, "NASA's Webb Delivers Deepest Infrared Image of Universe Yet," NASA, July 12, 2022, https://www.nasa.gov/image-feature/goddard/2022/nasa-s-webb-delivers-deepest-infrared-image-of -universe-yet.
15. L'Engle, *A Circle of Quiet*, 203.

16. L'Engle, 99–100.

17. L'Engle, 111–12.

18. Madeleine L'Engle, *Two-Part Invention: The Story of a Marriage* (San Francisco: Harper & Row, 1988), 145.

19. Scott Erickson, *Honest Advent* (Grand Rapids, MI: Zondervan, 2020), 39.

20. Phuc Luu, *Jesus of the East: Reclaiming the Gospel for the Wounded* (Harrisonburg, VA: Herald Press, 2020), 125.

21. Lisa Sharon Harper, *The Very Good Gospel: How Everything Wrong Can Be Made Right* (New York: WaterBrook, 2016), 32.

22. Robert L. Perkins, ed., *Upbuilding Discourses in Various Spirits*, International Kierkegaard Commentary, vol. 15 (Macon, GA: Mercer University Press, 2005), 254.

23. L'Engle, *A Circle of Quiet*, 179.

24. Walter Brueggemann, *Reverberations of Faith: A Theological Handbook of Old Testament Themes* (Louisville: Westminster John Knox Press, 2002), 57.

25. Michael Curry with Sara Grace, *Love Is the Way: Holding on to Hope in Troubling Times* (New York: Avery, 2020), 219.

26. Harper, *The Very Good Gospel*, 10.

27. Harper, 13.

28. Rich Villodas, *The Deeply Formed Life: Five Transformative Values to Root Us in the Way of Jesus* (New York: WaterBrook, 2020), xv.

29. Traci Baxley, *Social Justice Parenting: How to Raise Compassionate, Anti-Racist, Justice-Minded Kids in an Unjust World* (New York: HarperCollins, 2021), 139.

30. Frederick Buechner, *Beyond Words: Daily Readings in the ABC's of Faith* (New York: HarperSanFrancisco, 2004), 65.

31. Nouwen, McNeill, and Morrison, *Compassion*, 43.

32. Nouwen, McNeill, and Morrison, 47.

33. Baxley, *Social Justice Parenting*, 139.

34. Baxley, 156.

35. Sue Monk Kidd, *When the Heart Waits: Spiritual Direction for Life's Sacred Questions* (New York: HarperCollins, 1990), 202.

36. Dominique Dubois Gilliard, *Subversive Witness: Scripture's Call to Leverage Privilege* (Grand Rapids, MI: Zondervan, 2021), 101.

37. Baxley, *Social Justice Parenting*, 47.

38. Baxley, 61–62.

39. Jemar Tisby, *How to Fight Racism: Courageous Christianity and the Journey toward Racial Justice* (Grand Rapids, MI: Zondervan, 2021), 56.

40. Tisby, 55.

41. Tisby, 55–56.

42. Adapted from Kayla Craig, *To Light Their Way: A Collection of Prayers and Liturgies for Parents*, "A Prayer for Martin Luther King Jr. Day" (Carol Stream, IL: Tyndale House, 2021), 141–43.

43. Adapted from Craig, *To Light Their Way*, "A Prayer for Talking about Racism with Children", 86–87.

SPRING

1. Arnold Lobel, *Frog and Toad Are Friends* (New York: Harper & Row, 1970), 8.

2. Arnold Lobel, *Frog and Toad Storybook Treasury* (New York: Harper, 2014), 15.
3. John O'Donohue, *To Bless the Space between Us: A Book of Blessings* (New York: Convergent, 2008), 47.
4. "Seasonal Affective Disorder," Mental Health America, accessed November 7, 2022, https://www .mhanational.org/conditions/seasonal-affective-disorder-sad.
5. "A Spiritual View of Vulnerability with Pastor Mandy Smith," *Upside Down Podcast,* September 2018, podcast, episode 43, 45:54, https://open.spotify.com/episode/3FDvYGyT8bFnpWoTquSyXq?si =dbba5c31f4514f9f.
6. Mandy Smith, "Dance for the Healing to Come: The Strange Act of (Literally) Dancing in Lament," Missio Alliance, December 30, 2015, https://www.missioalliance.org/dance-healing-come-strange-act -literally-dancing-lament/.
7. Mandy Smith, *Unfettered: Imagining a Childlike Faith beyond the Baggage of Western Culture* (Grand Rapids, MI: Brazos Press, 2021), 67.
8. Mark and Jan Foreman, *Never Say No: Raising Big-Picture Kids* (Colorado Springs: David C. Cook, 2015), 133.
9. Vicki K. Black, *Welcome to the Church Year: An Introduction to the Seasons of the Episcopal Church* (Harrisburg, PA: Morehouse, 2004), 75.
10. Molly Baskette and Ellen O'Donnell, *Bless This Mess: A Modern Guide to Faith and Parenting in a Chaotic World* (New York: Convergent Books, 2019), 236–37.
11. Jan Richardson, *Circle of Grace: A Book of Blessings for the Seasons* (Orlando: Wanton Gospeller Press, 2015), xix.
12. Mary Oliver, "Low Tide," *Amicus Journal,* Winter (2001), 34.
13. Makoto Fujimura, *Art + Faith: A Theology of Making* (New Haven, CT: Yale University Press, 2020), 99.
14. Lisa Sharon Harper, *The Very Good Gospel: How Everything Wrong Can Be Made Right* (New York: WaterBrook, 2016), 42.
15. Henri J. M. Nouwen, *The Return of the Prodigal Son: A Story of Homecoming* (New York: Image Books, 1994), 106.
16. Madeleine L'Engle, *A Circle of Quiet* (New York: HarperCollins, 1972), 174.
17. Fujimura, *Art + Faith,* 130.
18. Traci Baxley, *Social Justice Parenting: How to Raise Compassionate, Anti-racist, Justice-Minded Kids in an Unjust World* (New York: HarperCollins, 2021), 102.
19. Baxley, 103.
20. Baxley, 108–9.
21. Miroslav Volf, *Exclusion and Embrace: A Theological Exploration of Identity, Otherness, and Reconciliation* (Nashville: Abingdon Press, 1996), 286.
22. Richard Rohr, *The Universal Christ: How a Forgotten Reality Can Change Everything We See, Hope For, and Believe* (New York: Convergent Books, 2019), 170–71.
23. Sue Monk Kidd, *When the Heart Waits: Spiritual Direction for Life's Sacred Questions* (San Francisco: Harper & Row, 1990), 148.
24. Fujimura, *Art + Faith,* 47.
25. Rohr, *Universal Christ,* 170.
26. Fujimura, *Art + Faith,* 48.
27. Justin Whitmel Earley, *Habits of the Household: Practicing the Story of God in Everyday Family Rhythms* (Grand Rapids, MI: Zondervan, 2021), 165.

28. Earley, 165.

29. Earley, 165.

30. Brenda Ueland, "Why Women Who Do Too Much Housework Should Neglect It for Their Writing," in *If You Want to Write: A Book about Art, Independence, and Spirit* (Saint Paul, MN: Graywolf Press, 1938).

31. O'Donohue, *To Bless the Space between Us*, 102.

32. O'Donohue, 104.

33. O'Donohue, 105.

34. Henri J. M. Nouwen, Donald P. McNeill, and Douglas A. Morrison, *Compassion: A Reflection on the Christian Life* (New York: Image Books, 1982), 99.

35. Frederick Buechner, *Beyond Words: Daily Readings in the ABC's of Faith* (New York: HarperSanFrancisco, 2004), 139.

36. Lisa Sharon Harper, *The Very Good Gospel: How Everything Wrong Can Be Made Right* (New York: WaterBrook, 2016), 34.

37. Harper, 41.

SUMMER

1. Laura Kelly Fanucci, *The Extraordinary Ordinary Time* (St. Michael: Mothering Spirit, 2022), 17.

2. Henri J. M. Nouwen, *The Return of the Prodigal Son: A Story of Homecoming* (New York: Image Books, 1994), 106.

3. Wendy M. Wright, *Seasons of a Family's Life: Cultivating the Contemplative Spirit at Home* (San Francisco: Jossey-Bass, 2003), 91.

4. Justin Whitmel Earley, *Habits of the Household: Practicing the Story of God in Everyday Family Rhythms* (Grand Rapids, MI: Zondervan, 2021), 200.

5. Sarah Bessey, *Miracles and Other Reasonable Things* (New York: First Howard Books, 2019), 175.

6. Morgan Harper Nichols, *Peace Is a Practice: An Invitation to Breathe Deep and Find a New Rhythm for Life* (Grand Rapids, MI: Zondervan Books, 2022), 39.

7. Vicki K. Black, *Welcome to the Church Year: An Introduction to the Seasons of the Episcopal Church* (Harrisburg, PA: Morehouse, 2004), 109.

8. Lisa Sharon Harper, *The Very Good Gospel: How Everything Wrong Can Be Made Right* (New York: WaterBrook, 2016), 183.

9. Dietrich Bonhoeffer, *Life Together: A Discussion of Christian Fellowship*, trans. John W. Doberstein (New York: Harper & Row, 1954), 68.

10. Michael Curry with Sara Grace, *Love Is the Way: Holding on to Hope in Troubling Times* (New York: Avery, 2020), 73.

11. "Read Martin Luther King Jr.'s 'I Have a Dream' Speech in Its Entirety," NPR, January 14, 2022, https://www.npr.org/2010/01/18/122701268/i-have-a-dream-speech-in-its-entirety.

12. Michael Curry, *Love Is the Way*, 73.

13. Madeleine L'Engle, *A Circle of Quiet* (New York: HarperCollins, 1972), 26.

14. Barbara J. McClure, *Moving beyond Individualism in Pastoral Care and Counseling: Reflections on Theory, Theology, and Practice* (Eugene, OR: Cascade Books, 2010), 235.

15. Bonhoeffer, *Life Together*, 99.

16. Dietrich Bonhoeffer, *God Is in the Manger: Reflections on Advent and Christmas*, trans. O.C. Dean Jr., ed. Jana Riess (Louisville, KY: Westminster John Knox Press, 2010), 2.

17. Shannan Martin, *The Ministry of Ordinary Places: Waking Up to God's Goodness around You* (Nashville: Nelson Books, 2018), 143.

18. Martin, 142.

19. "Frederick Douglass's, 'What to the Slave Is the Fourth of July?'" National Endowment for the Humanities, accessed November 10, 2022, https://edsitement.neh.gov/student-activities/frederick-douglasss-what-slave-fourth-july.

20. Harper, *The Very Good Gospel*, 21.

21. Harper, 172.

22. L'Engle, *A Circle of Quiet*, 98.

23. Brené Brown, *Atlas of the Heart: Mapping Meaningful Connection and the Language of Human Experience* (New York: Random House, 2021), 146.

24. Brown, 147.

25. Molly Baskette and Ellen O'Donnell, *Bless This Mess: A Modern Guide to Faith and Parenting in a Chaotic World* (New York: Convergent, 2019), 71.

26. Baskette and O'Donnell, 65.

27. Baskette and O'Donnell, 101.

28. Ruth Haley Barton, *Sacred Rhythms: Arranging Our Lives for Spiritual Transformation* (Downers Grove, IL: IVP Books, 2006), 34.

29. Baskette and O'Donnell, *Bless This Mess*, 131.

30. Rich Villodas, *The Deeply Formed Life: Five Transformative Values to Root Us in the Way of Jesus* (New York: WaterBrook, 2020), 25.

31. Villodas, 25.

32. Trevor Haynes, "Dopamine, Smartphones, & You: A Battle for Your Time," Harvard University, Science in the News, May 1, 2018, https://sitn.hms.harvard.edu/flash/2018/dopamine-smartphones-battle-time/.

ADDITIONAL RESOURCES

1. Michael Curry with Sara Grace, *Love Is the Way: Holding on to Hope in Troubling Times* (New York: Avery, 2020), 249.

2. Ruth Haley Barton, *Sacred Rhythms: Arranging Our Lives for Spiritual Transformation* (Downers Grove, IL: IVP Books, 2006), 14.

3. Barton, 147.

4. Curry, *Love Is the Way*, 251.

5. Barton, *Sacred Rhythms*, 95.

6. James Martin, *Learning to Pray: A Guide for Everyone* (New York: HarperOne, 2021), 152–53.

7. Inspired by "The Daily Examen," IgnatianSpirituality.com, accessed November 16, 2022, https://www.ignatianspirituality.com/ignatian-prayer/the-examen/?utm_source=substack&utm_medium=email; Dennis Hamm, "Rummaging for God: Praying Backwards through Your Day," Ignatian Spirituality.com, accessed November 16, 2022, https://www.ignatianspirituality.com/ignatian-prayer/the-examen/rummaging-for-god-praying-backward-through-your-day/?utm_source=substack&utm_medium=email; Martin, *Learning to Pray*, chapter 9.

8. Joan Chittister, *The Monastic Heart: 50 Simple Practices for a Contemplative and Fulfilling Life* (New York: Convergent Books, 2021), 57.

9. Though Lectio Divina is an ancient practice with many iterations, these steps are inspired by James Martin's book *Learning to Pray* and Joan Chittister's book *The Monastic Heart*.
10. Rich Villodas, *The Deeply Formed Life: Five Transformative Values to Root Us in the Way of Jesus* (New York: WaterBrook, 2020), xxiii.

Index

INDEX

About the Author

KAYLA CRAIG is a former journalist who brings deep curiosity and care to her writing and podcasting. She's the author of *Every Season Sacred* and *To Light Their Way*, and she's the creator of the popular Liturgies for Parents Instagram account, which was named an "essential parenting resource" by *Christianity Today*. Kayla's nuanced and accessible reflections, essays, and prayers are featured in various books, devotionals, and Bible studies. She has a regular readership of more than 70,000 people through her social media, newsletter, and weekly podcast, *Liturgies for Parents*, which is part of the Christian Parenting Podcast Network.

With the pen of a poet and the passion of a prophet, she has partnered with nonprofits like Bethany Christian Services and The Salvation Army in her writing; she regularly contributes to Dayspring's (in)courage and encourages an array of parents at PBS KIDS for Parents. Throughout seasons of her professional life, Kayla has worked in magazine publishing and for award-winning newspapers. Her work has appeared in The Upper Room Disciplines, Alabaster Co., and Propel Women.

When she isn't writing, Kayla is learning alongside her four wild, wonderful kids. As a parent to a child with Down Syndrome and global disabilities, she is learning to navigate and advocate for more equity and inclusion for everyone. Kayla lives in a 115-year-old former convent in her Iowa hometown, where she hopes to create spaces of welcome throughout the natural and liturgical seasons alongside her children, dogs, and husband, Jonny, who, in a gloriously full-circle moment, now pastors Kayla's childhood church.

Kayla writes for a more flourishing world for her family—and all of God's children. Connect on Instagram at @kayla_craig and @litgurgiesforparents or at KaylaCraig.com.